Dining with Leaders, Rebels, Heroes, and Outlaws

Dining with Destiny Series
as part of the Rowman & Littlefield Studies in Food and Gastronomy

General Editor: Ken Albala, Professor of History,
University of the Pacific (kalbala@pacific.edu)
Rowman & Littlefield Executive Editor:
Suzanne Staszak-Silva (sstaszak-silva@rowman.com)

The volumes in the Dining with Destiny series explore food biography, examining the private eating lives of icons from across the span of literature, art, music, politics, and revolution. If you've ever wondered what Lenin lunched on, whether George Orwell really swigged Victory Gin, or if there's such a thing as a Freudian supper, then the Dining with Destiny series is for you. Behind every great man and woman is a great meal. Their peccadilloes are explored anecdotally against the backdrops of history and culture, with accompanying recipes. Taste the disconsolate marriage of Marilyn Monroe to Arthur Miller, make red gravy and pasta Sinatra-style, or shake up the kind of chocolate malted that Woody Allen likes. How about a banana sandwich with Queen Elizabeth? Or a road trip picnic with Hemingway and F. Scott Fitzgerald?

Dining with Destiny is not just for all the "foodies" out there—the night-time cocoa will lie forgotten as you realize that Malcolm X entered the civil rights movement by rejecting anything piggy on his plate and as the Swinging Sixties are revealed through the hedonism and hashish cookies of Mick Jagger and Bob Dylan. The reader will dream of sitting at the table prepared by Hitchcock, Nelson Mandela, or Picasso. But beware: Dalí's lobster in chocolate sauce means that he has a desire to sleep with you rather than paint.

Each of these figures took part in landmark historical and cultural events that have shaped and defined our way of life—but they also had to eat. Now it is time to reveal the real man by looking in his fridge to discover what makes him a revolutionary, a hero, a rogue! Dining with Destiny lets you taste what's on Darwin's fork.

Dining with Leaders, Rebels, Heroes, and Outlaws

Fiona Ross

ROWMAN & LITTLEFIELD
Lanham • Boulder • New York • London

Published by Rowman & Littlefield
A wholly owned subsidiary of The Rowman & Littlefield Publishing Group, Inc.
4501 Forbes Boulevard, Suite 200, Lanham, Maryland 20706
www.rowman.com

Unit A, Whitacre Mews, 26-34 Stannary Street, London SE11 4AB

British Library Cataloguing in Publication Information Available

Library of Congress Cataloging-in-Publication Data Is Available
ISBN 978-1-4422-5229-5 (cloth : alk. paper) — ISBN 978-1-4422-5230-1 (electronic)

♾TM The paper used in this publication meets the minimum requirements of American
National Standard for Information Sciences—Permanence of Paper for Printed Library
Materials, ANSI/NISO Z39.48-1992.

Printed in the United States of America

Dedication

I would like to dedicate this book to these special people,
lost and found, and their food:

Marijke's lemon sponge

Liberata's Garibaldi (with Giuseppe forever young and
throwing sugared almonds with love)

Gareth's mass cook

Alastair Ross's fish and chips

Norman Levy's yellow Ford and his baked potato tea

Harry and Gill's game pie

Jim and Georgia McRobbie's tea trolley

Sarah Parry's tomato sauce, Eadie's brownies, and Johnny's guacamole

Moira Ross's coffee and crosswords (I knew Go-Getter would be your last clue)

Glenys Sanger's chocolate sponge cake

The Murray family's marag gheall and marag dhubh (plus The Aunt for a chat)

And well done to my great-great-auntie Lizzie Turner for not letting
Hitler get his hands on her hats . . .

Here's tae us; wha's like us?
Damn few, and they're a' deid!

—Robbie Burns

Contents

Acknowledgments

Like all books, this one is indebted to many people. I want to thank my kindly and talented editor, Ken Albala, for his advice and support. The library staff in the hot and dusty Upper Reading Room of the Bodleian Library has been wonderful, carting endless volumes of peculiar books from deep down in the stacks. Thank you to my dear friend Gillian Harrison for introducing me to the Bodleian and for all her fine companionship there in the golden hours. Thanks to my darlings, Moira and Alastair, for the brandy Alexanders and asparagus sandwiches and for feeding me so wonderfully for the first eighteen years of my life, from breast milk through to moules marinière. I'd also like to thank Margaret and Ken Conway for filming me while I curried a goat in their kitchen; Shelley Cooper for helping me roast a suckling pig on a makeshift spit in her back garden; and to the Allen and Harris property-renting agency for allowing me to marinate the aforementioned pig in the bath of the flat they rented to me. To Mary Birtill and Irene Tominey I owe a debt for inspiring me with the Going Foot and to all my Camino friends for walking the way with me. Jane Ganly has been a great help with ICT advice and her intimate knowledge of chocolate; also to Nathan Shelton of Bread and Butter Creative I owe eternal thanks for all his wonderful design work on my website and blog. To Yorick, Roberta, Octavia, Zoe Wilks, and Louise Guthrie I would like to express gratitude for all those mad dining experiments in the Allam Street kitchen, while Pompey hid bananas in her dog basket; and Jean and Richard Haigh I must thank for advice on the vast subject of vegetables. Thank you, Emily Gray, for letting me camp in your attic; and thank you to Willem, Max, Marijke, and Steve for so much laughter. Simon Saunders: I must thank you, dear friend, for your brilliant idea long ago that I write this book. You may have all of Roisin's sticks. Let us not also forget Oscar Hughes and his first scrambled eggs—they always taste best when thrown about. I'd like to send a kiss to Roisin Ross for being my best, kindest girl forever.

Finally, I'd like to express deep-hearted thankfulness to my dear husband and best friend, Gareth Sanger, for all the immense generosity, love, and belief he has shown in giving me a room of my own and £500.

Introduction

Let me take you back to Yalta, 1945, and that iconic black-and-white photograph of the "Big Three" world leaders, Winston Churchill, Teddy Roosevelt, and Joseph Stalin, seated in a row. Now, we all know that "Uncle Joe" Stalin was about to devour Eastern Europe; that Roosevelt was all set to die—he had a cigarette in his hand even then; that Churchill had foolishly decided Stalin could be trusted; and that both Churchill and Roosevelt's living quarters had been bugged *and* that a squad of female Soviet agents were listening to them whistle in the toilet . . .

But how can food help us to see each man more clearly? Not the most obvious or serious question, perhaps, but as you will find in the pages of *Dining with Leaders, Rebels, Heroes, and Outlaws*, the question is a relevant one nonetheless. Give me the supper, and I'll give you the man. Or, in this case, a goldfish. If you ever manage to make it to Churchill's old, bumbling, and beautiful country retreat, Chartwell, then you will find, among a prehistoric mess of violin-style ferns, a small greening pool. By the pool, tucked among the reeds is a dumpy little garden chair. This was Churchill's favorite seat, in which he'd doze, paint, and chase away the blues by watching the large, slick golden orfe fish (goldfish with six-packs) slip beneath the dappled water. The fish are still there to this day, goggling mindlessly up through the weeds, no longer privy to Churchill's worries. Here's the thing, then: when Churchill met up with Stalin, "Uncle Joe," being the perfect Communist host, housed Churchill in the glamorously named State Villa Number 7 (perhaps calling it Cherry Glade or Parson's Nibble would be too hedonistically capitalist), and outside State Villa Number 7 was a pool of rather handsome goldfish. Old Winston's admiring gaze was easily drawn, and at some point, perhaps that evening, over the vodka and pig's heads, while "Uncle Joe" was wrestling with a porcine cheekbone, Winston told him how pretty his goldfish were. Stalin grinned wolfishly at Winston and said something along the lines of, "Would you like one for breakfast? I can arrange it." And in that moment, I put it to you, the nature of each man is revealed: one wants the fish as pets, and the other sees everything as eatable and expendable. Brrrrrrrrrrrrr. And, of course, let's not forget Roosevelt. Now he, I suspect, wouldn't have wanted to eat a goldfish (though he was in the clutches of Mrs. Nesbitt, his grim White House cook), but he would have shaken you up one of his breath-taking Haitian libation cocktails (a dusky muddle of brown sugar and dark rum), while Eleanor Roosevelt scrambled your eggs.

This brief comparison, then, sets us on the culinary trail of all three leaders, and there is revelation in that. *Dining with Leaders, Rebels, Heroes, and Outlaws* and indeed all of the Dining with Destiny series tracks such culinary trails to expose the secret eating lives of icons, and in this volume the focus is on our leaders, our heroes, our outlaws, and our rebels. Unexpected insights into the course of history are exposed at the dinner dates and power lunches of the political brokers, geniuses, gurus, and explorers who have shaped our time. You can taste the dreams of Martin Luther King Jr. through his beloved soul food (plus learn about his way to find the perfect wife) and savor the great revolutionary epochs through Lenin, Marx, and Castro. The Palestinian-Israeli conflict takes on a different flavor when the late-night visits of Yasser Arafat show the true nature of his taste buds. . . . Readers can enjoy rare insights into the behind-the-napkin politics of great dictators like Chairman Mao or Mussolini. Stalin loved to spook you out by serving you chicken—carved—nice and slowly—by himself. Einstein claimed to his first wife that what bound them irrevocably together was not only their "dark souls" but a common interest in sausage and coffee. His second wife, the wild-haired Elsa, was known to trade intimate "audiences" with Albert for a reasonable slice of Sachertorte. You will almost hear the singing at Captain Scott's last birthday party before setting out for the South Pole, and you'll have the chance to analyze how Freud's subconscious worked when it came to food. I have drawn from many different sources to discover the dining habits of the individuals in this volume. Memoirs, letters, and diaries give a flavor of the food experiences of such heroes as Lawrence of Arabia, from gazelle through to rose sherbet. Mahatma Gandhi's advice, set out in his "Guide to London," for other Indians and especially vegetarians who happen to turn up looking for a bite to eat in late, meat-laden Victorian London, is full of insight. Many of those cooks who manned the kitchens of the great American presidents have assiduously recorded their recipes—but these only tell a silent tale of food biography. Now it is time to reveal the real man by looking into his fridge to discover what makes him a revolutionary, a hero, a rogue! What I have tried to do is to anecdotally re-create the eating lives of icons, in part by creating, tasting, and re-creating recipes as close as possible to their originals, whether that be in substance or mood. All the recipes in the Dining with Destiny series are my own, made in my kitchen, with weighing scales which have a mind of their own. But they have turned out jam tarts to please Karl Marx and pecan pies for Malcolm X.

1

Dining with the Leaders

Apparatchiks and their appetites will appeal to all those readers with a transcontinental interest in behind-the-napkin politics. Candidates include Golda Meir; Lyndon B. Johnson; Boris Yeltsin; Jimmy Carter; Margaret Thatcher; Richard Nixon; Winston Churchill; Bill Clinton; Mikhail Gorbachev; Ronald Reagan; and John F. Kennedy.

GOLDA MEIR AND HER KITCHEN CABINET

Golda Meir, the future female president of the newly emerging state of Israel, began life in a miserable, frost-bitten shtetl in Eastern Europe, near Pinsk, a city in Belarus, on the fringes of the Russian Empire. The distant, gilded tsar ruled over his vast kingdoms, and the life of one of his subjects, little Golda Meir, was nipped by hunger and the constant threat of burly Cossack hordes thundering over the Pinsker Blotte, a muddy swamp, on their horses (this was such a disturbing childhood memory for Golda's younger sister, Zipke, that she let out a loud wail of "The Cossacks are here!" when mounted police pranced past at the Labor Day parade in Milwaukee—the family had emigrated there). Food was scant in the Russian Empire, and Golda always felt frozen on the outside and empty on the inside; one of the few comforts was the steamy magnificence of a bowl of her mother's warming gruel. Her parents, Moshe and Blume Mabovitch, kept a kosher kitchen, in which Golda's older sister, the formidable Sheyna, held revolutionary meetings with a huddle of fellow dissidents on Saturday mornings, plotting the overthrow of the tsar. Blume stood outside fretting, sobbing, and looking out for tsarist spies while little Golda squeezed into a warm space above the coal stove to spy on them, clutching a notebook for doodling and listening uncomprehendingly to their plans. Nevertheless, this motif of the kitchen as a place fit for politics was to define Golda's government in Israel.

On Friday nights, the kitchen was given over to the Sabbath meal, when Blume, a very good cook, taught her daughters how to conjure up toothsome, simple, sustaining Jewish food, food which was at the core of the family's history and experience. They were made of stern stuff: Golda's grandfather served with the Russian army but never ate nonkosher food (*treyf*) and survived on raw vegetables and bread (he also favored a stone for his pillow). Meanwhile, her maternal grandmother, Bobbe Golde, refused sugar in her tea, opting instead for a spoonful of salt, because, she said, "I want to take the taste of the *Goless* [Diaspora] with me into the other world." She had to keep up this habit for quite some time, as she didn't die till her ninety-fourth year. It was at her mother's side where Golda learned to cook and bake, but always as entry points and expressions of their Jewish faith and community; Blume was always baking for bazaars, listening to the woes of friends, the kitchen air warm with the smell of bagels. For Sabbath, Blume and her girls prepared rich chicken soup, gefilte fish, a delicious stew of braised meat and onions, with tzimmes of coin-shaped carrots (symbolizing wealth) stewed with plump, black prunes, and both family and guests gathered around the table. Much later, in Tel Aviv, Golda's son, Menachem Meir, recalled Golda's home on Thursday nights, which sounds like a lovely, respectful echo of Blume's: "Thursday nights were special, as they were over all of Tel Aviv; the small apartment filled with the aromas of Shabbat cooking—freshly baked challah, chicken soup, gefilte fish, all the traditional Jewish foods, which my mother prepared for us, for father, and the many guests who inevitably dropped in."

Challah

½ tbsp. dry yeast
½ cup warm water
3½ cups all-purpose flour
2 large eggs
1 tbsp. granulated sugar

1 tbsp. runny, dark honey
¼ cup sunflower oil
1 tsp. kosher salt
1 to 2 cups chopped, dried dates,
   apricots, and raisins

TO GLAZE
1 egg white
1 tbsp. olive oil
⅛ cup milk

½ tbsp. sugar
2 tsp. mixed finely chopped almonds,
   sesame seeds, and poppy seeds

Challah (*continued*)

Put the yeast into a bowl with the warm water. Stir and then leave this in a warm place for 15 minutes until the yeast-water mixture froths. Sieve 1 generous cup of flour into a large, deep mixing bowl; make a well in the center of the flour and gradually add the warm yeast-water, combining it with your fingertips until the yeast-water and flour are mixed thoroughly into a rubbery ball of dough. Cover the dough, put it in a warm, snug place, and leave it to rise and bubble for 1 hour.

After 1 hour—with the exception of the remaining flour—combine the eggs, sugar, honey, oil, salt, and dried fruit with the mixture. Put the dough on a lightly floured surface. Roll up your sleeves. Begin to add the remaining flour a little at a time until you have smooth, elastic dough. Knead vigorously—if the dough sticks to the bowl, then add a little more flour. Stop adding flour as soon as any stickiness vanishes. Now knead for a further 10 minutes.

Lightly oil a bowl and, when you have thoroughly slapped the challah dough about, place it in the bowl, cover it again, and return it to the snug, warm spot for a full 2 hours.

After 2 hours, prepare a lightly floured surface and divide the challah dough into 3 equal-size portions. Roll the each portion into a 12-inch-length rope. Make the ends thinner than the main body of each strand. You are now going to braid your challah. This is the complicated bit. Line the strands up vertically, parallel to each other. Take the right strand, cross it over the central strand, and let it lie in the center. Take the left strand and drape it over the middle strand. Keep repeating this until the challah is braided to the very end. When finished, gather the braid ends together. *But* you will see that the top end of the challah has unbraided. Turn the challah over so that the unbraided stands are facing you and repeat the same process with the strands.

Lightly oil a baking pan and place the challah in the pan; cover, return the challah to the warm, snug spot, and leave to rise for just under 3 hours.

After this time, preheat the oven to 180 degrees centigrade. Make the challah glaze by whisking together the egg white, olive oil, milk, and sugar. Sprinkle with the finely chopped almonds, sesame seeds, and poppy seeds. Now put the challah into the oven and bake for about 40 minutes, until the challah is a deep golden color and sounds hollow when tapped on its base. Cool; eat the same day with a cup of bitter black coffee and imagine you're in Golda's kitchen!

Gefilte Fish

FOR THE FISH STOCK

2 tbsp. olive oil
1 onion, finely sliced
3 shallots, finely sliced
2 celery stalks, plus leafy tops, sliced
1 leek, finely sliced
3 lb. fish heads, bones, and
   trimmings

1 bunch flat-leaf parsley
1 small bunch fresh thyme
1 scant tsp. finely chopped garlic
1 bay leaf
½ pint dry white wine
pinch of sea salt
8 whole peppercorns

FOR THE GEFILTE FISH

1 medium onion, chopped
½ tbsp. finely chopped dill
1 tbsp. finely chopped parsley
1 tsp. crumbled fresh thyme
2 eggs
1 tsp. kosher salt
pinch of freshly ground black pepper

1 tsp. sugar
¼ cup fresh bread crumbs
1 lb. boned minced white fish,
   such as pike or cod
2 pints fish stock
2 carrots, sliced

Begin by preparing the fish stock. In a deep, heavy-based pan, warm the olive oil. Add the onion, shallots, celery, and leek; cover with a dish of buttered, grease-proof paper and let this sweat on a gentle heat for about 10 to 15 minutes—but they must not brown! Now add the fish heads, bones, and trimmings with the parsley, thyme, garlic, and bay leaf. Add the wine, sea salt, and peppercorns, top up with enough cold water to just cover the fish, and simmer gently, uncovered, for 30 minutes. Skim any fat or scum off the surface. Finally, strain the fish stock through a muslin cloth and cool.

Now for the fish quenelles: in a food processor, combine the onion, dill, parsley, thyme, eggs, salt, black pepper, and sugar. Process to a mush. Empty this into a large bowl and fold in the bread crumbs and minced fish. Refrigerate this for 30 minutes. Pour the fish stock into a deep pan with the sliced carrots and heat to simmering point. Using your hands, shape a tablespoon at a time of the fish mixture into quenelle shapes. Plop these into the stock and simmer for about 20 minutes. Then remove the quenelles and carrot disks from the pot with a draining spoon and allow the quenelles and carrot disks to cool. Return the stock to the heat and reduce it by half. Arrange the quenelles in a serving dish, place a disk of carrot on top of each quenelle, pour the fish stock over them, and refrigerate overnight. The next day, the gefilte fish will be beautifully jellied and ready to eat, while each carrot disk guarantees prosperity.

Carrot and Prune Tzimmes

2 lb. carrots, peeled and cut into
  1-inch pieces
1 cup orange juice
½ cup honey
1 tsp. cinnamon

¾ cup chicken stock
generous pinch of sea salt
freshly ground black pepper
6 oz. pitted prunes

Put the carrots in a deep, thick-based pot. Combine the orange juice, honey, cinnamon, chicken stock, sea salt, and black pepper. Pour this into the pan on top of the carrots. Over a medium heat, bring the tzimmes mixture to a simmer, stir once, and then cover the pot and reduce the heat to a soft simmer. Half an hour later, stir once and add the prunes. Cook on a very low heat for a further 10 minutes. Now the tzimmes is ready to serve.

Economic migration took the Mabovitches to the United States and the railroads of Milwaukee, where Moshe found work, while Blume ran the local grocery story. But Socialist Zionism had hooked Golda's imagination and heart, and, when she met and fell in love with Morris Meyerson, a precondition to their marriage was emigration to Palestine.

Accompanied by the ever-fiery Shenya and her children (Shenya's husband joined them later, along with Moshe and Blume), they hauled up at Tel Aviv in the summer of 1921, bedraggled and exhausted, to a dispiriting welcome: they roomed with Mr. and Mrs. Barash, whose tatty beds were already occupied by a team of lively and diligent bedbugs. Jews already settled in Palestine gave them a big hug and said, "Thank God you millionaires have come to us from America. *Now* everything will be alright!" The flyblown fruit and vegetable markets of Tel Aviv made them long for the sanitized soda parlors of Milwaukee and Denver. The stifling heat and listless, dusty, half-built streets were a far cry from the diaphanous Palestine of their dreams. Even when friends from Jerusalem turned up to console them, things didn't get any brighter: the consolation involved telling them of the terrible ordeals they would face in the future in Palestine, and, when they tried to cheer Golda and Shenya up by feeding them "American" hamburgers, these tasted of soap and left a foamy sensation in their mouths . . . it turned out soap had fallen into the ground meat.

Nevertheless, Golda experienced the wonderful awe of living for the first time in a Jewish state in Palestine—undefined and unnamed as yet—but where it was normal to be Jewish, where every man was her brother or sister within Judaism. As her

son Menachem put it, "Tel Aviv was the first . . . Jewish city in the whole world."
Joining a kibbutz, Golda decided, was the best way to chip in, to test out socialist
ideas of communal living, and to clear and develop the land for a Jewish state in
Palestine. Kibbutz Merhavia was the answer to her dreams: a mishmash of malarial
black swamps and scorched patches of earth. Golda took to life in a kibbutz with
joy—she proved herself a skilled chicken handler and was sent on chicken-rearing
courses for the kibbutz. The rearing of livestock, farming, reclamation, irrigation,
and, of course, food were the main business of the kibbutz. When Golda first arrived, on the table was chickpea mush, tinned bully beef the British had forgotten
to take back with them, endless amounts of "fresh" herring in tomato sauce for
breakfast, and sour cereals supplemented by a type of unrefined oil their Arab
neighbors supplied them with, carried in goatskin bags; this means of transport
imparted a piquant but not cheering astringency to the oil. Golda couldn't wait for
kitchen assignment so she could shake it all up. First, she struck off herring from
the breakfast menu; oatmeal was in order instead. Oatmeal, the others muttered,
was one of Golda's fancy American ideas. Gone were the chipped, reused enamel
cups: Golda introduced glasses and tablecloths. Herring turned up at lunchtime
instead, and Golda decreed that the herring's obstinate skin be removed—almost
everyone on the kibbutz had only one eating utensil: you had a knife *or* a fork *or*
a spoon, so skinning herrings was a mucky task, and you often had to wipe sticky,
oily herring residue from your fingers onto your overalls. On Saturdays, the Sabbath, the kibbutz could not transport its milk to Haifa, so Golda instigated milk
Sabbaths, in order to consume the produce. They had coffee with milk, and crafted
their own leben, a delicious thick and savory yogurt, and lebeniya, a jazzed-up,
enriched form of leben.

Destiny wasn't to keep Golda with her chickens in the kibbutz, but she remained
faithful to its ideals; even when she set up an Israeli embassy in Moscow in the
Soviet Union in 1948, it was run along the lines of a kibbutz, as Golda hoped Soviets might drop by for a slice of cake and cup of tea in much the same way as you
would on a kibbutz. Needless to say, it didn't happen. The Soviets weren't ready
for Golda's kitchen diplomacy. Representing a cash-short, fledgling new nation,
the Israeli delegation tended to be a bit low on rubles, so Golda organized shopping
expeditions to get food at cheap markets and, rolling up her sleeves, made communal meals. Future foreign diplomacy gradually became more comfortable, but
eating what was on offer remained pretty complex, albeit in other ways. When she
visited Burma in 1963, Golda loved everything, apart from the food. Choice Bur-
mese delicacies were challenging; she quailed at the prospect of roasted leopard;
declined the 1,000-year egg on her plate; blanched at their sharp, salty fish pastes;

and, when offered a spoonful of birds' nest soup, shook her head. Meanwhile, on her visits to the United States—and Washington, in particular—Golda was asked about *her* style of cooking: "Your grandson Gideon says you make the best gefilte fish ever. What's your recipe, Golda?" called out one reporter. Golda replied with the promise that the next time she came, she'd make gefilte fish for all of them. She was inundated by 40,000 requests for her recipe for chicken soup—given that she wasn't convinced her chicken soup was much good, she worried a little about 40,000 versions of it, bubbling away in pots across America.

Here, straight from the Israeli national archives comes Golda's recipe:

Boil the chicken with parsley, celery, cut-up carrots, peeled onion, salt, pepper, a pinch of paprika, until the chicken is tender.

If you like rice, you may add it after straining the soup, bringing to boil for another quarter of an hour.

Mrs. Meir generally serves chicken soup with KNEIDLACH which she prepares as follows:

The matzos (unleavened bread) are soaked in cold water until soft, then squeeze them dry, crush with a fork and add fried onions and a little oil, some parsley, salt, pepper and two beaten eggs. Add some matzo meal for binding. Make into small balls, set aside before serving for 1 hour. Half an hour before serving, drop the balls into the boiling soup and cook for half an hour.

Back in Israel, Golda ran an open house for any members of her cabinet who might want to pop in for a quiet chat; as she put it, "Now and then, different members of my cabinet dropped in so that we could talk about specific problems in a relaxed and informal way. These were not official meetings, and no decisions were ever taken at them, of course. But I am convinced that they helped to make the process of government more efficient just because we could talk things out over a cup of coffee or a bite to eat around my kitchen table." Slowly but surely, Golda's kitchen meetings gathered in fame, and those who sipped coffee there were renamed her Kitchen Cabinet. Some members of the Knesset objected to the domesticity but also jealously begrudged the visits of others to Golda's kitchen; were they being excluded from an inner circle? Golda joked she could start running a kibbutz-style kitchen. Endless cups of strong, dark Turkish coffee were about—cold, lukewarm, or piping hot—and baggy-eyed, wise Golda puffed away on her Chesterfields while the smoke curled about the pots and pans. In her apron, she baked up cakes with a sprinkling of politics. Homemade cheesecake or apple strudel might appear and was sliced up on her green Formica table, with a wedge or two for the likes of Moshe Dayan.

Kitchen Cabinet Apfelstrudel

Forget about wussy sheets of filo pastry: in the old versions of apfelstrudel, the pungent and sweet cinnamon apples are encased in a tunnel of unleavened pastry . . .

FOR THE STRUDEL DOUGH
300 g. (2½ cups) strong,
   white bread flour
½ tsp. crumbled sea salt
200 ml. dry, kosher white wine

1½ tbsp. butter, melted
2 tbsp. melted butter for brushing
   the dough

FOR THE DOUGH BREAD CRUMBS
3½ tbsp. unsalted butter

100 g. freshly made white bread
   crumbs—from unleavened bread!

FOR THE APPLE FILLING
2¼ lb. cooking apples
1 unwaxed lemon, zested
   and juiced
3½ tbsp. vanilla sugar
1½ tsp. ground cinnamon

1 tsp. freshly grated nutmeg
1 tsp. ground cloves
2½ tbsp. raisins, macerated for 3
   hours in 2½ tbsp. kosher white wine
2½ tbsp. toasted, flaked almonds

FOR THE APFELSTRUDEL GLAZE
1 egg white, beaten
2 tbsp. apricot jam, warmed and
   melted to glaze

powder-white confectioner's sugar
   for dusting

FOR SERVING
homemade vanilla custard

The apfelstrudel is a funny old creature of a cake, which you make from the inside out, as you'll see. About 3 hours before you are going to begin to make the apfelstrudel, soak the raisins in the white wine: this requires forethought, of which many of us—I for one—am not always capable. Three hours later, and possessed of forethought, you begin by preparing the many other different elements of the apfelstrudel filling. First you are going to make the buttery bread-crumb sprinkles that you'll use to line the dough. In a small frying pan, heat 3½ tablespoons of unsalted butter until it foams. Throw in the 100 grams of freshly made white bread crumbs and toast them in the butter, stirring constantly, until they are a medium brown color (yes, the color of toast!).

   Assemble the apple mixture that will make up the scrumptious core of the strudel. Peel and core the apples, then chop them up. Pour on the lemon juice and lemon zest and stir to coat the apples. Next, add the vanilla sugar, cinnamon,

Kitchen Cabinet Apfelstrudel (*continued*)

nutmeg, cloves, raisins fat with rum, and toasted almonds. Reserve this lovely, chunky apple goo.

Now it is time to make the strudel dough. Brace yourself. Sift the flour and sea salt into a large, wide bowl. Get a wooden spoon, make a small well in the center of the flour, and begin to add the white wine, stirring it through the flour. Now add the melted 1½ tablespoons of butter. Using your hands, knead the dough for about 5 minutes until it is smooth, silky, and blisters slightly. Brush the dough with the remaining 2 tablespoons of melted butter, cover with a clean cloth, and leave in a warm place for 1 hour.

After the hour is up, turn the pastry out onto a large, flour-dusted board. Lightly flour a clean dish towel and tip the pastry onto it. Using your floury fingertips, gently press and stretch the dough into a rectangular shape, thinning it—but not so that it is newspaper thin, which many strudel recipes suggest, as this may well break and let the rich, musky apple juices leach out, ruining the dough and diminishing the succulence of the filling. Instead, the dough should be *reasonably* thin. Very thick edges should be trimmed off, still retaining a rectangular shape on top of the floured cloth that lies beneath it.

Get ready a baking tray. Butter it lightly and then flour it. Position the tray immediately beside your pastry, ready to have the completed strudel placed on it. Drain off any excess liquid that may have formed in your apple mixture.

It is now time for the fried, buttery bread crumbs. Sprinkle these over the pastry; you want to leave on all sides a space of about 1 inch, so you have a smaller rectangle of bread crumbs on top of a larger rectangle of pastry. Directly on top of the bread crumbs, load the edge of dough nearest to you with the scrumptious apple goo, forming a rectangle of apple—and not *too* close to the edge. Leave an inch spare. Fold in the top and bottom of the rectangle. Very carefully, using the cloth to help you manipulate the dough, begin to roll the apfelstrudel into a long Swiss-roll shape. Begin, of course, with the edge *with* the filling. Roll up completely. You should now have an apfelstrudel that resembles in shape a Swiss roll. Again, using the cloth, shift the apfelstrudel gently onto the baking tray, shaping it now into a crescent shape. Put this in the fridge and chill for 10 minutes.

Preheat the oven to 200 degrees centigrade. Brush the apfelstrudel with more melted butter. Place it in the oven and bake at 200 degrees centigrade for 20 minutes. Turn down the oven to 180 degrees centigrade, use a brush at this point to pick up any juice that may have seeped out, and spread this over the apfelstrudel. Peek in every so often to check that the pastry is not darkening too much—if it looks as if it might be, then cover the apfelstrudel with tin foil. Cook for a further 40 minutes.

Remove the strudel from the oven, brush the top with melted hot apricot glaze, and sprinkle with powdered sugar. Slice and serve with warm vanilla custard.

HIGH ON THE HOG WITH LADY BIRD
AND LYNDON JOHNSON

Lyndon B. Johnson was a Scotch and soda man all the way through who was not embarrassed to be caught in his underpants and perfectly happy to pee while chatting to his aides. And if a flash of the president's willy wasn't enough, he was pretty proud of the large stomach scar he had after his gallbladder was dragged out in 1965 and happily gave visitors a flash of that. Lechery was also supposedly the name of the game with Lyndon—he was nicknamed "ball nuts" by his staff. Meanwhile, his guests certainly had to have ball nuts when he took them out for a drive to see the Pedernales River; Lyndon would drive his blue car straight in, pretending that the brakes had failed, as his guests (the secretary for health in one case) gave end-of-life wails and scrabbled for the latch—the big joke was that the car was amphibious. What a wheeze. An insomniac, Lyndon flitted about the house, whether it was the White House or his ranch at Pedernales, at all hours of the night, switching out the lights. Intent on saving money, Lyndon left people in darkness if he didn't realize they were in the room. Yet this punctiliousness was not observed in other matters; Lyndon was not always on time for dinner and often foxed his cooks by getting the number of dinner guests wrong.

When they arrived at the White House, the Johnsons inherited a very sophisticated French chef from the Kennedys, one René Verdon, but were less than impressed by his fancy ways—not surprising, given that Lyndon had no concept of the sort of finesse a chef like René could offer: he bellowed at a chef for serving his guests raw meat, when actually it was medium-rare steak . . . steak was either cooked or raw in Lyndon's culinary world. Another time, when René painstakingly prepared tournedos Rossini for a state luncheon, Johnson, unaware that the noisome, plump filet of beef came perched on a wad of creamy foie gras, choked on his first mouthful. "The steak's spoiled. Don't eat any of it!" Lady Bird warned her table of dignitaries. They put down their forks. Where, René must have lamented, was Jackie Kennedy and her sophisticated palate? Instead, Lyndon sent demands to the kitchen for chili con queso, which René acidly renamed "chili con-crete." Fortunately for Lyndon, lest René set about killing him some more, he had with him his own chef, Zephyr White, one of the many brilliant black cooks who have served American presidents over time. So, when Lyndon returned René's version of his adored tapioca pudding to the kitchen, uneaten, with the instructions that he let Zephyr teach him how to do it, René grumbled that Zephyr must pour glue into her tapioca to please the president, adding, bitchily, "The President eats so much tapioca pudding that Zephyr doesn't even cook it herself. She has the pot washer do it."

Tapioca (. . . courtesy of the pot washer)

⅓ cup of small pearl tapioca
2½ cups of full fat milk
2 egg yolks, beaten
⅓ cup of granulated sugar

Pinch of sea salt
Vanilla seeds and pulp from
 one vanilla bean
Pinch of cinnamon

In a medium sized mixing bowl, soak the pearls of tapioca in the milk for half an hour. Now add the egg yolks, sugar, salt and vanilla. Combine thoroughly. Transfer this mixture to a saucepan; stirring constantly, bring the tapioca to the boil and then turn the heat down to a very gentle bubble. Stir regularly and cook for a further 20 minutes. Remove from the heat and pour into individual serving bowls. Sprinkle each with cinnamon and then leave to cool and set in the fridge (this will take a couple of hours).

René, however, always masterminded the large, grand state dinners—except in the case of King Faisal of Saudi Arabia, who had a delicate stomach and was frightened by reports of LBJ's love of chilies and barbecues. Panicking, Faisal suggested that his own chef should make the state dinner, as a gift to the Johnsons. It was a no-go. Instead, King Faisal's chef and royal taster turned up with four briefcases, each containing a course. Each briefcase was opened, its contents revealed and then subsequently tasted.

Barbecues were to the Johnsons what peanuts were to the Carters. Barbecue diplomacy was born. The Johnsons loved to make smoke on the roof of the White House with Texas barbecue, served alongside chili soup. Lady Bird sunbathed up there too. Even grander, mythic barbecue fare was dished up at the Johnson's ranch near the Pedernales River: this was the sort of food that makes it into American mythology (indeed, had JFK not been shot in Dallas, he was due to attend a Johnson barbecue that evening). A local barbecue aficionado called Walter Jetton often swept in to cater for the Johnsons on large-scale occasions, producing Minotaur-size whole spit-roast cattle; hams; barbecued, sticky pork and railway tracks of beef ribs; knobs of yellow butter melted over cobs of corn; coleslaw (when Lyndon served barbecue to a German delegation, the joke went around that they'd tried to barbecue sauerkraut); pickles; Texas toast; potato salad; and Texas-style baked beans. Bubblingly sweet fried peach pies were served to those desperate to consume good-old-boy authenticity along with Western hats, the jingle of spurs, singers in the dust, and historical reenactments of the-Spaniards-meet-the-Indians. There were generous, plate-sized pecan pies and big simmering pots of red sauce, all eaten balanced on paper plates.

BBQ Spareribs and Red Sauce

4 lb. beef spareribs

FOR THE RED SAUCE

3 tbsp. beef dripping

6 onions, chopped

8 cloves garlic, finely chopped

2 cans tomatoes

1 cup tomato puree

3 red chilies, coarsely chopped

1 tbsp. smoked paprika

2 tsp. ground cumin

2 tbsp. mustard

2 tbsp. brown muscovado sugar

2 tbsp. brown malt vinegar

2 tbsp. Worcestershire sauce

sea salt

freshly ground black pepper

While the barbecue coals heat up, go red, and whiten, prepare the red sauce. In a deep, heavy-bottomed frying pan, heat the beef dripping. To this, add the onions and garlic and fry gently until they are a warm gold color. Add the tomatoes, tomato puree, chilies, paprika, cumin, mustard, muscovado sugar, brown malt vinegar, and Worcestershire sauce. Salt and pepper. Bring to a boil and reduce until the red sauce is thick and sticky.

Place the ribs on the barbecue about 5 inches from the heat and barbecue them for about 45 minutes—take care that they never burn. Now, begin to baste them thoroughly with the sticky, pungent red sauce. Reapply the sauce every 5 minutes or so and continue for about half an hour, until the ribs are a deep, rich brown red and sticky with glazed red sauce.

And if that didn't fill you up for the next ten years, Lady Bird was ready at breakfast, with the offer of scrambled eggs, spicy deer sausage, and a smile. For smaller, family-oriented meals Zephyr sizzled up sliced sirloin and mushrooms, a plate of asparagus slippery with hollandaise sauce, and all finished with scrumptious strawberry meringue. "I have yet to find," wrote Lady Bird in her diary, "a great chef whose desserts I like as well as Zephyr's." On the ranch on New Year's Eve in 1966, the Johnsons were "hungry as bears" at the prospect of Zephyr's ham and black-eyed beans, which were going to make 1967 a lucky year, with delicious warm cornbread and buttermilk. The good luck spell worked, at least food-wise, as on New Year's Day Zephyr served turkey, burnished to a dark gold, with sweet potatoes topped with marshmallow and a zippy cranberry sauce. Lady Bird sighed dreamily, "Nobody in the world makes better dressing than Zephyr."

Barbecue eating is, generally, a good redneck political flag to wave, and the Johnsons, perhaps more than any other president and first lady, understood the connections between food and politics, campaigning through food, showing understanding of the voter's soul through food, but also reaching out to the voter through food: indeed, Lyndon B. Johnson was fond of dishing out earthy aphoristic food metaphors. "Don't spit in the soup," he'd warn opponents. "We all have to eat it." Lyndon's "Great Society" would be drawn together through food, no more seen than on Lady Bird's legendary rail journey.

Southern cuisine, Lady Bird figured, was the arrow that would shoot you straight to America's heart. Everyone wanted to have a bite of the president's food, in this case, one of Lyndon's special treats, Pedernales River Chili, distributed on a card, which was "almost as popular as the government pamphlet on the care and feeding of children." The original can be found in the LBJ archives and reads as "Mrs. Lyndon B. Johnson's Recipe for Pedernales River Chili," but in truth it should read as Zephyr White's. Here's a more modern version, but using Lyndon's preferred deer meat.

Pedernales River Chili

2 red peppers
½ lb. coarsely chopped rump steak (beef or venison)
1 large chopped onion
2 cloves garlic, minced
2 tbsp. chili-infused olive oil
1 tbsp. suet (optional)
1 tsp. oregano
1 tsp. ground cumin
1 tsp. chili powder

1 tbsp. tomato puree
1 can chopped tomatoes
1 tsp. scarlet paprika
1 large, dried chili (Anaheim or New Mexico)
cracked black pepper
2 dashes Tabasco
pinch of rubbed sea salt
2 cups beef stock
1 can pinto beans

Preheat the oven to 210 degrees centigrade. Rub the 2 peppers in olive oil and then roast them. When they shrivel and blacken slightly, remove them from the oven and strip them of their skins. They will add an intense, subtle sweetness to the final chili.

In a Dutch oven, gently fry the meat with onion and garlic in the olive oil and suet until the meat is lightly browned and the onions soft and golden. Add the oregano, cumin, chili powder, tomato puree, tomatoes, scarlet paprika, large dried chili, black pepper, Tabasco, sea salt, and beef stock. Bring just to a boil; lower heat and simmer, covered, for approximately 1 hour. Drain and add the pinto beans. Cook for a further 10 minutes.

Serve with cornbread and guacamole.

Cornbread Made in a Skillet

2 tbsp. bacon fat
1¼ cups white or yellow cornmeal
¾ cup all-purpose flour
1¼ cups buttermilk
2 eggs, beaten

3 tsp. brown sugar
good pinch of sea salt
2 tsp. baking powder
½ tsp. bicarbonate of soda

Begin by frying up some streaky bacon in a little oil; press the bacon against the pan to release the grease. When the streaky bacon is thoroughly cooked, drain off the fat and reserve. You will need 2 tablespoons for the cornbread.

Preheat the oven to 200 degrees centigrade. Melt the bacon fat until it is sizzling in an ovenproof skillet. In a bowl, combine the cornmeal, flour, buttermilk, eggs, sugar, salt, baking powder, and bicarbonate to make a batter. Pour in the hot bacon grease. Make sure the skillet is still hot and pour the cornbread batter into the hot skillet. Place in the oven and bake for half an hour, until it is golden brown.

Guacamole

2 large ripe avocados (to check
   ripeness, the flesh of the avocado
   should yield gently when pressed)
½ red chili, finely chopped
½ red onion, finely chopped

½ tbsp. chopped fresh cilantro
½ tbsp. olive oil
juice of 1 lime
sea salt
coarsely ground black pepper

Skin and stone the avocados. In a medium-size bowl, mash them with a fork until they pulverize into a pea-green gloop, though a few tiny blobs of solid avocado work well in terms of texture. Add the red chili, red onion, and fragrant cilantro. Drizzle the olive oil over, stirring to make it meld with the avocado mix. Squeeze the lime over and fork in. Finally, salt and pepper to taste.

Should you want to give this a garlicky undertone, rub the mixing bowl with a clove of garlic, pressed into salt: this will leave delicate garlicky oil on the bowl.

As Lyndon haughtily observed, "Chili concocted outside of Texas is usually a weak, apologetic imitation of the real thing. One of the first things I do when I get home to Texas is to have a bowl of red." Lady Bird understood this and the South: she was raised there and, indeed, in 1964, spent four days in place of Lyndon rattling along on the *Lady Bird Special* train on a whistle-stop campaign trail covering

1,628 miles through eight states of the seething, restless South. It was thought too dangerous for Lyndon to go himself; the Civil Rights Act had been passed just months before to great controversy. The Jim Crow laws were ground into the dust, and many Southern whites saw their very way of life destroyed, rebuked, and discarded. A November election loomed, and Lyndon's advisors figured the Southern Democrats might bolt. Brilliantly, food came to Lyndon's aid . . .

Lady Bird invited key politicians on board the train for a bite to eat, ushering them on with her team of fifteen sunny-faced, welcoming hostesses. Meticulously, she planned every step of the trip: she wanted to speak to those voters who never went near an airport or a depot—she was heading to where "the pavement runs out." Playing on her soft Southern voice, femininity, and food, Lady Bird was determined to court the South. As the *Lady Bird Special* wheezed into each state, Lady Bird had cooked up a menu to fit: Texas found her sizzling up her famous deer meat sausage; shrimp and avocado dip beckoned Florida; Louisiana was served okra and shrimp creole; in Kentucky the aroma of slow-cooked burgoo stew and biscuits wafted its way off the train. Lady Bird handed out "her" recipes to desperate crowds (like the temperance homilies favored by the Plymouth Brethren). Privately, though, Lady Bird felt a little squirm of doubt when handing out some of the recipe leaflets—for instance, later in 1967, in the case of the dodgy pound cake recipe the Johnsons sent out after their daughter Lynda's wedding. Complaints poured in of pound cakes collapsing. Would a bad pound cake cost them Democrat votes? Lady Bird fretted.

But there was no stopping the *Lady Bird Special* in 1964. Finger-burning hot, battered hush puppies were deep-fried in Carolina, and Virginia bit into beaten biscuits and ham. Opposition to integration was staunch in Georgia, so a delicious ham, basted in apple and orange juice and ginger ale, then cooked in a couple of inches of Coca-Cola, was baked there. Printed copies of the recipes flew off the train and into the hands of potential voters; even the congressmen traveling on board the train began to use food analogies in their speeches, to disarm hecklers and quiet the boos. And she was right: a local politician introduced Lady Bird to the expectant crowd as "as much a part of the South as [. . .] peanuts and red-eye gravy." There's an endorsement for you! One congressman, Hale Boggs from New Orleans, traveling with Lady Bird, got straight to the point: "You're not gonna turn your back in the first Southern-born president in a hundred years?" Lady Bird was reaching out to the hearts and stomachs over a half a million Southerners, and this type of food-meets-politics was dangerous: intelligence picked up that a bomb may be planted on the *Lady Bird Special*.

Various health issues, from gallbladder problems through to heart attacks, meant that Lyndon should have stuck to a low-cholesterol, monitored diet. Lady Bird watched what she ate all the time, lunching on salads and clear soups—although she found it hard to resist crabmeat crepes; Lyndon, however, was his own worst enemy. Try as she might to steer Lyndon away from hors d'oeuvres tables, Lady Bird always noted his tendency to linger about the vol-au-vents there. "These have way too many calories; are you trying to kill me?" he'd ask when she put extra slices of watermelon on his plate. As much as Lady Bird tried, Lyndon was always rebelling by stealth: he got his secretary to smuggle bottles of Cutty Sark onto his private jet, whispering, "Make sure Lady Bird doesn't know about the booze." You almost get the feeling that a similar sneakiness worked with Lyndon's secret lady friends on the side: they were all just Cutty Sark. Comically, Lady Bird hid food from him in odd places; when her plane was dramatically struck by lightning on her way from Washington to Cleveland, the first thing she did when she made it back to the White House was rummage under her bed for the peanut brittle she'd hidden from Lyndon and eat it all. Though the combined forces of Zephyr and Lady Bird tried to keep his calorie intake down to a very lean 1,100 daily, Johnson drove everyone crazy moaning about grated carrots, low-fat soufflés, and the lack of gravy in his life: "What's a broiled veal chop?" he sighed. "Those old green beans, same old squash, tossed salad—I'm against anything that's tossed." In the end, only low-fat tapioca pudding was bearable. If his weight went up, he didn't let his doctor look at the scales, and when it was down, he'd sashay about in baggy suits pointing out how pinched his waistline was. Eventually, though, Lyndon put on so much podge that he took to wearing a girdle. Zephyr was driven to scribble out a checklist of fat, carbohydrates, and protein contained in each meal; maddeningly, Johnson called these Zephyr's "love letters" to him. One of Zephyr's "love notes" reads as follows: "Mr. President, you have been my boss for a number of years, and you always tell me you want to loose [sic] weight and yet you never do much to help yourself. Now I am going to be your boss for a change. Eat what I put in front of you and don't ask for any more and don't complain."

Lyndon and Zephyr had a long and complicated history together. His close reliance on her cooking, right from the early days before he became president, gave him his first real insight into America's Jim Crow laws and forged his commitment to civil rights, as Johnson acknowledged in his memoirs. The Johnsons had two black key staff members: Sammy, their chauffeur, and Zephyr for the kitchen. The director of the U.S. Information Agency, Leonard Marks, was at lunch with the Johnsons when Lyndon told Zephyr and Sammy to "get ready to go to Austin."

"Senator, I'm not going to do it," blurted out Zephyr, desperate to avoid its "whites only" prohibitions. "When Sammy and I drive to Texas and I have to go to the bathroom, like Lady Bird or the girls, I am not allowed to go to the bathroom. I have to find a bush and squat. When it comes time to eat, we can't go into restaurants. We have to eat out of a brown bag. And at night, Sammy sleeps at the front of the car with the steering wheel around his neck, while I sleep in the back. We are not going to do it again."

Lyndon certainly listened. Later, in 1964, when Lyndon put his signature to the Civil Rights Act, he drew Zephyr aside and pressed the pen he had used into her hand. "You deserve this more than anybody else," he said.

HUNTING BORIS YELTSIN

Forget about any image you have of Boris Yeltsin as a boozehound. In his down-time he was to be found hunting and fishing. He learned to hunt in Sverdlovsk, and it was love at first blast. Yeltsin liked to track game with small, intimate circles of suitably bloodthirsty fellow hunters, not with large packs of men, particularly in Zavidovo, one of his official residences, in the spring. Hidden deep in the un-dergrowth till dawn, Boris listened for the mating call of the wood grouse. Then, when the wood grouse stood in silhouette against the rising sun, his song of love rising from his plumed throat: BANG. Boris found it terribly exciting. Apart from the amorous grouse, the forests of Zavidovo held wild boar, stag, and Siberian deer.

As a real stress buster, Yeltsin, equipped with a map, might take off with his fishing gear to one of the islands on the lakes of Zavidovo. There he could fish, have a nap, and best of all make his beloved *ukha*, fish soup made to a rare recipe known to hunters. Once, he decided to take someone he obliquely referred to in his memoirs, *Midnight Diaries*, as a "foreign guest" on a boat around the Zavidovo lakes. Yeltsin's black briefcase slid around the bottom of the boat—one can only ask *why* he had this with him, as did the "foreign visitor" who kept glancing ner-vously at the briefcase and seemed to feel safest perched dangerously close to the edge of the boat. Clearly, he thought the briefcase contained some nuclear mate-rial. How the foreign visitor laughed when they got to the island and the briefcase was opened to reveal . . . gherkins and two bottles of vodka! The nuclear material, Yeltsin confided jokingly, was on the second boat, under guard. Perhaps they ate ukha afterward, cooked the way Yeltsin describes:

"You take a big pot and boil a dozen different types of fish together. Then, after you've added some huge tomatoes and other ingredients, you drop in a sizzling piece of wood from the fire. It gives the soup the flavor of wood smoke and gets rid of that fish-fat taste."

At home, far from the lands of the hunt, Boris liked to watch thoughtfully while his wife, Naina, cooked: it was as if, he thought, Naina was trying to protect her family through food. Her many-layered cakes were acts of sheer kindness, and her many meatballs a symbol of her generosity. Most of all, Boris loved it when she baked blini at New Year's Eve at their dacha. Naina made these in an ancient Rus-sian oven that nested beneath an overhang outside the dacha; the family ate blini outdoors as Naina miracled them out of the stove. She dished them hot onto the table even as it snowed, and the table was ringed by hot plates of steaming blini set among small drifts of snow.

Ukha (. . . as told to me by a Zavidovo hunter)

FOR THE FISH STOCK

2 cups onions, finely sliced
1 carrot, chopped
2 bay leaves
8 black peppercorns
generous pinch of
   sea salt
1 bunch parsley

1 rib celery, complete with leaves,
   chopped
twist of lemon peel
glass of white wine
3 lb. fish trimmings (spines, heads,
   and tails!)
2 egg whites

FOR THE SOUP

2 huge tomatoes, chopped
1 lb. mixed white fish fillets
1 lime, thinly sliced

1 tbsp. finely chopped dill
lump of burning wood (optional)

In a deep stockpot, combine 4 pints of water with the onions, carrot, bay leaves, peppercorns, sea salt, parsley, celery, lemon peel, white wine, and fish trimmings. Bring this to a boil and then lower the heat, partially cover the pot, and simmer gently for 30 minutes. Next, strain the stock through fine mesh, bearing down with a metal spoon on the vegetables and fish to extract their last trickle of flavor and goodness. Return the stock to the pan.

Now it is time to clarify your stock. Beat the egg whites to a froth, add them to the stock, and bring the stock to a hard, rolling boil, stirring constantly with a whisk. The stock will froth and threaten to overflow—now is the time to remove it from the heat and let it sit for 5 minutes. Get a sieve and line it with muslin or some other fine material (I use a jam-making jelly bag). Pour the stock into the sieve and place over a bowl; leave this entirely undisturbed to drain slowly into the bowl. One drained, discard the soil-like mess in the sieve. Taste the stock; you may need to add more seasoning.

This is the final stage in making ukha. Pour the stock back into a deep pan and bring to a boil. Throw in the huge tomatoes. Gently slip the white fish fillets into the broth and turn the heat to low. Simmer for about 4 minutes, and then remove the now opaque fish fillets from the broth. Slice the fillets into 2-inch pieces; arrange in the base of individual soup bowls. Now is the time to decide if you want to throw a chunk of burning wood in; it will make the soup sizzle! Finally, pour the fish broth over the fish and then decorate with slices of lime and chopped dill.

IT WASN'T ALL ABOUT THE NUTS:
JIMMY CARTER

Granted, Jimmy discovered the power of nuts early on in life. His mother, Lillian Carter, grew and farmed pecans; Jimmy and others shook them off the trees, and his mother picked them up, saying it was like "picking up money off the ground." One of his earliest occupations was selling peanuts in Plains, Georgia, but, in case this makes the Carters sound as if they were simple nut eaters, they liked their food far fancier than that of the majority of inhabitants of Plains. A truckload of grapefruit was once dumped on the road near the Carters' house, and all the local people went out to help themselves. But only the Carters had *any* experience of eating grapefruit and briefly became grapefruit consultants; people grumbled that they just couldn't get along with grapefruit, even when it was . . . boiled!

Christmas at the Carters' home meant that Jimmy's aunt Ethel made endless amounts of cake; if it wasn't upside down, or angel or coconut, it was Jimmy's adored Japanese fruitcake. His mother, Lillian, was a pragmatic, no-nonsense cook, whose starring dessert at Christmastime seemed biblically inspired, called ambrosia, and served after turkey and sweet potato soufflé. Ambrosia involved Jimmy piercing coconuts by hammering nails into their "eyes" (he loved this), drinking their milk, and biting into their glossy white flesh. Ambrosia, for the uninitiated, is a heavenly pile of sugared oranges and flakes of fresh coconut. But it was over to Jimmy's father, James Earl, for the really big gestures in cooking; he would conjure up waffles or battercakes for breakfast and a remarkable "special occasion" conglomeration called sousemeat of pigs' faces, ears, feet, and "other parts," which was boiled into a gloop, richly seasoned, and then shaped into a loaf. James Earl liked to crack: "There are two things you never want to see being made: sousemeat and laws." Sousemeat was produced whenever visitors were in the offing, and the Carter children suspected it was their father's way of trying to keep visitors at bay.

At Christmas, though, James Earl made Lane cake, with buttery raisins, white icing, and drenched with bourbon. His eggnog too was legendary, involving a whole family effort with everyone beating eggs and whisking cream; the aim was to have as little "loose" liquid at the bottom of each glass of eggnog, and the children had their eggnog in alcohol-free bowls.

Daddy's Eggnog

18 eggs, chilled
1½ cups sugar
1 pint whiskey, rum, or
   bootlegged moonshine

1½ pints double cream
ground nutmeg

Separate the egg whites from the yolks; cream the yolks until they thicken, slowly adding the sugar and spirits. Set aside in the fridge. Now, using an electric whisk, beat the egg whites until stiff; do the same with the double cream. Gently fold these together and then fold in the egg yolk mixture. Serve in glass eggnog cups. Sprinkle with grated nutmeg.

Ambrosia (Warning: This recipe contains some scenes of violence toward coconuts.)

1 to 2 fresh, hairy coconuts, enough
   for 3 cups of coconut meat (shake
   them to make sure you hear the
   slosh of milk inside)

2 tbsp. white confectioner's
   sugar
12 oranges, peeled and sliced

Pierce the top of the coconut and drain off the coconut milk. Smash the coconut using a hammer. Prise the white meat out of the shell. It will still have a brown skin on it, which you need to strip off. Now grate the coconut finely until you have about 3 cups. Now combine the confectioner's sugar and oranges in a bowl. Get a large glass or crystal bowl and put a third of the oranges in the base of the bowl. Top this with 1 cup of coconut. Repeat twice more. Cool in the fridge and then serve.

When Jimmy made it to the presidency and the White House, he invited Lillian to visit and asked the chef and kitchen staff if they could rustle up some lovely, homely Southern cooking. The cook snootily replied, "Yes [. . .] we've been fixing that kind of food for the servants for a long time." Hmmm. Jimmy was to play a Southern-eating card, with his push for pork chops and corn bread, ham, grits, and red beans and rice at the presidential table. As the Carters' chef testified: "The Carters didn't want to live high on the hog [. . .] They wanted to live like the average American." Mrs. Carter was bowled over by being able to order anything she wanted for breakfast in the White House, while Jimmy, frugally, asked the head chef to trim the food bill. The Carters had a shock when their food bills for the first ten days in residence turned up. It came to a total of $600 and was the first time they discovered that the president pays his own food bill, a tradition started by Hoover (damn him), which must have been tough on Hoover's pocket, given that he and "Mother" liked to dine on seven-course meals even when it was just the two of them. Perhaps the most frugal of White House reigns was under the sway of Mamie Eisenhower, who liked to monitor the fate of any leftovers at the table: when three visitors left their guinea fowl at the side of their plate, the fowl was reincarnated as a chicken salad, on Mamie's orders. Famously, she redeployed secret servicemen to nip off to the grocery store to redeem coupons she'd clipped out of the morning paper. At White House dinners, the Carters, perhaps pushing their stock, liked to serve visiting dignitaries Southern peanut soup.

Southern Peanut Soup (. . . to be served before the boiled grapefruit)

8 tbsp. chilled, unsalted butter, cut into sticks
1 onion, finely chopped
2 stalks celery, finely chopped
3 tbsp. all-purpose flour
4 pints homemade chicken stock

2 cups peanut butter
1 tbsp. lemon juice
generous pinch of sea salt
1 tbsp. roughly crushed peanuts
1 tbsp. chopped lovage (or celery leaves)

Melt the butter in a large, deep pan. Soften the onion and celery in the melted butter, allowing them to sweat. Now add the all-purpose flour and, stirring quickly, blend with the buttery mixture. Still stirring, pour in the chicken stock, one warm golden sloop at a time; still stirring, bring gradually to a boil. Reduce the heat and simmer for 30 minutes. Remove from heat and cool till gently warm. Drain the soup, pressing down on the vegetables to extract their goodness. Now put the peanut butter in a large mixing bowl and, using a whisk, add the soup stock slowly, blending together as you go. Now add the lemon juice and a pinch of salt. Taste and adjust seasoning as you wish. Return the soup to the heat and warm through.

To serve, sprinkle with crushed peanuts and the bright green chopped lovage or celery leaves.

MIDNIGHT SNACKS WITH MAGGIE THATCHER

When their eyes met over dinner on a blind date at the Dartford Conservative Club, it wasn't just physical allure that drew Margaret Roberts to Denis Thatcher; it was a shared politics and their mutually held conviction that socialists the length of Britain were up to all sorts of low criminal activity. He whisked her home in his car, and their courtship engulfed the next two years, conducted in the bistros of Chelsea or the eating dens of Soho.

After marriage, motherhood arrived (brilliantly, when Margaret presented the twins to Denis for the first time he exclaimed, "My God, they look like rabbits!"). A young mother, Margaret knitted the twins blue jerseys and baked them pancakes, themed birthday cakes, or her adorable ginger cake (once, distracted by a phone call on parliamentary business, she baked her measuring teaspoon into the cake), and rustled up cozy Conservative dinners for Denis's colleagues and friends from the legal world.

Iron Lady Ginger Cake

250 g. self-raising flour
1 tsp. bicarbonate of soda
1 tsp. ground cinnamon
1 tbsp. ground ginger
150 g. butter, softened
8 orbs sticky stem ginger, drained
    of their syrup, but reserving 6 tbsp.
    of the russet gingery syrup

100 g. molasses (black treacle)
100 g. golden syrup
100 g. dark muscovado sugar
200 ml. milk
2 eggs
100 g. light muscovado sugar
    (for the cake's top)

FOR THE BUTTERCREAM ICING

5 oz. soft butter
10 oz. confectioner's sugar

2 tbsp. freshly squeezed lemon juice
2 tbsp. finely grated lemon zest

Preheat the oven to 160 degrees centigrade. Sieve the flour, bicarbonate of soda, cinnamon, and ginger into a large bowl. Add the softened butter and rub it into the flour using your fingertips, until the mix has a bread-crumby texture. Roughly chop the orbs of stem ginger and sprinkle these into the flour mixture.

In a saucepan, place the molasses, syrup, the ginger syrup, the dark muscovado sugar, and the milk. Heat gently, and stir until the sugar has dissolved. Now increase the heat until the mixture is just below boiling point.

Iron Lady Ginger Cake (continued)

Pour this milky, treacle mixture slowly into the flour mixture, combining the two with a wooden spoon. Beat the 2 eggs and then add these to the mixture and combine.

Butter a baking tin, pour in the rich ginger cake mix, sprinkle the top with the light muscovado sugar, and bake in the preheated oven for 50 minutes. The cake should be firm to the touch when ready. Should the cake require longer in the oven, then protect the top from burning with aluminum foil.

When the cake is ready, remove it from the oven, leave the cake to stand for 10 minutes, and cool on a wire rack.

Meanwhile, make the butter icing. In a large bowl, beat the butter until it is soft. Add the first half of the confectioner's sugar; beat and then repeat with the other half until the icing is smooth. Add the lemon juice and zest and beat until well combined.

Using a palette knife, spread the icing thickly over the ginger cake. Leave no one alone with the cake—one taste of the icing and it will not be safe. Lock the kitchen door and hide the key . . .

Margaret's penchant for ginger goes back to her Grantham childhood. Her mother, Beatrice Roberts, was a skilled cook, produced shelves of baked goods for the family twice a week, and was famed for her Grantham gingerbreads (the ginger being supplied no doubt by Mr. Roberts's grocer's shop). These tasty biscuits are much paler than the customary British ginger biscuit, as they are made without molasses. Showing the sort of wartime resolve that she prided herself on in the several wars she waged on Britain's behalf in the course of her premiership, young Margaret scoured the country lanes of Grantham for blackberries and rosehips and liked to debate the pros and cons of World War II in the Grantham fish-and-chip-shop queue.

Woe betide Margaret if any garlic should have snuck itself into those early Thatcher family meals—Denis loathed the stuff, and the kitchen door *had* to be kept shut when onions were fried. Lobster flan was the young housewife's pride, as were elegant marquises with their scaffolding of sponge fingers. Denis sounds a bit stodgy when it comes to grub. Salmon steak with peas and chips followed by steamed sultana pudding constituted his number one meal (though he was also partial to lemon soufflé, which he had for his seventieth birthday).

Grocer's Grantham Gingerbreads

8 tbsp. softened, unsalted butter
4 tbsp. granulated sugar
1 egg, separated
2 cups all-purpose flour

pinch of baking powder
1 tbsp. minced, crystallized ginger
1 tbsp. ground ginger

Heat the oven to 150 degrees centigrade. In a bowl, cream together the softened butter and the sugar. Add the egg yolk and mix thoroughly. Sift the flour over this; add a pinch of baking powder, the crystallized ginger, and the ground ginger. Mix thoroughly. In a separate bowl, whip the egg white until it forms into peaks. Fold the egg white into the biscuit mix. Lightly shape the mixture into circular biscuit shapes.

Butter a baking tray, or line with greased paper. Put the biscuits on the tray, leaving at least 1 inch between them, and bake for about 35 minutes.

Steamed Sultana Pudding

8 oz. self-raising flour
2 tsp. baking powder
pinch of sea salt
4 oz. butter, cut into little cubes
2 rounded tbsp. vanilla granulated
  sugar

6 oz. plump raisins
2 eggs
1 tsp. vanilla essence
2 tsp. grated zest of lemon
a little milk

Sift the flour and baking powder into a large bowl. Add a pinch of sea salt. Add the cubed butter and rub it into the flour, until the mixture is crumbly. Stir in the vanilla sugar and the raisins. Whisk the eggs. Using a wooden spoon, stir the eggs into the mixture. Add the teaspoon of vanilla essence and the grated zest of lemon. Keep stirring, working toward a smooth consistency, adding the scant amount of milk if necessary. Eventually, the mixture should have a dropping consistency.

Butter a Pyrex heat-proof basin. Pour the sponge mixture in and cover in the following way: butter a foot-square piece of grease-proof paper. Fold two 1-inch pleats into the center of it. Repeat this process with aluminum foil of the same size (but unbuttered!). Place these, grease-proof paper first, foil as the outer layer, over the top of the pudding basin. Make sure they are at right angles to each other (this will let the pudding rise and "grow"). Secure these homemade "lids" with string, tightly knotted around the rim of the bowl. Steam for 1½ hours. To do this, simply fill a third of a large saucepan with boiling water, lower the pudding in, cover the pan, and cook for about an hour and a quarter. After this time, remove the string, foil, and grease-proof paper and tip the pudding out onto a plate (best done be covering the pudding basin with a plate and then turning the whole lot over, holding the plate tightly against the bowl, and not allowing slippage).

Serve with custard.

Happy Birthday Lemon Soufflé

This delicious lemony soufflé should be eaten on the same day that you make it, as it gradually begins to sink as soon as it's ready.

½ oz. gelatin
5 tbsp. cold water
4 organic medium-size eggs
8 oz. vanilla granulated sugar
finely grated rind of 3 lemons
juice of 2½ lemons
½ pint rich double cream

hazelnuts, toasted and chopped
pistachio nuts, toasted and split to
    reveal their pea-green souls
finely chopped almonds
1 twinkling glass or crystal soufflé dish,
    about 6 inches in diameter

Get the soufflé dish ready. Measure out a length of grease-proof paper long enough to go around the outside of the top of the soufflé dish. Fold this in two, doubling it up. This band must be a couple of inches (about 3 or 4) deep. Now tie it around the outside rim of the soufflé dish, securing it with a piece of string. Its open edge must face you and must stand about 2 inches above the dish, like a crown, and will help your finished soufflé to stand proud, about an inch above the edge of the soufflé dish. Once your soufflé is ready to serve, you will remove this crown by warming a palette knife in hot water and then very gently and carefully drawing the blade of the palette knife around the groove space between the dual grease-proof paper layers.

Fill a pan (large enough to have a Pyrex bowl placed inside it) a third deep with water. Bring to a gentle boil. Place the ½ ounce of gelatin in 5 tablespoons of cold water. Separate the eggs, reserving the yolks and white separately. Whisk the egg yolks and mix these in a heat-proof bowl with the sugar, finely grated lemon zest, and juice. Place the bowl over the heated water (the bowl should not touch the water). Whisk the egg mixture continuously until the sugar dissolves. The mixture will thicken a little. When the sugar has dissolved, take the basin out of the pan and place on the work surface. Continue to whisk until the mixture (and the basin) becomes cool—if you stop before it's cool, the mixture may well scramble! But its temperature should *never* be below room temperature.

Next, pour the gelatin and the water you've been soaking it in into a pan and place over a low heat. The gelatin will quickly melt into the water. Prepare a large bowl of cold water studded with ice cubes. Keep to the side. Whisk the double cream until it begins to thicken—the texture of the cream should be such that it leaves a clear, raised trail across its surface when you lift the whisk. Now fold it into the egg mixture. Add the gelatin water. Make sure the mix you're adding the gelatin to isn't too cold; otherwise you'll be left with strands of gelatin going through your soufflé. Place this bowl of mixture into the larger bowl containing the iced water.

Now it is time to use the egg whites. These you must now whisk until they are firm and stiff (though they should never be whipped to the point of becoming desiccated and dry). Using a metal spoon, fold and cut the puffy egg whites gently and carefully into the egg mixture. Stir very gently.

Pour this soufflé mixture into the soufflé dish and place it in a cool, quiet place to set. This will take up to 4 hours.

When you are almost ready to serve, remove the grease-proof paper and decorate the top of the soufflé with concentric circles of the hazelnuts, pistachios, and finely chopped almonds.

Margaret (aka The Boss) worked incessantly; rumor had it at Atlas Preservative Co. (Denis's place of work) that he dithered about there after hours to give Margaret room to work. Indeed, Denis was very good at tucking himself away: the night of Margaret's election as prime minister in 1979, while Margaret shared a well-deserved Chinese takeaway with her staff in 10 Downing Street (she'd taken to chain-eating biscuits on the campaign trail), Denis dined alone on baked beans on toast. Margaret, hair chiseled out by the hairdresser, like an aureole of political power, could never shake off a secret awe of fate—it wasn't good to chance it, and thus it was that Margaret never kept champagne on ice at the end of any personal or political contest. So no champers that night, perhaps? In the two-weeks lead-up to her arrival in Number 10, Margaret went on a murderous egg diet of twenty-eight eggs per week (there is something almost epic and Greek about the idea of the Iron Lady preparing for power by eating unfertilized embryos), plus the odd grapefruit thrown in for good measure, as she didn't want to cut a tubby figure for reading her Saint Francis speech at the grand photo call on entry to Number 10.

The Downing Street flat was pretty basic and lacked luxuries. This was the way Margaret liked to live "over the shop," as she called Number 10. Often it was ten or eleven in the evening when Margaret popped into the kitchen to rustle up something quick (she knew every conceivable combination of eggs and cheese). There was never ice for drinks (Denis said it impaired alcohol to dilute it), Margaret didn't take it in her favorite tipple of whiskey and soda (a nightcap often fixed for her by Denis), and frozen lasagnas and shepherd's pies were the order of the day. There was always, as Margaret put it, something to cut at in the fridge (and we're not talking Geoffrey Howe here). When stuck without any help from staff, Margaret rustled up food for any minister working after hours with her (a poached egg on Bovril toast was one of her specialties), until one MP grew so frustrated in their discussion by Margaret hopping up and down to look at her frozen peas that he mutinied. Thatcher also surprised Indira Gandhi at lunch when she started sweeping away their plates after eating, like a bossy dinner lady—while continuing to talk seamlessly about global political issues.

Poached Egg on Bovril Toast (. . . a prime minister's midnight snack)

splash of vinegar	butter
1 medium egg	½ teaspoon Bovril
½-inch-thick slice of sourdough bread	freshly ground black pepper
	timer

Half fill a medium-size pan with water. Bring to a boil and then lower the heat slightly to a medium simmer. Add a splash of vinegar. Break the egg into the

Poached Egg on Bovril Toast (*continued*)

simmering water and cook for 1 minute—set the timer. Do not cover the pan. Now take the pan off the heat and leave the egg to sit in the hot water for 10 more minutes—use the timer again. After 7 minutes is up, toast the sourdough bread. Once toasted, butter immediately, so that there are little pools of butter on the toast, then add a scraping of Bovril across the toast. Remove the egg from the water with a slotted spoon, shake the spoon gently to remove water, and place on top of the toast. Pepper and serve.

Enter the frozen meals, prepared by the lunchtime cooking staff. That way Margaret could bolt her food the way she liked it. Both Margaret and Denis were gauche in their own ways; for instance, when she was at Buckingham Palace for tea, Margaret quickly turned over the side plates to check their origin, while Denis at state dinners could run short of things to say to visiting dignitaries and once resorted to asking the foreign wife of one official, "Likey soupy?" One of the reasons Denis so liked Ronald Reagan was because he found him easy to talk to. Perhaps boarding school was to blame, but Denis liked people and food to be reliable . . . reliably the same, again and again and every day. Particularly when it came to chunks and breakfast: marmalade had to have chunks, as did fresh grapefruit, each chunk easily detachable from the whole. If cherry jam were on offer, it had to have chunks of cherry. Perhaps that way he could be sure there were no Trade Unionists hiding in his jam, or any of the "bloody BBC poofs and Trots" that he so detested. Denis was also a stickler about the way his meat was cooked, and he considered any lamb chop that didn't look as though it had died in the flames of a cockpit to be underdone. "I'll still be able to taste the wool," he'd sigh, sending his chops back. At one point, served a perfectly respectable tournedos of beef, he called the waiter back and prodded the steak with a fork, while making a long, low mooing sound. If a portion of poultry looked suspicious to him, he ordered a cheese roll, squashed it into a chicken breast shape, and ate that. Restaurant menus were lost on Denis—if his eye wasn't caught by salmon steak or charred chop, his options were seriously limited. Once, his family took him to the glamorous restaurant at the Hotel Walserhof in the exclusive Swiss ski resort of Klosters (a treasured eating hole of Prince Charles). Desperately, Denis scanned the menu for something edible and happened on émince de veau. Once it was dished up, though, he barely tasted it. When asked why, he could only reply, as if summing up the essence of all things: "It just wasn't mince."

It was common practice to present Margaret Thatcher as either the Iron Lady or as an explosive sexual lure to her male political allies; hence the magnetism or chemistry that the British press breathlessly reported between her and Gorbachev (*and* Reagan—the hussy). When Thatcher and Gorbachev met in Chequers in December 1984, their lunch dessert of oranges in caramel was quickly forgotten as they sparred over political ideologies, their interpreters stumbling to keep up. Meanwhile, Raisa Gorbachev was left to muse with Michael Jopling (then agricultural secretary) over whether the USSR or the UK came tops on recipes for potatoes.

Détente Oranges in Caramel

4 large seedless oranges

FOR THE CARAMEL
4 oz. granulated sugar   ⅛ pint warm water
⅛ pint cold water

Pour the sugar and cold water into a thick-based pan. Dissolve the sugar over a very low heat, but do not stir. The water must come to a boil after the sugar has dissolved, so as soon as the sugar has melted, raise the heat a little. Boil steadily until a dark, rich caramel has formed. Remove from the heat momentarily and carefully—put on oven gloves—pour the warm water into the caramel. Return the pan to the heat and melt the caramel into the water. Transfer into a bowl and leave to cool.
    Grate 2 teaspoons of zest from the oranges and pop into the cooling caramel. Peel the oranges, removing all peel and pith, slice them finely, and lay the slices in a glass bowl. Pour the caramel over and serve.

Not all of Margaret's encounters with foreign politicians have been as pleasurably charged with tension. It was 1991, and Margaret was in Beijing—John Major had succeeded her as prime minister. She enjoyed some delightfully odd moments in Beijing, one being when the Communist Party general secretary, Mr. Jiang, caroled a Romanian folk song to her and chatted chirpily about Shakespeare. But that was later, after her encounter with one Mr. Rong Yren . . .
    Her host for some time in Beijing was the redoubtable Yren, deputy chairman of the People's Congress, who enjoyed an opulent lifestyle in his Hu Tong traditional courtyard house in Beijing. Margaret's joy in her surroundings was tempered when she caught sight of Yren's stuffed dog, which gazed back moodily at her from its glass case. The glassy stare of a dead dog seemed, however, to be the only eye contact Margaret was destined to have: the Chinese liked to have everyone sit in a row for formal discussions, and Margaret was irritated at having to crane around to

look at whoever was speaking. Could it be, she ruminated, a sneaky Oriental ploy to avoid direct eye contact? Things went from worse to worse when Yren valiantly suggested that women in the West should be encouraged to seek advancement (nervously hoping to curry favor with Margaret). She finally managed to lock him into a hard stare—this was a woman, after all, who thought women were best armed with handbags.

Yren must have been relieved to hear the dinner gong, but for Margaret, it presaged an unusual culinary hell. A huge table filled a small room, and specialties from Yren's home province arrived in unstoppable waves at the table. A large platter of giant foot-sole-gray prawns arrived, bug-eyed in their sauce. Taking her cue from the Chinese diners, Margaret followed the customary way of eating these, chewing through the horny shell, which then, robbed of its gelatinous core, had to be dropped from the side of the eater's mouth; the sort of dining ritual, in short, that many of us associate with the onset of senility. She breathed a light sigh of relief when the table was cleared—but wait! A bath-like tureen was brought in, meaty steam billowing forth. The lid was lifted. Within bobbed something large and white. A substantial ham, coated thickly in a scarf of soft white fat. The next course had arrived.

Thatcher, then, was no stranger to the politics of eating and used her cunning knowledge of French gluttony to cut French president Giscard d'Estaing down to size in Strasbourg in 1979. It was Margaret's first European Council meeting and—at least as Margaret would have it—Britain's reputation was in tatters. Her chief opponent on European budgetary policy was Giscard, and it was nearing 7 o'clock in the evening . . . Giscard, desperate for his dinner, suggested they postpone discussion of budgetary issues till the next morning. No, said Margaret and stood her ground, knowing, with deep feline cunning, that Giscard would be much more amenable to her ideas on an empty stomach with his mind "turning to the prospect of French *haute cuisine* and *grand crus*." Sure enough, she had him nailed and won the day. Her heart swelled with pride when she overheard a foreign official say: "Britain is back."

TAKING TEA WITH "TRICKY DICK" NIXON

Dick Nixon's food memories stretched back beyond the presidential dinners, beyond his cottage cheese and pineapple lunches as a young lawyer, to the early Quakerish poverty of the first Nixon home in Orange County, California. His mother, Hannah, worked endlessly, not just baking pies but also making strawberry ice cream, which Richard delivered. Old Mr. Nixon and the boys cooked the meals: tinned spaghetti, pork and beans, tinned chili, burgers, and fried eggs. Young Richard's main role was in the mashed potato department: he could mash them so smooth that right into middle age, Nixon was known in his family as a wonderful masher of potatoes. Those foodstuffs all stayed favorites, like familiar friends. Local politics were hotly chewed over at the dinner table, but prayers and Bible verses were part of mealtimes then too . . . although Richard and his brothers prayed hard that something bad would happen to their goat, as their mother had put them on an intensive goat milk diet, having read somewhere of its health benefits.

Perhaps the memory of his adored mother carried Nixon through the dark times of Watergate and impeachment: Hannah Milhous loved making angel food cake, but it was only good, she told her son, if she could beat some of the cold early morning air into it before it went in the oven. There she'd be, framed by the doorway in the blue predawn air, beating and beating the angel food batter with a wooden spoon.

All the jittery years of the Nixon presidency, of "Tricky Dick" and "Plastic Pat," began far more innocently and romantically for Richard and Pat Nixon. In the small town of Whittier, twenty-five miles from Los Angeles, a young lawyer, Richard Nixon worked through lunch at his desk, supplied by his secretary with pineapple malteds and burgers from the local drugstore. Acting in an amateur dramatic production of the play *The Dark Tower*, Nixon had become entranced by the winsome Pat Ryan, who taught business and carried an air of flowery glamour about her. Pat played Daphne Martin, a bitter, cast-off mistress whose language rocketed on stage; her performance was watched by the Quakerish Hannah Milhous, who observed purse-lipped her son's paramour on stage. What was she to make of it? Pat had perfumed red-gold hair and was cool and strong with slightly sulky, peachy skin. Dick asked her for dates again and again, and she finally agreed to go on a date with Dick at the Kiwanis Young Professionals Club ladies' night (note, young professionals were *not* ladies). Gradually Pat succumbed to Dick's advances, inviting him around so she could—perhaps euphemistically— "burn a hamburger" for him.

This was followed up by tea at the Nixon family home on a Sunday afternoon, as Nixon still lived with his parents, right up to becoming a partner in a law firm. The air was tense as Quaker sensibilities clashed with new woman values. Hannah poured the coffee and offered around her home-baked, special-recipe strawberry shortcake. Finally, Pat bonded with Hannah by getting up at 5 a.m. to hop around to the Nixon house to help Hannah make the fifty pies she made each morning; she was the pie supplier to the Nixon Market (pies made very good return, and cherry pie was her best seller), and Pat *never* trod on anyone's toes by interfering with Hannah's special pie recipe.

Mother-in-Law's Cherry Pie

FOR THE CRUST

½ cup shortening, chilled and diced

6 tbsp. chilled butter, diced

1½ cups all-purpose flour

½ tsp. sea salt

3 to 4 tbsp. ice cold water

FOR THE FILLING

2 cups fresh cherries, stoned and halved

½ cup sugar

2 tbsp. cornstarch, combined with water to form a thin paste

1 small can of sour, morello cherries

1 tbsp. butter

2 tbsp. milk

In a pan, combine the cherries and the sugar. Bring to a boil, stir in the cornstarch paste, and remove from the heat. Cool. Preheat the oven to 190 degrees centigrade. Now make the pie crust by rubbing the shortening and butter through the flour and sea salt until the mix has a bread-crumb-like, crumbly consistency. Now pour 3 tablespoons of the iced water over the mix and combine into a ball. If it's too crumbly, and the dough doesn't stick together, then add the fourth tablespoon. Wrap the dough up and let it chill for an hour in the fridge.

Butter an 8- or 9-inch pie dish. Combine the poached cherries with morello cherries.

Now roll the pastry out on a floured surface and line the pie dish with the pastry, reserving pastry for the lid. Trim the excess dough off the edge. Prick the base of the pastry with a fork. Fill the pie base with aluminum foil topped with baking beans and bake blind in the oven for 12 minutes. After this, remove the tinfoil and beans and bake for a further 2 minutes. Remove from the oven and cool. Meanwhile, roll out the lid for the pie shell.

Now pour the cherry filling into the crust and dot the surface with butter. Brush the edge of the crust with milk and place the lid on top. Seal with a fork. Brush the top with milk, sprinkle with sugar, and bake in the oven for about 30 minutes.

Hannah was suspicious, though: was this Pat's way of getting her claws into young Dick? Little did she realize that it was Dick doing all the chasing; Pat refused to sleep with him and kept dodging the subject of marriage whenever it came up. But slowly, gradually, Pat fell in love with Dick, and their togetherness was signaled by home-cooked spaghetti dinners and trips to the movies. Finally, she agreed to become Mrs. Nixon when he proposed at sunset, and the lovers were bathed in pink and gold light, which seemed to melt into the Pacific.

The Nixons had very little money; the Great Depression had just started to lift, and every penny counted. Hannah baked their wedding cake, and they took their own food with them on their Mexican honeymoon: a case of canned foods, from which the labels had been peeled off—this made for interesting savory breakfasts and fruity evening meals. Back home in Whittier, the newlyweds lived in a rented apartment, and on Sundays Pat baked biscuits and served them with Dick's favorite honey and jams. Entertaining at home made them feel even more married; they invited Evlyn Dorn, Nixon's secretary—the same one who trotted about with pineapple malteds—and her husband for their very first dinner party. Pat cooked up a pot of spaghetti with meat sauce while Dick made the salad and mixed the drinks—later, when the Nixons took people out for dinner, he liked to order Spanish and Mexican food but also insisted on ordering for everyone there. He was always "the highlight of the party because he had a wonderful sense of humor," Pat later recounted. "He would keep everyone in stitches." He also pitched in to help prepare the rest of the meal. "Remember the time when you even made the chop suey?" Pat wrote him during World War II of the fun they'd had at those dinner parties. "I never shall forget how sweet you were . . . the night I had the teachers for a wiener roast—you [. . .] helped with the salad, bought the pies." Pat always washed up her dishes before she went to bed, and Dick dried them down.

On their first wedding anniversary on June 21, 1941, they sped through the desert by night in their car to get to New Orleans for a romantically glorious meal of oysters Rockefeller before catching a boat bound for Panama. They knew they would be separated by war; Dick was called up after the Japanese bombed Pearl Harbor, so the Nixons went to Cape Porpoise, Maine, and spent the weekend picking blueberries and eating lobster.

The presidency and its scandals lay ahead of them. Avarice, pride, and deceit proved far greater challenges than any wartime separation. Time could be found to relax in the Nixons' retreat, the "Western White House," La Casa Pacifica, which Nixon "bought" in 1969. So relaxing was it that once, when the TV was on and Nixon was feeding biscuits to his dogs, one of Nixon's security detail watched mutely as Nixon absent-mindedly popped a dog biscuit into his mouth. Oddly enough, though, when Nixon walked on the beach, he chose to remain in one of his navy blue suits, dress shoes kicking through the sand. Nor did the heat persuade him to don swimming trunks: even in high summer, Nixon insisted on a log fire.

While Nixon rarely drank before the Watergate scandal hit him, he began drinking more heavily as the pressure took its toll, downing a martini or a Manhattan.

"All he could handle was one or two," a Secret Service agent recalled. "He wouldn't be flying high, but you could tell he wasn't in total control of himself. He would loosen up, start talking more, and smile. It was completely out of character. But he had two, and that was that. He had them every other night. But always at the end of business and in the residence. You never saw him drunk in public."

It was August 9, 1974, and Nixon recognized the emotional resonance of his last day as president in the White House: his resignation was to take effect at noon, following the crippling Watergate scandal. Instead of sticking to his usual wheat germ and coffee, Nixon, barefoot and in his pajamas, turned up in the kitchen and pushed the boat out for breakfast by ordering a poached egg and corned beef hash. An odd choice for a last breakfast, a shift away from the cosmopolitan self-consciousness of wheat germ . . .

Corned Beef Hash

4 floury potatoes, diced into ½-inch cubes, skin still on
3 tbsp. groundnut oil
1 large onion, halved and sliced
1 clove garlic, pulped
¼ tsp. dried thyme
freshly ground black pepper

sea salt
¼ tsp. cumin
10 oz. tinned corned beef, crumbled
1 tbsp. Worcestershire sauce
Tabasco
1 tbsp. parsley, finely chopped
2 tbsp. scallions, minced

Three-quarters fill a medium-size saucepan with water; add a pinch of salt and then the diced potatoes. Simmer until the potato cubes just yield to a fork—about 5 minutes from boiling. Drain and set aside on a plate.

In a frying pan heat 2 tablespoons of the groundnut oil. When it is very hot, add the onion and garlic and fry for 3 minutes—the onions should blister a little. Push the onions to one side of the pan, add another tablespoon of oil, let it warm, and then add the potatoes. While they brown, add the thyme, black pepper, sea salt, and cumin. Keep moving and turning the potatoes and onions around the pan. After about 5 minutes, add the corned beef, Worcestershire, a dash of Tabasco, parsley, and scallions. Keep stirring and frying the hash for about 5 minutes and then serve.

Poached Egg

1 very fresh egg
½ tsp. white wine vinegar

Take a saucepan and fill it with about 4 inches of water. Bring it to a boil, and when you see fine, small bubbles beginning to form on the base of the pan, add half a teaspoon of vinegar to the water, stir the water to a swirl, and drop the egg into the very center of the pan. Switch a timer on for 2 to 2½ minutes and simmer very gently. Remove with a slotted spoon and serve on top of the corned beef hash.

Angel Food Cake

125 g. all-purpose flour
375 g. granulated sugar
12 egg whites
1 tsp. cream of tartar

1 tsp. vanilla extract
½ tsp. almond extract
2 tsp. grated lemon zest

Preheat the oven to 190 degrees centigrade. Butter a deep cake tin and dust with flour. Sift the flour and half the sugar together into a bowl. Keep to one side. Place the egg whites in a very large bowl and begin to whisk. Add the cream of tartar and vanilla and almond extracts and continue to whisk until the whites are in soft peaks. Add the remaining sugar and whisk until the whites are thick, glossy, and stiff. You will now have what resembles an elephantine white cloud in the bowl: don't panic, it will reduce in size when you fold in the flour and sugar. Now, using a large flat spoon, gently fold the flour and sugar into the egg whites. Scatter the lemon zest in too. Pockets of flour will form, so keep folding through the flour and sugar—but gently does it. This is the point when you should stand in your doorway in the early morning light to capture the cold new air in the angel food cake. Finally, pour the fluffy cloud of mixture into the tin. Bake for 30 minutes or until a toothpick inserted in the cake comes out clean. Cool on a wire rack.

Chapter 1

TUMMY TIME WITH WINSTON CHURCHILL

Winston Churchill was a creature of delightful, bluff food eccentricities: he always smoked a cigar in bed after breakfast—which ended at 9 a.m.; his ashtray was right next to his wastepaper basket, so there was always the danger of fire. He never inhaled his cigars, though, and liked to chew on the cigar when deep in thought, collecting his cigar ends for the pipe of his gardener. This was helped along by a postbreakfast whiskey and soda to moisten his throat—served an hour after breakfast.

And all this happened in bed. The cigars, the whiskey, British policy, the battle against Hitler, and breakfast. The day began when Churchill was immediately handed his glass of orange juice. It was always bottled—he didn't like freshly squeezed—and if it was raining, he'd roundly swear at the weather. He always slept with his own pillow; wherever he went at home and abroad he carried it with him, with his black satin eye mask tucked under it. Clad in his baroque black silk dressing gown with silver dragons, he'd brace himself for the day to come with a substantial English breakfast of cold chicken, or partridge and grouse when in season—though he was very partial to a grilled sole too. But he always had something hot with something cold (the cold was generally reserved by him the night before for his breakfast)—if breakfast was bacon and eggs, then he had to have a slice of ham accompanying it, racks of hot toast with lashings of butter, and jams and jellies. All with a pot of hot tea and an outsize cup. Wiping the last toast crumb from his lips, Winston perched in bed, his arms propped up with sponges, placed at each of his elbows to elevate his arms (he said the breakfast table hurt his elbows), and read the newspapers—including the Communist *Daily News*.

If there was no cabinet meeting at 11 a.m., Winston worked through till lunch in bed. Pets were never far from Churchill's bedside: his poodle Rufus, whose breath could wither flowers, was close by, panting gently through decayed gums. At the start of any meal at Chartwell, Rufus's bowl of dog food was brought in on a small mat and laid by Churchill's chair. The assembled company were not served till Rufus had polished off his nosh, and, in later years, Churchill's budgie Toby might be about, ready to do crash landings on people's heads and argue with himself in the breakfast silverware. A friend suggested to Churchill that he should teach Toby his telephone number in case he got lost, to which Churchill replied, "I don't know my telephone number."

Churchill's personal servant for some years was Norman McGowan, who took up the mantle of responsibility when one brilliantly named Fred Raven injured his leg. Norman went to Mrs. Churchill, Clementine or Clemmie as she was affectionately known, for his instructions; Winston stood alongside, rather like a demonstration model. Mrs. Churchill had few stipulations, but these were to prove comically difficult to enforce. "See that he is on time for meals and appointments. See that he wears an overcoat when it is cold." Very quickly, Norman found that Churchill was forever bolting outside without a coat. Privately, Clementine came to an arrangement with Norman that he trick Churchill into being on time for lunch. "Lunch will be at 1:45 p.m.—but tell Mr. Churchill the meal will be served at 1 p.m." Norman passed this on: "Lunch will be at 1, sir," and Churchill smiled darkly and turned up at 2. Clemmie tried fiddling with the clocks in his bedroom to trick him into punctuality, but Winston, bright with suspicion, insisted on sticking to the time as displayed on his watch.

If lunch was at Chartwell, Churchill's country house, it was often made by Churchill's ever-faithful cook, Mrs. Georgina Landemare (Clementine and Winston cheekily nicknamed their first cook "Dan Leno," after a burlesque cross-dressing pantomime dame); Norman used to try to prise him out of bed by various ingenious means, such as running downstairs to clang the front doorbell and then rushing back up to breathlessly declare, "The guests have arrived!" But then, instantly, Winston insisted on taking a bath, which he executed with a number of foibles, running his toes under the taps, blowing bubbles in the water, and making a "whale blowing" noise when finished. He was also rather fond of muttering in the tub; when Norman first heard Churchill holding forth in the bath, he asked if Winston were talking to him. The reply came, "I wasn't talking to you, Norman, I'm addressing the House of Commons."

The kitchens of Chartwell were dominated by a vast black coal range, full of glowing coals, crumbling and scarlet, and on top of the stove bubbled a seemingly bottomless stockpot. Mrs. Landemare could never go wrong if she served Winston what he called "good red beef," symbolizing England. During the years of rationing, Churchill grew tired of chicken and ducks at the table, as they were always a reliable source of protein in times of rationing, but even more so because Churchill was forever wondering if it was a bird he was on friendly terms with. He made a honking noise when he was in one of the meadows at Chartwell, and a bar-headed goose from Canada waddled excitedly toward him, and, keeping pace with Churchill but at a respectful webbed foot or two behind him, surveyed the Chartwell lakes with him, seemingly helping his inspection: he named it his "Flag Lieutenant"—once, earlier, in the lean times of World War I, he refused to carve a goose, telling Clemmie, "You'll have to carve it, Clemmie. He was my best friend." In the winter Churchill and his men went wooding, clearing scrubland and then building a big, roasting bonfire. They baked large potatoes in the embers, which the children cradled in their hands, steaming hot. The potato skins were bitter with charcoal.

Dinners at Chartwell were always fun: Charlie Chaplin might be there, fresh from the premier of *City Lights*—Churchill was very taken with him. Raiding the coat cupboard for a hat and coat, Chaplin did wonderful impersonations of Napoleon. Lonely Lawrence of Arabia turned up during the Christmas of 1933, roaring up the drive on his motorcycle, scattering gravel. He came under the alias Aircraftsman Shaw, as he was shy and hated publicity. Churchill's daughter, Mary, burst into the dining room to find Lawrence transformed into a prince of Arabia, dressed in flowing robes. Winston, who really enjoyed dressing up, would have found this great fun. Then they would all stay up most of the night, doing the fox-trot under the stars.

If lunch was to be had at Number 10 Downing Street (still with Mrs. Landemare as its cook), Clementine and Winston liked to lunch together, often with a few guests—Churchill loved having guests at meals. Cream always had a number one spot on the menu; as Winston sagely advised: "You should eat plenty of cream. It coats the sheaths of the nerves." Churchill's medical knowledge was equal to his own ability to cook: once, when he was threatening to leave Downing Street for Chartwell, deep in the English countryside, in order to get some real work done, Clementine told him this was impossible, as there was no one there to make him food. He protested, "I shall cook for myself. I can boil an egg. I've seen it done." An amazed silence followed.

After lunch, Winston trotted off to the House of Commons, returning for an afternoon nap later, often throwing his clothes off in a trail leading to the bed. He'd slip into a long silk vest—his skin was delicate, and he always favored silk underwear—pop a sleeping pill, and be out for the count for two hours. After? He'd dress again, have dinner, and then begin the real business of the day, often working through till 3 or 4 a.m., with a weary secretary alongside, her head falling into her dictation pad. Despite his late hours, Churchill boasted to a private secretary that he had few sleepless nights during World War II, thanks in part to the "red pills" his doctor supplied him with and his blue rubber hot-water bottle—with the exception of one gloomy sleep-tossed night when the Japanese sank two ships and the Germans took Crete. "What do you do in these circumstances?" asked the private secretary.

"Well, I just turn out the light, say bugger everybody, and go to sleep," Churchill replied.

In the popular imagination, Churchill seems to remain permanently in his sixties, arrested at the age he was when he led the British in World War II. It is easy to forget then that he had lived the life of a great adventurer, writer, and politician before that. When he arrived in Cuba with the 4th Hussars in 1895, in order to observe and report on their defense of the island with the Spanish, he thought he had stepped into the pages of *Treasure Island*. Gone were the sticky buns of his old public school, Harrow. Instead there were great quantities of oranges to be eaten while looking out for revolutionary insurgents—which Churchill did, glancing about the vines, the palms playing tricks with light and shadow, expecting to hear a bullet whistle past his ear at any point. But nothing happened, and the 4th Hussars had to stop for breakfast. The general's aide de camp offered Churchill a beguiling drink called "runcotelle," contained in an elongated metal bottle. Whatever it was, it was very agreeable to Winston. Only years later did he discovered that this was, after all, rum cocktail. Then the 4th Hussars and Churchill all took a nap; Churchill was to swear by the restorative power of a nap after lunch ever afterward and, on this occasion, the 4th Hussars snored away for four hours.

Fortunately, they were more awake at the end of lunch a few days later, despite the exhaustion of working with machetes to cut their way through the emerald green Cuban jungle. Churchill sat down against his horse and started to eat a very skinny half chicken when, suddenly, a burst of gunfire rang through the trees. A chestnut horse nearby—not his horse—started forward, a bullet having lodged itself between his ribs; just, Churchill, reflected humbly, as he looked at the widening red circle on the horse's burnished chest, within a foot of where his own balding head had been resting . . .

Runcotelle (Prepare for a nice, long nap afterward.)

½ pint dark, añejo rum	½ tsp. ground nutmeg
2 tbsp. sugar	½ tsp. ground cinnamon
1 pint water	

Pour the whole lot wildly into a flask, shake up, quaff, and hope you don't wake up in a jungle!

Three years later, Churchill was caught up in the whirlwind of war at the Battle of Omdurman in Sudan. While this battle has gone down in history as a bloodied example of British military superiority and Kitchener's brutality in massacring a near medieval army of Sudanese dervishes, from the ground, Churchill offered a prebattle view, which, of course, involves lunch. The merciless sun beat down on the British forces on their nine-day march across the desert to meet up with Kitchener and fight the fearsome Dervish army. The Nile looked as if it were made of molten steel or brass but offered a cooling, refreshing draft of water to the tired soldiers, who had spent the day chasing illusions of gleaming water on the ochre-yellow desert sands, while clad in pith helmets, padded clothes, and spine pads.

Churchill was ordered to set out on horseback to reconnoiter with Kitchener and his infantry troops. He cantered six miles across the Sudanese desert, only to spot the Union Jack and a very sunburned, red-faced Kitchener, who stared at Churchill over his heavy mustaches and listened to his report. The Dervishes, Churchill gasped, were on the advance. Kitchener asked, "How long do you think I have got?" To which Churchill replied, "You have got at least an hour." Kitchener nodded gravely, and Churchill worried if he'd got his timing wrong: would the bloodthirsty hordes of Dervishes be upon them before then? Then, out of the blue, came a cheery voice, "Come along and have some lunch!" All thoughts of death and responsibility sailed out of Winston's mind as he was happily led to a "low wall of biscuit boxes" over which was draped a white oilcloth. There were many bottles "of inviting appearance" and platters of bully beef and pickles. Kitchener vanished, but Churchill no longer cared: all he wanted was lunch. With great concentration he applied himself to the bully beef and the refreshments, watched by a vulture, which made longing, gurgling noises. It was like, Churchill said, "a race luncheon before the Derby."

Having won a seat for the Liberals in Dundee in 1908, Churchill was already an MP by the time he married Clementine Hozier and wrote to her mournfully on his visits to Dundee, on one occasion in October 1909 from the Queen's Hotel: "This hotel is a great trial to me. Yesterday morning I had half eaten a kipper when a huge maggot crept out and flashed his teeth at me. To-day I could find nothing nourishing for lunch but pancakes. Such are the trials the great and good men endure in the service of their country!" Even worse than maggoty kippers, Dundee held suffragettes who tailed Winston's movements in a motor car, until they were pelted with mud by ploughmen. Thank goodness, then, for London and its clubs. Considered too radical for membership at The Club, a political dining club, Churchill and his friend, the pugnacious Conservative MP F. E. Smith (who was to die early in life of cirrhosis of the liver!) founded their own dining club, The Other Club, in May 1911. It met fortnightly in private rooms at the Savoy Hotel; for years after, Churchill, a rug tucked over his lap, rolled up in his long black car, which he called "the Bullock Cart" because it was driven by his stoical chauffeur, Joe Bullock. Should the number of members at the Other Club table turn out to be thirteen, a large stuffed black cat named Kaspar was seated at the table, a napkin was draped about his neck, and he was served a full dinner and champagne. Eventually Kaspar vanished, and one member claimed to have caught sight of him in Hong Kong. Invariably, Winston's plate was heaped with roast rib of beef or, even better, an Irish stew with lots and lots of tiny onions and not too much gravy. Mostly, too, Churchill tended to go his own sweet way when ordering dessert and liked nothing so much as a gooey, blue-pitted wedge of Roquefort cheese alongside the honeyed curve of a peeled pear and a little pot of mixed ice cream.

By December 1915, Churchill was away at war, in the trenches in France, now Major Churchill, watching with increasing horror events unfold (this is a man who wrote to Clem that the most significant thing was the pointless barbarism of war). Churchill explored No Man's Land by moonlight, the only safe(ish) time to roam, and became familiar with the surreal sight of two bright red Belgian Tamworth (an English variety) pigs who could be seen trotting through the mud of No Man's Land, rooting about. The pigs survived shells and shots and never became anyone's bacon. Churchill's command found that they could sneak right up to the German wire and cut sections of it out as souvenirs for home; if this sounds foolhardy, it was even less of a bright idea to leave a Union Jack hooked to the wire as a calling card. The Germans were alerted to their presence and promptly decided to shell them, hitting two officers out of five. Churchill told Clemmie: "It was odd gobbling bacon & marmalade in the dugout, while the doctor bandaged the gt raw wounds of our poor officer a foot or two away!" Rationing made things tight, and during another fierce attack on the Western Front, Winston told Clemmie he had hastily seized the marmalade before taking cover. The lack of food set the tone for some of his early correspondence with Clementine. He pleaded that she send some "useful and practical" items which he could contribute to the officers' mess, such as peach brandy. Then the brandy became a "small box" with potted meat, a chocolate or two . . . perhaps a sardine. "Begin as soon as possible," he added. The *small* box had expanded in proportions two days after, when he asked for two bottles of brandy and a bottle of peach brandy. But two months later in January it had reached removal box size: "the sort of things I want you to send me are these—large slabs of corned beef: stilton cheeses: cream: hams: sardines—dried fruits: you might almost try a big beef steak pie: but not tinned grouse or fancy tinned things. The simpler the better: & substantial too; for our ration meat is tough & tasteless: & we cannot use the fire by daylight. I fear you find me vy expensive to keep. [. . .] With fondest love my own darling, your ever loving and devoted—greedy though I will fear you say."

Churchill well understood the immensely cheering effect food could have on others—it had that effect on him. By the time he was minister for munitions in 1918, he managed to change the entire atmosphere of a dinner on the Western Front with key military and political figures—just through his perspective on food! The first course was laid on the table, stolid and unappealingly wholesome to the appetites of the assembled company: a shepherd's pie. "Ah!" said Churchill, "minced meat under a glorious cloud of mashed potatoes!" Everyone's appetite picked up.

All through his life, Churchill was a bluff and hale dining companion. Anthony Montague Brown, who was Churchill's private secretary for the last ten years of Winston's life, remembered Churchill always egging him on to enjoy himself even more, trying to bully him into having champagne, or brandy, or at least a cigar. When Anthony refused all, Churchill said grumpily, "It's a great mistake to miss doing yourself good while you're still young." They went to Boodles Club together, where, after Winston wept a little (or blubbed as he preferred to call it) at those who had died in the service of their country from the Boodles' Roll of Honor, they went on to have a magnificent supper of lamb cutlets and ice cream while perched in the bow windows of the club, which look out onto St. James' Street. Passers-by looked twice when they caught sight of the venerable old prime minister about his supper in the window. They managed no less than sixteen brandies—but many of these were bought for other old boys in the club. Winston looked misty eyed around Boodles' dining room and admired the "decent county gentlemen" who ate oysters there. Anthony pointed out that at least three of the members they could see were stockbrokers. Churchill blustered: "You shouldn't say such things about your fellow-members! Really, my dear, you must avoid this penchant for pessimistic judgement."

Ice cream was a subject that remained close to Churchill's tummy. He cherished it; ice cream really was one of his most prized desserts, and he even went so far as to hazard a daring rescue of it from the misery of bureaucracy in World War II. Churchill got wind of the terrible news that ice cream was no longer available at the Savoy as the result of a tedious government ruling that banned restaurants and hotels from serving ices—by all means, they could offer diners the same ingredients in mousse but not frozen form. Churchill drilled Santorlelly, the maître d'hôtel at the Savoy: could this be true? No ice cream was to be had for dessert at the Savoy? Churchill set out to investigate this gross injustice and discovered the truth: the embargo on ice cream was intended to apply only to huge ice cream producers, not hotels. The order was tweaked, and ice cream returned once again to the bowls of the Savoy. Ice cream, though, had an effect on Churchill's figure, and Clementine worried about his health. He was getting too chubby, and his notion of a convalescent diet after any bout of ill health was champagne, oysters, pâté, and mouthfuls of steak. It was high time, Clemmie decided, for Winston to embark on an exercise regime, and she asked Norman to pin the regime onto Churchill's mirror. The valet, having innocently heard a young new mother speak about doing very similar exercises, asked her what they were. "They're prenatal," she informed him, and so that is how Norman chose to define Churchill's regime, entitling it "prenatal." Churchill went to the mirror, adjusted his tie, and then asked slowly, "Norman, do I look pregnant?"

Mrs. Landemare had always cooked for the Churchills sporadically, but in 1939, she made it her full-time occupation, donning her apron and entering the kitchen of Number 10 Downing Street as their full-time cook, to do her duty for the war effort. As she told an interviewer, "I was doing my best to look after him." Wartime rationing wouldn't put her off; she just rolled up her sleeves and, armed with her whisk, set about to feed the leader, staying up to make sure Winston got his jellied beef and veal consommé in the wee small hours and rising bright and early to boil eggs and make steaming pots of tea for breakfast. They fed themselves on rations at No. 10, but if anyone special was coming, Churchill used his diplomatic coupons to feed them. He had a terrible weakness for Mrs. Landemare's Irish stew and, after General Ike Eisenhower praised its crust and gravy, he always told her to make it whenever Ike visited—with "plenty of onions and not much broth" and perhaps too with the fresh, buttered peas Winston loved. He tried to get Mrs. Landemare to hoard the stew for the next day too, but she knew it never survived a reheat, so her Irish stew mysteriously vanished overnight.

Irish Stew

1 leek, finely sliced
20 small pickling onions
3 carrots, sliced into
    ¼-inch disks
6 medium-size potatoes,
    peeled and cut into
    ¼-inch slices

3 lb. very lean lamb (preferably neck, with all fat trimmed off and diced into 1-inch chunks)
generous pinch of sea salt
1 tsp. fresh, crumbled thyme
freshly ground black pepper
½ pint lamb stock

Get a large, heavy-bottomed casserole dish with a close-fitting lid. Line the base of this with ½ the sliced leek and 10 small onions. Now add a layer of carrots. Layer half the potatoes on top. Place all of the diced lamb on top. Sprinkle with a good pinch of sea salt, the thyme, and plenty of ground black pepper. Place a final layer of leek and pickling onions on top of this. Now add a layer of carrots. Arrange your last layer of potatoes on top. Salt and pepper again, and then pour on the lamb stock.

Place the casserole over a high heat, then, once you hear a boiling, bubbling noise, turn the heat down to its very lowest and cover the casserole very tightly. Let it to cook undisturbed for 1½ hours.

At the end of the 1½ hours, you can serve portions of this delicious, plain, and yet aromatic stew.

Churchill's wartime diet was helped by his moderate, though keen, appetite; if he had a cutlet at night, he wouldn't always eat the whole thing and might save what was left for his breakfast.

The worry of the war took a toll on Churchill, but Mrs. Landemare never found it put him off his food, though the great loss of life caused him deep grief. One day Churchill was hunting down Mrs. Landemare in Number 10 to show her a guest list for dinner, calling out for her and eventually tracking her down in the servants' hall. He stopped short before a photograph hanging there of young men who had gone to serve as bombers. Tears filled his eyes and he said to her, "I saw them all go out, and very few came back." "I couldn't have managed without you through the war," he told Mrs. Landemare on Victory in Europe night, leaving his ministers behind to shake her hand while the bells pealed across London and fireworks lit up the skies. It sounds, however, as if Georgina also owed her life to Churchill. On the evening of October 15, 1940, Churchill was had been enjoying dinner at 7 or 8 o'clock in the evening with guests in the garden room of Number 10 (Churchill had been late for dinner, as usual) when the wail of sirens broke the quiet. Churchill, however, was not alarmed, as the garden room was secured against bomb damage by steel shutters fixed to the windows. Mrs. Landemare and the kitchen maid were working in the spacious, high-ceilinged kitchen of Number 10, their figures framed by the twenty-five-foot-high and magnificent plate glass kitchen window. Mrs. Landemare was watching carefully over her soufflés rising in the oven.

The wail of air raid sirens rose above the cobbled streets. Suddenly realizing the danger the kitchen window posed to the kitchen staff, Churchill strode to the kitchens, ordered his butler to put the dinner on a hot plate, and demanded that the cook and her staff make their way to the Number 10 air raid shelter. Mrs. Landemare didn't think the German bombers were overhead: nothing was allowed to spoil the light and airy texture of her dessert. "Sir, the soufflé isn't done!" she protested, as Churchill hustled her out.

No more than three minutes later, a bomb smashed through Downing Street, exploding the glass and sending deadly shards and blocks of rubble through the air. The glass would have shredded the cook to pieces, and Churchill led Mrs. Landemare back into the kitchen to show her the damage. True to form, what upset her most was the wretched mess the Germans had made of her kitchen. Mrs. Landemare showed similar solidity on that desperate and sad afternoon in July 1945 when the news broke that Churchill was not reelected as prime minister. Churchill's daughter, Mary, found her in the kitchen making some honey sandwiches. "I don't know what the world is coming to," Mrs. Landemare lamented, "but I thought I might make some tea."

Georgina stayed on with Churchill until 1954, and her work was certainly cut out for her, but she could cope. Once a scullery maid, she went on to cook for sixteen kings in Churchill's service and was married to the renowned Ritz chef Paul Landemare, who, rumor has it, invented the macaroon. Churchill's eating habits were ruled by when his appetite peaked—what he called "tummy time," which Mrs. Landemare tried to fill with the good plain cooking Churchill's tummy liked, jam pudding or sole Colbert, for instance . . .

Sole Colbert (You need to begin making the veal stock for this about 2 days in advance.)

FOR THE DEMI-GLACE SAUCE

10 lb. veal bones
3 onions, chopped

2 carrots, chopped
white of 1 leek, chopped

FOR THE ESPAGNOLE SAUCE

1 tbsp. butter
2 onions, very finely chopped
1 carrot, very finely chopped
1 rib celery, very finely chopped
1 tbsp. all-purpose flour

2 tbsp. tomato puree
3 cups veal stock
1 bay leaf
½ tsp. fresh, crumbled thyme
3 branches parsley

FOR THE MAÎTRE D'HÔTEL BUTTER

200 g. unsalted, softened butter
3 tbsp. very finely chopped parsley
1½ tbsp. very finely chopped scallions

1 tsp. finely grated lemon zest
sea salt
freshly ground black pepper

FOR THE SOLE

2 fresh, skinned on-the-bone sole
all-purpose flour
2 eggs, beaten
freshly made brown bread crumbs

sea salt
freshly ground black pepper
4 tbsp. lard

TO FINISH

2 tbsp. demi-glace sauce

2 teaspoons chopped fresh tarragon

Unusually enough for a fish dish, sole Colbert begins with meat in the form of the construction of a rich, brown demi-glace sauce. Heat a large, deep roasting pan in the oven as it climbs up to 250 degrees centigrade. Now remove the roasting pan from the oven and place the veal bones in the pan. Return to the oven and cook for 1 hour and 15 minutes. Now add the onions, carrots, and leeks to the pan. Cook for a further 50 minutes, until they are colored a deep brown.

Now put the bones and browned vegetables into a deep pan and set to one side. Place the roasting tin over a medium heat and pour onto it about 2 cups of water, using a wooden spoon to scrape up and blend with the water all the delicious, sticky veal residue from the base of the roasting tin. Pour this on top of the veal bones and cover with cold water. Bring to a boil slowly and then simmer on a medium to low heat for at least 14 hours, skimming for impurities frequently in the first hour and then about every half hour after this. Strain the stock through muslin and cool. Reserve 3 cups of the veal stock for the espagnole sauce.

Sole Colbert (*continued*)

The next day, you are ready to transform this veal stock into a demi-glace sauce. First, make the espagnole sauce, which will eventually combine with the veal stock to make a delicious, classical demi-glace sauce. Melt the butter in the base of a deep saucepan. Add the onion, carrot, and celery. Turn down the heat to low, cover with some lightly buttered grease-proof paper, and sweat gently for 15 minutes. Next, remove the grease-proof paper, take the pan off the heat, and add the tablespoon of all-purpose flour, stirring thoroughly to form a roux. Return this to a gentle heat and, still stirring, let the roux brown. Incorporate the tomato puree with the roux, and then, using a whisk to agitate the sauce, slowly add the veal stock to the roux. Bring to a boil, stirring continuously. Add the bay leaf, thyme, and parsley and simmer for a further 40 minutes, or until the espagnole sauce has reduced to ½ pint. Now strain the espagnole sauce; you should be left with a generous ¼ pint of sauce.

Finally, it is time to make the demi-glace sauce. Return the veal stock combined with the espagnole sauce to the stove and simmer for at least 4 hours until the stock is reduced to 2 cups.

Make the maître d'hôtel butter next, as you can keep this cool in the fridge. In a mortar and pestle, cream together the butter, parsley, scallions, and lemon zest. Season with sea salt and freshly ground black pepper, then refrigerate the beautifully green and yellow herby lump that is your maître d'hôtel butter. Next, make the maître d'hôtel sauce—this essentially begins as a béchamel sauce to which you add some glorious extras. You must first prepare the sole so that they can be split open once they are fried. To do so, run the point of a sharp knife along the back of the spine of each fish, so that it will be easy to detach later. Put the flour, beaten egg, and bread crumbs each, separately, on 3 flat plates. Season the flour with salt and black pepper. Take the sole and dip it first in flour, then egg, and finally in bread crumbs. Heat the lard in a spacious, wide frying pan until it goes silent. Now cook the fish in the hot lard for approximately 15 minutes; you must turn the fish when one side looks golden and crisp. Remove from the heat and drain on oil-absorbent paper. Using a clean knife, detach the spine from the sole. Now pop a generous yellow nugget of the maître d'hôtel butter into the cavity. Pour a tablespoon of warm demi-glace over this and a teaspoon of fresh tarragon. Serve immediately.

Woe betide Mrs. Landemare, though, if Churchill's meat was overdone. She timed putting chops, grouse, or plover in the oven by listening for the sound of Churchill running his bath above her in Number 10. He liked plain food—but liked it just right. Once when hosting a formal dinner party for a Russian delegation (including Molotov) at his formal country prime ministerial residence of

Chequers, Churchill was served aged, dry quail. He complained: "Tell Cruikshank [the cook] that these miserable mice should never have been removed from Tutankhamen's tomb!" (One of the housemaids was all distressed to find a loaded revolver in Molotov's bed, and he was to surprise the doughty housekeeper by answering his bedroom door with it pointed toward her.) Fortunately the Russians seemed oblivious.

Churchill was no great adventurer when it came to food. His doctor, Lord Moran, remembered him grumbling about some deviled chicken; why on earth was it necessary to mess up some perfectly fine chicken with odd saucing? Churchill also described himself as having "a grievance against the tomato" and showed insight when it came to sandwiches: the bread should never overpower the sandwich filling but should be "nothing more than a vehicle to convey the filling to the stomach." Churchill had been recommended sandwiches before bedtime by a gastroenterologist in 1938, so he obligingly tried to practice this, standing firm by the belief that no gentleman eats ham sandwiches without mustard.

Despite his own food faddism, food fads were generally suspect, he opined, when congratulating Lord Woolton on his skepticism toward the Scientific Committee's 1940 report on rations for British soldiers: "nut-eaters and the like" all seemed to die young, but only after a spell of "senile decay." Let the British soldier stick to his instinct for beef and nothing but beef. "The way to lose this war is to try to force the British public into a diet of milk, oatmeal, potatoes etc., washed down on gala occasions with a little lime juice." Always partial to a prime piece of British beef, Churchill felt like a mouthful of this, slightly underdone but sticky with a thin ream of rich fat on the outside, was quintessentially British and brave. It made a man of you. The same went with a good beef consommé. Churchill detested creamy soups; when he visited Roosevelt at the White House, he was subjected to reams of cream soups—and pigs' knuckles. When Roosevelt's chef tried to serve him clam chowder, Churchill balked, asking for Bovril: "If you haven't any clear soup, please bring me a plate of Bovril, double strength." This request had Americans scratching their heads. Roosevelt mixed martinis that could make your bones break; one special one was made with a knock-out vermouth from Argentina. His notorious martinis brimmed with huge quantities of vermouth and a smaller amount of Gordon's Gin. Even Stalin was to refuse one of these, and Churchill, not liking cocktails, turned up just before dinner with Roosevelt in order to avoid the embarrassment of refusing his kindly host. Never one to forget the British subjects he led, Churchill stuck to his food-rationing habits in the deliciously food-rich Washington, D.C.: he'd always try to save half his supper for the next day. Churchill's delegation were again surprised by the food wealth on display in Moscow in October 1944: to the ration-bound Brit, the Kremlin food seemed magnificent, but each meal was, in essence, exactly the same. So every day was partitioned by the same circular, repetitive meal, and lunch and dinner took three hours apiece; three-course breakfasts of caviar, smoked salmon, and suckling pig were resurrected at lunch and dinner to become caviar, salmon, pig followed by soup, fish, game or chicken, stewed fruit, and ice cream.

Any troubles and misunderstandings with Stalin, Churchill held, could have been avoided if they had been able to have lunch together once a week; but he may have come to regret this hasty sentiment when he visited Stalin in Moscow in 1942. Stalin was desperate for Churchill to open up a Second Front. Churchill, now sixty-seven, stayed at the invitingly named State Villa Number 7 and hung about there, hoping for a proper audience with Stalin, who, being Stalin, was all set to be intractable and wily. Churchill expressed himself as very willing to fit in with Stalin's schedule (being a dictator is very time-consuming), and so their meetings tended to start around 10 p.m. Churchill didn't roll back to State Villa Number 7 until the wee hours of 3, 4, or 5 a.m., rousing sleepy employees who were a third his age. Diplomacy, Stalin-style, meant that Churchill at his first state meal with Stalin (plus devotees) had to endure twenty-seven toasts over dinner; intoxicated Russians in the inner circle were always falling in a slump to the ground after too many yellow vodkas, though the more devious ones seemed to become more and more sober. Even worse, as Churchill told his doctor, Charles Moran, afterward, "the food was filthy." This was followed by more intimate drinks with Stalin the next day, which became an intimate dinner—albeit with interpreters. Dinner began with a radish or two but very quickly elephantine trays of food appeared—enough to feed at least thirty people. There were two chickens, the obligatory suckling pig, haunches of mutton and beef, plus an assortment of fish. Stalin sampled one or two platters. Four hours into this, Stalin stopped toying with his potatoes and launched an attack on an eyelashed, shiny pig's head (after offering it to Churchill). It was if he almost had a preternatural knowledge of Churchill's pro-piggy sentiments. First, Stalin rapped his knife against the skull, grating against the bone, and he cleaned out the pig's brain, popping gobbets into his mouth. Then it was on to the cheeks; these he chopped up and devoured with his fingers. It was a six-hour dinner in total. Oh joy—why did foreign allies always want to impose pig on Churchill—Stalin with the head, Roosevelt with the knuckles—given Churchill's fondness for the creature. His letters to Clemmie always had pig cartoons on them, and his nickname was "the Pig"; she was "the Cat." They even called out for each other, going "Wow, wow!" to which the other replied, "Wow, wow!"

Indeed, Churchill loved animals, furred, feathered, or flat-footed. His affections even stretched to amphibians: he had a pool full of gleaming foot-long golden orfe fish at Chartwell; he called to them at feeding time and loved to see them flock toward him. Almost as good as the pig dissection was the marked difference between Stalin and Winston when it came to pets. On one Kremlin visit, Churchill told Stalin how handsome he found the goldfish swimming in his villa pool (presumably Number 7 again?). Stalin brightened up and solicitously replied, "If you like, you are welcome to take some as your breakfast." Fond as he was of whiting (served with its tail in its mouth) and whitebait, goldfish were strictly pets. This same brutishness was clear in Stalin's attitude to France; after one conversation together, Churchill wondered perplexedly if Stalin ever read books, as he spoke of France as if she had no past. An interestingly chilling observation . . .

Chapter 1

FRENCH FRIES FOREVER: BILL CLINTON

The watermelons of Hope, Arkansas, symbolize Clinton's food beginnings. Born to a family of modest means who often supplemented their daily diet with what they could grow on small plots outside of town, the distinctions between which was sweeter, red or yellow melon, loomed large in young Clinton's life. In fact, edges of Clinton's youth have moments of Dorothy from *The Wizard of Oz*; take Auntie Em out of the equation and replace her with Uncle Buddy and Aunt Ollie, and you have young Clinton, hair smoothed, sitting down in Hope for a weekend dinner (lunch) with his extended family, courtesy of Auntie Ollie (now doubt they've been out square dancing the night before and have been gospel singing that very morning). It was a world in which, according to Clinton's memoirs, "men hunted and fished" and Bill shelled peas. They'd drink long drafts of iced tea from goblets, and the table might be set with dark yellow, warm cornbread, collard greens and peas, a large ham, bowls of steaming mashed potatoes, lima beans or green beans, and, best of all, a sugar-flaked, golden-crusted fruit pie with homemade ice cream; hopefully peach, Bill's childhood favorite. Willing Bill helped crank the ice cream maker and prepare the lunch.

But even Hope had its dark side: Clinton's stepfather, Roger, was only just keeping his head above the alcoholism that threatened to drown him, and although his mother, Virginia, doted on Bill, he also worried about the sweets consumption of his younger brother, Roger, writing dolefully, "Sometimes I think the whole house will sink into a heap of sugar."

The apple of his mother's eye, young Bill was academically gifted, and Virginia would have nothing stand in his way, even food-wise. She always stocked up the house with his favorite food: luscious peach ice cream in the freezer, tuna salad in the fridge for him to slap on some rye, bananas and peanut butter on hand so he could rustle up his beloved peanut butter and banana sandwiches. Awestruck friends watched with admiration the speed with which Bill could slice banana for his sandwich. Indeed, even when he was president, a top late-night speechwriting snack was a banana with peanut butter smeared on it. Even with a banana, Bill could charm the crowds; he wooed his first girlfriend, Denise Hyland's, family by teaching her little sister the secret art of making peanut butter and banana sandwiches, wrestling with her brothers, and then—holy of holies—drying the dishes after dinner.

Far from Hope and at university in Georgetown, Washington, Clinton went downhill food-wise; left to his own devices and the constraints of a student budget, Clinton ate on a dollar a day, stashing cash for taking girls out for dinner at weekends. On Thirty-Sixth Street he'd pop into Wisemiller's Deli for coffee and doughnuts. The coffee must have tasted of youthful dynamism—it was the first coffee Clinton ever had. Midday found Clinton biting into a Hostess fried pie—cherry or

Peach Ice Cream

4 large, ripe peaches
1 cup organic full-fat milk
1 pint double cream
½ tsp. salt flakes

150 g. vanilla granulated sugar (keep
a pot of granulated sugar in your
cupboard with at least 2 long black
vanilla pods embedded in it)
6 egg yolks

Remove the skin from the peaches by making a + incision in the skin and plunging them very quickly into enough boiling water to immerse them. Then rinse the peaches in very cold water; let them cool and then slip their skins off. Remove their pits, then cut them into chunks and stew them gently in a closed saucepan. When the peaches have softened, blend half of the mix and dice up the remaining peach-mess of chunks into small pieces. In a medium-size saucepan, gently warm the milk, HALF of the cream, salt flakes, and vanilla sugar. When the milky mix is warm and the vanilla sugar has dissolved, remove the pan from the heat, cover it, and leave it to rest for about half an hour.

When the 30 minutes is up, place the egg yolks in a bowl and whisk them. Slowly add the warm milky cream to the eggs yolks—keep whisking—and then return this to the pan. Warm over a medium to low heat, using a wooden spoon: when the custard is ready, it will coat the spoon. Don't stop stirring or the eggs may scramble. Now combine this with the remaining HALF of the cream. Put the cold cream in a large bowl and, constantly stirring, add the custard. Now add the pureed peach. Cool for 30 minutes.

When it is cooled, start to churn the ice cream following the ice cream maker's directions. When the ice cream is almost set, add the peachy chunk mess; this will give delicious morsels of peachiness to the peach-scented ice cream.

apple—with a Royal Crown Cola. Dinner was either a substantial roast beef sandwich at eighty-five cents or, if financial desperation had taken hold, a giant tuna on rye sandwich for thirty-five cents at the Hoya Carry Out, topped off with another basin-size soft drink. But the biggest pull of Hoya's Carry Out was the shapely, curvaceous, and beehived Rose, who, if you ate your huge sandwich really slowly, shimmied around in a very tight sweater, jiggling those soda taps . . .

Dinners at university afford us glimpses of Clinton's political idealism: at college he was a scruffy, brilliant bear, given to reciting whole sections of Martin Luther King's "I Have a Dream" speech over dessert. Acquaintances often found Bill sleeping on the sofa and drawing up a chair at the dinner table. On his Rhodes Scholar trip through the Eastern Bloc, coming back from Moscow, he stayed in Prague with the family of his friend Jan Kopold (in Jan's absence) and rapidly became a surrogate son; he'd have an intimate breakfast with Kopold's grandmother and then roll up his sleeves for a dinner of home-cooked pork, cabbage, and bread dumplings with Kopold's parents. Back in Oxford, he stayed in the student den at Leckford Road; the kitchen had a scuffed green linoleum floor, and the front door could not be locked, so people just came and went. The American students celebrated Thanksgiving there: two of them cycled into Oxford's Covered Market and came back with the turkey in their bike basket, feathered, beaked, head tucked in, and scaly legs poking out. Then Brooke Shearer, a dynamic young sophomore from Stanford (and the possessor of the bike basket), decided that everyone should do fifteen-minute shifts basting the turkey while she—get this—read *Mrs. Dalloway*. Bill and a friend were on first shift but got so carried away talking about politics that they ended up doing it all. At Yale, Clinton had buckled down a little more, but had moved now to a beachside house where hip music throbbed out, the air spiced with marijuana. But Bill puffed away on his pipe, and his housemates rustled up coq au vin. All of which paved the way for the spaghetti dinners and charged conversations about politics that Bill had with his lithe, bespectacled girlfriend, Hillary Rodham, in their first flat together.

While still a law student at Yale, Bill, new to Texas politics, was working on the Texas campaign team for George McGovern. Bill stayed in Austin, Texas, and couldn't get enough of Tex-Mex food and the buttery, perfumed taste of mango ice cream, which he adored. He made friends with strong, zippy liberal Democrat Billie Carr, and it was over such a lunch in Houston that Clinton glowingly described his future. As he dug into a plate of enchiladas, Clinton looked Billie in the eye and said, "I love Arkansas. I'm goin' back there to live. I'm gonna run for office there. And someday I'm gonna be governor. And then one day I'll be callin' ya, Billie, and tellin' ya I'm runnin' for president and I need your help."

The Enchiladas of Ambition

FOR THE TORTILLAS
7½ oz. masa harina   ½ pint cold water
generous pinch of sea salt

FOR THE FILLING
6 dried ancho chilies   1 tsp. oregano or ½ tsp. epazote
6 ripe, bright red tomatoes   ½ tsp. crumbled thyme
1 onion, roughly chopped   generous pinch of brown sugar
2 cups chicken stock   pinch of sea salt
2 tbsp. tomato puree   freshly ground black pepper
4 cloves garlic, crushed   2½ oz. lard
2 tsp. cumin   2 eggs

The Enchiladas of Ambition (continued)

225 ml. double cream
6 chorizo sausages, skins removed
  and diced
1 oz. Parmesan cheese

1 cup grated Monterey Jack cheese
1 cup grated strong Cheddar cheese
1 onion, finely chopped

TO GARNISH
4 scallions, sliced
small bunch cilantro, finely chopped

½ cup sour cream

Tear the ancho chilies into strips and clean out their seeds. Heat a skillet and dry-fry the ancho chilies for about a minute each side. Now soak them in a small bowl of boiling water—about 225 milliliters—for half an hour. Peel and deseed the tomatoes, then coarsely chop them. Now pour the chilies and their water into a blender and whizz. Add the onion, tomatoes, chicken stock, tomato puree, garlic, cumin, oregano or epazote, thyme, brown sugar, sea salt, and black pepper. Puree: you now have a dynamite enchilada sauce base.

Now melt ½ ounce of the lard over a high heat in a large frying pan. Add the enchilada sauce, turn down the heat a little, and let the sauce bubble away for 7 minutes. In a small bowl, whisk the eggs and cream together. Remove the pan from the heat, and, stirring constantly, add the egg and cream mixture. Pour into a bowl, cover, and set aside.

In a large frying pan, melt another ½ ounce of the lard and then fry the crimson, diced chorizo sausage. Fry the chorizo until it has browned and released its crimson fats. Drain, discard the fat, and put the chorizo in a bowl with ½ cup of the enchilada sauce and the Parmesan cheese. Wash the large frying pan!

Now make your tortillas. Sift the masa harina and salt into a large mixing bowl and then add the water a little at a time, kneading the mixture until it is no longer sticky. Flour a surface for rolling out the tortillas and divide the dough up into 4 batches. Roll out each batch—the dough should be pretty thin—and then, using a saucer about 5 inches in circumference, cut out the tortillas. Stack them between layers of grease-proof paper. Get a dry frying pan and place it on a moderate heat. Cook each tortilla separately for about 2 minutes on each side or until such time as the tortilla blisters and goes golden brown. Stack the tortillas up in piles of 5 and keep them warm under a clean tea towel.

Now preheat the oven to 180 degrees centigrade. Get a large, wide baking dish, spread a thin layer of enchilada sauce in its base, and keep it by your side. Dip each tortilla in the enchilada sauce and then stuff with a generous dollop or two of the chorizo mix, roll the tortilla up, and transfer it to the baking dish; make sure each tortilla is lying on its seam. Repeat until all the tortillas are stuffed, rolled, and in place. Now pour the remaining, delicious enchilada sauce over the tortillas and top with the cheese and raw onion. Bake in the oven for about 20 minutes until the cheese is bubbly and beginning to brown. Scatter scallions, cilantro, and dollops of sour cream on top.

However Clinton might adore McMuffins, he and Hillary still had to pay service to fine dining at the White House—but not always successfully. As ever with American presidents, their ambitions and pretensions can be measured in their White House menus, and the Clintons' kitchen produced complex and, at times, unpleasant food, particularly when experimenting with less familiar international foods. One witness, with a little verbal shudder, found it hard to forget the Darjeeling tea–smoked chicken in a chilled pea sauce that was served at the banquet for Indian prime minister Atal Behari Vajpayee in 2000. Shouldn't they just have stuck to Hostess fried pies?

Notably, Clinton's waistline was to be ruined by his fondness for campaign-trail hamburgers and doughnuts—after one tuck-in, he grandly declared, "[I] feel like a sow in the sun!" Indeed, he has shared his food insights with the nation, reflecting: "I don't necessarily consider McDonald's junk food. You know they have chicken sandwiches, they have salads." French fries were forever on his lips. Gluttonous binges always left Clinton feeling guilty, though. He was like an "accordion" in the way he would rapidly expand and contract and expand again. He was famous for gorging himself on junk food; cinnamon buns and enchiladas, jalapeño burgers, and pork barbecue. He has had to have plates of cupcakes snatched from his hands. Arkansas journalist Bob Lancaster used to run into him at the movies, where he was amazed to see Clinton order "triple buttered popcorn." "I had never seen that before. I asked him one time, how does that work?" Clinton showed him. "They would fill the popcorn bag about a third of the way, and they would just load it down with butter, and add a third more popcorn, and then load it down with butter, and pour on the top third, and load it down with butter, so he had triple-buttered popcorn." The press made jokes like, "Is the forklift with the governor's lunch here yet?" This all seems much less of a wheeze now, after Clinton's heart surgery. A born-again vegan, he attributes this diet to saving his life. Before we get too somber, though, his favorite vegan meals are lasagna and . . . enchiladas! Maybe Clinton was always heading in the vegan direction though.

Even in the throes of his first magnetizing encounters with Monica Lewinsky, he managed to get her to fetch him two slices of *vegetarian* pizza and self-consciously sucked in his tummy when she first unbuttoned his shirt.

MIKHAIL GORBACHEV LIKES IT DÉTENTE

Mikhail Gorbachev grew up on a Cold War diet—not only this, but the sort of diet you get on a postwar Communist collective farm that spans miles and miles of the Ukraine and is miles away from anywhere else. It doesn't raise the spirits, does it? The markets of Stalingrad and Rostov were, of course, also miles away, and the Gorbachevs were always short on everything . . . but why? Given that they lived and worked on a farm, you'd imagine that there was farm produce in abundance, and even more so when there was a glut of delicious produce at harvest time. Here's how it goes, though, on the Soviet-style diet: fifteen-year-old Mikhail would thresh thirty hectares a day during the harvest, and this, according to the "rules," entitled him to a "parcel." A food parcel, no less, which Mikhail described as "Not just a 'parcel,' but a gift from God. . . . A feast indeed!" He'd rummage through it quickly. With dreary certainty there was vodka, an eye-watering liter, which Mikhail had no interest in; thank goodness, because if it had put too much of a gleam in his eye, the Berlin Wall might still be intact. But what he seized upon with delight—remember he was heralded as the politician who put butter before guns—was Ukrainian butter dumplings. Or stewed meat. Or, glory of glories, a pot of honey.

And it was over food that Gorbachev could cement his political loyalties and forge his own version of glittering, liberating *perestroika*: when they both holidayed at the Krasnie Kamni Sanatorium in the late sixties and early seventies, Gorbachev and KGB chairman Andropov set off on joint family excursions to the mountains, staying up late at night to cook shashlik around a bonfire. With no one to listen except the vast, starry expanse of the southern skies, they could talk openly at last . . .

Butter Dumplings (Galushki)

Serve hot with sour cream poured over them. Pork fat or salt pork may be substituted for butter. Dice the pork finely and render; pour over the galushki together with the cracklings.

2½ cups all-purpose flour	2 eggs
1 tsp. sea salt	½ cup water
3½ oz. butter	

TO GARNISH

2 tbsp. butter, melted	1 cup sour cream

Sift the flour and sea salt into a large bowl. Make a well in the center of the flour. Melt 3½ ounces of butter in a small saucepan. In a second bowl, whisk the eggs, add the water, and then add the melted butter, still whisking. Pour this into the well

Butter Dumplings (*continued*)

in the flour and work the mixture through the flour, kneading it eventually into a smooth, flexible dough. Pull off sections of the dough and shape these into small, walnut-size balls (dumplings or galushki). In a large, deep saucepan bring salted water to a boil. Pop the galushki into the boiling water and cook for 10 minutes. The galushki will rise to the surface of the water when cooked.

Remove them from the pan and drain.

In a frying pan, melt 2 tablespoons of butter and fry the galushki in this until they become golden brown. When serving them, drizzle with the nut brown butter and then the sour cream.

Collective Meat Stew

3 tbsp. butter
4 medium-size potatoes, peeled
　and quartered
1 lb. beef, diced
2 onions, finely chopped
2 parsnips, quartered
1 celeriac, diced
2 carrots, roughly sliced

3 cloves garlic, crushed
sea salt
freshly ground black pepper
1 pint strong, dark beef stock
1½ tbsp. dill, chopped
2 tbsp. parsley, chopped
2 tbsp. sour cream

Preheat the oven to 170 degrees centigrade. In a frying pan melt 2 tablespoons of butter and fry the potato chunks until they are golden. Remove and drain. Fry the diced beef in the pan and brown in the butter. Remove and drain. Next, melt 1 tablespoon of butter in a deep and large, heavy-based pot and fry the onion gently until it has softened and darkened. Now add the meat and potatoes to this, followed by the parsnip, celeriac, carrots, and garlic. Season with a large pinch of sea salt and finely ground black pepper. Cover with the beef stock, bring to a boil, and place in the 170 degree centigrade oven for 2 hours. Ten minutes before serving, add the dill, parsley, and sour cream.

You'll find the shashlik recipe with Stalin . . . what else would you expect?

ANTI-COMMUNIST EATING WITH RONNIE AND NANCY

When it came to food, Nancy Reagan was like Ronnie's prison warden, drilling him in the art of eating healthily . . . but, out of sight, Ronnie liked to sneak in forbidden, contraband old treats like macaroni and cheese. Trouble loomed for Ronnie if Nancy got there first and spied mac and cheese on the menu: "You're not eating that," she'd tell him firmly. Nancy's tight rein slackened temporarily after Ronnie was shot in 1981, and she arranged for delicious hamburger soup with hominy and split pea soup to be transported from the White House kitchens into the hospital.

Nancy was always much more drawn to the glamour of high-class foods and schmaltzy side dishes than Ronnie; she learned at the elbow of her favored sidekick, Betsy Bloomingdale, wife of the sexually errant multimillionaire, Alfred Bloomingdale, and presumed "authoress" of the esteemed and modestly titled: *Entertaining with Betsy Bloomingdale: A Collection of Culinary Tips and Treasures from the World's Best Hosts and Hostesses*. Perhaps even Nancy penned a tip or two? Johnny Carson jibed that Nancy's favorite junk food was caviar, and she was criticized in her first year in the White House for ordering fancy dinner sets just at the point when the government announced that tomato ketchup counted as a vegetable in school dinners. Indeed, when Ronnie was at the receiving end of negative press about being a food snob like Nancy, the Reagan PR machinery went into overdrive to establish that hamburger soup was dear to his heart (was the hospital delivery part of this exercise?). Even the signature jar of jelly beans that Ronald Reagan kept on his desk at the Oval Office had a subtler purpose—"You can tell a lot about a fella's character by whether he picks out all of one color or just grabs a handful," claimed Reagan. Politics and food had a way of mixing themselves up with the Reagans' private family life too: their daughter Patti had a typically odd political childhood. For instance, one evening, just after having lost to Kennedy, Nixon came for dinner and used her room to change in. Patti went upstairs to find his clothes on her twin bed. Poor Patti.

Public Relations Hamburger Soup

2 tbsp. butter	2 carrots, sliced
2 onions, finely chopped	1 tbsp. tomato puree
1 stick celery, chopped	2 pints good, rich beef stock
1 green bell pepper, diced	1 pint fresh, chopped tomatoes
2 cloves garlic, crushed	small bunch parsley, chopped
1 lb. minced beef	1 tsp. oregano
freshly ground black pepper	2 tsp. cayenne pepper
sea salt	5 oz. hominy

Public Relations Hamburger Soup (*continued*)

Melt the butter in a deep, large pan. Add the onions and sauté for 5 minutes, and then add the celery, green pepper, and garlic. Sauté gently for a further 5 minutes. Add the beef mince and brown it. Season with black pepper and sea salt. Now add the carrots. Sauté for a few minutes more, and then add the tomato puree and pour the rich beef stock over the vegetables and meat. Add the chopped tomatoes, parsley, oregano, and cayenne. Let the soup simmer on a medium to low heat for 30 minutes, at which point you should add the hominy. Simmer for a further 10 minutes, season to taste, and serve.

Ronnie was a simpler, albeit unhealthier, eater than Nancy. He loved his desserts so much that he was always nervous that speech making might mean he'd miss pudding; it might be whisked away around about paragraph four of his speech. Wine, coffee, or tomatoes never held any allure, though, and Brussels sprouts made him shiver—when he was holed up in England filming *The Hasty Heart,* he stayed at the Savoy Hotel, where the English made him eat so many sprouts that he developed a lifelong aversion to these tufted green globes. There were other nasties lurking too. When Reagan sat down for his first meal in the Savoy, he opted for the romantic-sounding "pheasant under glass," thinking it would be gourmet's heaven, but was horrified when they served him a bird with a feathered ruff, head still on and yellow legs still attached.

Nancy Reagan was a tough cookie, with high standards, a stare that could freeze your blood, and an offhand, regal manner. With Betsy Bloomingdale as her guru, Nancy's attitude to personal thrift was never going to impress the average American; after all, Betsy's reply to the issue of energy conservation in the 1970s was, blissfully, "I ask my servants not to turn on the self-cleaning oven until after seven in the evening." Copying Betsy's hair, outfits, lipstick, and manners, Nancy was foul-tempered with her maids, who were considered ever-disposable, leaving at short notice with their bags on account of their poor cooking skills. Even gardeners vanished—one because he asked for a glass of water and got mud on the house floor (it turned out later he was having a heart attack). She was also comically shockable—according to her biographer, Kitty Kelley, Nancy covered her son, young Ron's, eyes lest he see some neighboring Democrats painting flowers on their bins. She managed to suck all the life out of state dinners, tasting sample dishes and using her pronounced "visual" flair to determine the exact arrangement and position of green beans on a plate. Snapshots were then taken of rubber-stamped dishes, so that kitchen staff could replicate them. Watch out, anyone who got Nancy's favorite dessert of brown Betty wrong . . .

A surefire way, Patti Reagan claimed, to get Reagan's attention at dinner was to mention the word "Communists"—who, in Reagan's world, could usually be spotted because of their beards. Meals with Cold War opponents like the Gorbachevs were, then, always beautifully complicated and show that even supper or a cup of tea can be a battleground. When Nancy met Mrs. Gorbachev in Geneva in 1985, she was very wary of the diminutive Raisa, with her startling red hair and job lecturing in Marxist philosophy (akin for Nancy to teaching honors in Satanism) at the University of Moscow. First, Nancy wasn't quite sure what to call her; there isn't a Russian word for "first lady," and the wives of presidents of the USSR weren't usually very public figures: no one knew Andropov even had a wife until she showed up for his funeral. Raisa and Nancy drank decaffeinated almond tea together, and Raisa perched on a chosen chair—apparently she'd spent five minutes clicking her fingers to have the KGB bring her one chair after another—droning on about Communism.

The next day she invited Nancy to tea at the Soviet mission. Again, Raisa appeared odd to Nancy: why was she wearing a stern black tie? Tea was served at a long table. "Welcome," said Raisa grandly. "I wanted you to see what a typical Russian tea looks like." The table groaned under the weight of blinis with caviar, blueberry pie, cabbage rolls, honey and jam, chocolates, cookies . . . Nancy added in a catty aside in her memoirs, "It was a beautiful spread, but if that was an ordinary housewife's treat, then I'm Catherine the Great."

The Gorbachevs couldn't deliver on ambience either when they paired up with the Reagans for dinner at the office-like Soviet mission (though cheekily Raisa was later to compare the White House to a museum). The building was stone cold and wearily impersonal. There were no concessions to pleasure in terms of lighting: the overhead lights lit the room up with industrial brightness. Dinner began with fruit juice; there was no loosening up with cocktails. Gorbachev's policy was to curb vodka consumption in the USSR, and he was, depressingly, leading by example. Brisk Russian fare was served, none of which impressed Nancy.

Like competitive suburban neighbors, the Reagans extended hospitality for the next night, inviting the Gorbachevs to the columned and elegant eighteenth-century Maison de Saussure, where they were holed up and which was the Aga Khan's home. They banked up the soft lighting, laid out bowls of sumptuous soft fruits, and got the house chef to dish up what appears, in hindsight, to be a disproportionate number of soufflés and mousses: a delicious lobster soufflé, followed by supreme de volaille périgourdin—a moreish breast of bread-crumbed chicken—green salad, then lo and behold a cheese mousse with avocado, all rounded off, for dessert, with a hot lemon soufflé with raspberry sauce. Nancy felt they'd scored a victory for the West when Gorbachev said of the lemon soufflé: "I *like* this. What do you call it?" He had never ever tasted a soufflé before; such were the privations of life behind the Iron Curtain.

Lobster Soufflé

½ oz. softened butter
1 tbsp. grated Parmesan cheese
⅜ pint hot milk
1 blade mace
½ cup white wine
2 small lobster tails
1½ oz. butter
1 oz. flour

pinch of sea salt
freshly ground black pepper
¼ tsp. paprika
4 egg yolks
6 egg whites
½ cup finely grated Gruyère cheese
1 tbsp. grated Parmesan cheese

Preheat the oven to 200 degrees centigrade. Butter the bottom and sides of a 3- to 3½-pint soufflé dish. Add a tablespoon of grated Parmesan cheese and tip the soufflé dish to line the bottom and sides with Parmesan. Warm the milk, with the blade of mace, in a small saucepan. As soon as it begins to steam, turn off the heat and leave the mace to infuse the milk. In another saucepan, bring the white wine to a boil, add the lobster tails, and cook very gently until they are opaque (6 to 8 minutes). Now remove them from the wine, cool, and, using a food processor if necessary, cut into very fine pieces.

Next, melt the butter in a second saucepan, remove from the heat, and, stirring, add the flour. Combine the butter and flour thoroughly to form a roux. Salt and pepper this, then add the lobster meat, the paprika, and then gradually add the milk (blade of mace removed). Return the pan to a low heat and cook, stirring constantly, until the sauce begins to boil. Now remove the sauce from the heat and beat in the egg yolks, one by one, blending each thoroughly with the sauce before adding the next. Now set this sauce to the side.

In a large, clean bowl, whisk the egg whites until they are stiff; stir a large spoonful of the whisked egg white into the sauce. Now stir in the half cup of Gruyère. With a spatula or metal spoon, fold the egg white into the sauce; make sure you fold, not stir.

Carefully and gently pour the soufflé mixture into the soufflé dish. Smooth the surface and sprinkle the top with the remaining tablespoon of grated Parmesan cheese. Place the soufflé in the center of the oven and turn the heat down to 190 degrees centigrade. Cook for just over half an hour.

Things never went smoothly between Raisa and Nancy, though: when Nancy couldn't make the next Gorbachev-Reagan summit in Reykjavik in 1986, she still sat glued to the television, fuming about the amount of media coverage Raisa got. When Raisa was handing out pins of Lenin to small schoolchildren, the interviewer asked her why Nancy wasn't there. Raisa shrugged indifferently and quipped: "Perhaps she has something else to do. Or maybe she is not feeling well?" Oh puh-lease! fumed Nancy.

Hot Lemon Soufflé with Raspberry Sauce

generous knob softened butter
5 tbsp. vanilla sugar
4 egg yolks
4 tbsp. finely grated lemon
   zest

1 tbsp. all-purpose flour
1 cup milk
4 tbsp. freshly squeezed
   lemon juice
5 egg whites

FOR THE RASPBERRY SAUCE
2 cups fresh raspberries
1 tbsp. sugar
2 tbsp. water

1 dessert spoon raspberry
   liqueur

Line up 6 ramekins and butter them. Pour a little vanilla sugar into each ramekin and tilt them to coat the base and inside of each ramekin.

Whisk together the egg yolks, 2 tablespoons of the lemon zest, flour, and 1 tablespoon of the vanilla sugar until you have a smooth paste.

Warm the milk and then, whisking all the time, add the milk in a thin trickle to the egg yolk mixture. Put the combined mixture in a pan and bring to a boil, stirring constantly. When this has become a thick custard, remove from the heat and add the lemon juice. Cool completely in the fridge. When cool, stir in the remaining 2 tablespoons of lemon zest.

Preheat the oven to 200 degrees centigrade.

In a large, clean bowl, whisk the egg whites into a soft froth. Now slowly add the remaining vanilla sugar, whisking constantly until the egg whites form glossy, stiff peaks. Take a tablespoon of the egg white and stir it into the cooled custard—this helps to loosen the mixture. Now, using a spatula or metal spoon, gently fold the egg whites into the custard.

Now divide the soufflé mixture equally into the ramekins. Put them in the oven and immediately reduce the heat to 190 degrees centigrade. Bake them in the oven for about 15 minutes, until they are risen and golden.

Meanwhile, make the raspberry sauce. In a pan, combine the raspberries, sugar, water, and raspberry liqueur. Stir, cover the pan, and cook for 4 minutes. Remove from the heat and cool.

Determined to wow Raisa on her visit to Washington in 1987, the Reagans served champagne that was created solely for the dinner. The Russians, however, had their own ideas and refused to wear tuxedos, those rank symbols of bourgeois capitalism. Hopefully, though, Mikhail enjoyed the honey ice cream dessert.

Chapter 1

DINING IN CAMELOT: JFK AND JACKIE

Jackie Kennedy was no cook—if she laid hands on a rolling pin, it only made people groan. Indeed, the whole recipe-exchanging culture of Senate wives made her shudder; she couldn't bear its dowdiness. Congressmen's wives' prayer meetings made her shudder, and, when she was first lady, she'd ask her chef to supply her with deliberately ornate French recipes that she could hand out, minus one instruction or ingredient, just to bedevil the Senate wives. Very ungenerously, she thought Lady Bird Johnson was a "pigeon" who'd scoot down the road stark naked just to advance Lyndon's career. Mind you, when presidents and their first ladies do cook at the White House, they always tend to add their own inimitable touch, for better or worse. Eleanor Roosevelt used to scramble eggs for her guests at the table, and the staff called her dish "scrambled eggs with brains," as all of Eleanor's focus was on policy and not on the eggs. Roosevelt fancied himself a bartender and liked to mix drinks in his private study; he just loved the equipment. His specialty was a dry martini. As an aside, Roosevelt also managed to address the prim, boyish-looking niece of the Chinese emissary as "my boy," and then, realizing his error, claimed he called all young people this. After card games, Eisenhower liked to invite everyone up to the roof of the White House for a cookout of burgers and Kansas City steaks, plus he boiled up a pot of stew. For the sake of the public, this was called "Ike's stew," but in truth it was known among staff as "Moaney's stew" as Sergeant Moaney (his long-serving valet, harkening back to Eisenhower's days as a general) had to cut up all the ingredients—the meat and vegetables—assemble all the spices—"parsley, paprika, garlic"—and then stand alongside Ike handing him ingredients one by one, which Ike then cast into the pot. Moaney was like a nurse assisting a surgeon.

When, as a result of Addison's disease, JFK's body fat seemed to slip off, leaving him at a lean 140 pounds, he joked to his sister, Eunice: "Don't worry. It's nothing serious. Just a result of Jackie's cooking." Jackie, however, was meticulous in making sure Jack had three meals a day, regular as clockwork, and not the sort of rubbish he might shovel down in a hurry. She liked to have a hot lunch from home delivered to him at his office when he was a senator. Nothing, Jackie was determined, was going to go amiss with her housekeeping—she even consulted the odd annual. There would always be good food and drink stocked up in the house, and she froze down large quantities of Jack's favorite fish chowder to make sure he never went short. Pearl Nelson, who was to be partially ousted in the White House kitchen by French chef René Verdon, was the Kennedys' Georgetown cook, and it was Pearl who made many of the dishes close to Jack's heart: his favorite chowder, the hot fruit dessert he was partial to, and his baked seafood casserole, which might even follow him on his travels.

Fish Chowder

2 pints milk
2 bay leaves
1 blade mace
2 lb. haddock, smoked or unsmoked,
  depending on your preference
1 lb. bacon, finely chopped,
  or diced salt pork
2 medium-size onions, sliced

1½ tsp. garlic, crushed
3 large potatoes, chopped into 1-inch
  pieces
3 ribs celery, finely sliced
freshly ground black pepper
pinch of sea salt
2 tbsp. butter

In a saucepan, warm the 2 pints of milk with the 2 bay leaves and the mace. Now add the haddock fillets and simmer for 5 minutes. Turn off the heat and leave these delicious flavors to infuse the milk. In a deep pan, fry the bacon or pork until it is crispy. Remove with a slotted spoon and set aside on some kitchen roll. Now slowly sauté the onion and garlic in the bacon/pork fat until the onions have turned a rich gold. Now add the fish and milk—the fish will break up naturally on its own. Add the potatoes and celery, plus plenty of black pepper and a pinch of salt—less if you have used smoked haddock. Simmer for 25 to 30 minutes; the starch from the potatoes will thicken the soup and produce a rich creaminess. Finally, remove the bay leaves and mace. Add the generous 2-tablespoon knob of butter at the end and sprinkle each bowlful of the chowder with the crisp bacon or ham.

Baked Seafood Casserole

2 lb. mixed, cooked shellfish such
  as lobster, crab, and shrimp
240 ml. mayonnaise
1 green pepper, finely chopped
1 small to medium onion, finely
  chopped
3 ribs celery, finely chopped
1 tbsp. tomato puree

generous pinch of sea salt
1 tsp. cayenne pepper
freshly ground black pepper
1 tbsp. Worcestershire sauce
2 tsp. Tabasco
2 cups crushed, plain potato chips
1 cup grated Cheddar
1 tsp. paprika

Preheat the oven to 200 degrees centigrade. In a large mixing bowl, combine the shellfish, mayonnaise, green pepper, onion, celery, tomato puree, sea salt, cayenne pepper, black pepper, Worcestershire sauce, and Tabasco. Empty this into an ovenproof baking dish and top with a layer of crushed potato chips with paprika shaken over them. Bake in the oven for about 15 minutes and then serve.

Hot Fruit Dessert

3 oranges
3 lemons
1 cup demerara sugar
2 tins peaches, in their own juice
2 tins apricots, in their own juice

2 tins pineapple chunks, in their own juice
2 tins destoned dark purple sweet cherries, in their own juice
freshly grated nutmeg

Preheat the oven to 200 degrees centigrade. Get a large baking dish. Finely zest the oranges and lemons, then remove all the skin and pith from these, cut them into very thin slices, and remove all seeds. Take the citrus zest and mix it through the demerara sugar. Now layer the fruits in the baking dish, interleaving each layer with a sprinkling of the zesty demerara sugar and a good grind of fresh nutmeg. Finish with a sprinkle of demerara and nutmeg. Bake in the oven for 20 to 30 minutes, until it is very hot. Pearl would have served it with sour cream. Now call for the president!

JFK and Jackie were very different, and when Jack was a senator, their house in Georgetown showed this. Jack liked playing to the crowd and was careless about his appearance—he could go out with mismatching shoes. He loved table-thumping conversations about politics, mashed potatoes, and boisterous fun, while Jackie was shy, elegant, and refined, sipping daiquiris by candlelight and edging her conversations with polite, remote references to Baudelaire and the ballet—she was a bit of a whisperer, so you had to strain to hear her. Everything about her eating style was European in a very contained and refined way; fresh fruit and some delicious cheeses were her choice of dessert, while JFK, in a wrinkled suit, raided the kitchen cupboard for chocolate sauce and the freezer for vanilla ice cream, which he wolfed down unceremoniously. But they were united in some things, to the cost of their guests—they loved playing Categories, trouncing their guests with their expertise: Jackie in fashion, and JFK in everything from tennis to history.

There was one JFK category, though, that Jackie had to learn to turn a blind eye to: ladies. He was too fond of poolside lunch at the White House, swimming naked with some lovely; if she arrived for dinner at the White House and stayed the night, Jack turned up first thing in the morning, tray in hand, to supply a very steamy breakfast in bed. One ex-lover described JFK as looking for a mirror in women that could reflect back how special he was. If Jackie was about, she'd have a grilled cheese sandwich in bed at lunch before having a nap. JFK finished work at 1:30 every afternoon, and then liked to swim nude in the pool—hopefully alone—and then get into bed and eat lunch, mostly a hamburger or a glass of Metrecal from a tray. He and Jackie enjoyed some alone time until 3 p.m.

Jackie revamped the White House and its kitchens, introducing fine French cuisine to the table, through her new French chef, René Verdon, although Pearl remained in the background. French cuisine, Jackie averred, was part of her proud French Bouvier heritage, and she had been enchanted by France when she lived there for a year in 1949. René and Jackie pored over French menus, and non-French-speaking guests at the White House had to decipher their dinner. This wasn't helped by the fact that state dinners in the White House often featured Cuba libres in enormous tumblers, which made everyone foggy-headed.

Impatiently, when she was criticized for using French on her menus, she rather satirically hacked off the French in any menu: the indigestible "eggs mollet" replaced the lyrical *oeufs mollet* à la Reine. One thing the kitchen couldn't quite get right was the mix for her beloved daiquiris, so Jackie used Scotch tape to plaster her instructions on the kitchen wall: "2 parts rum, 3 parts frozen limeade, 1 part fresh lime juice. Add a few drops of Falernum as sweetener." In a dark-lady rather than first-lady move to economize, she canceled the food parcels the White House kitchen sent to orphans and commanded that these supplies be reworked into their family dinners. Charity began at home, even if your home was the White House. When her sister, Lee Radziwill, turned up for a visit, the White House was shaken down; only the best would do. This once, René and the kitchens were not enough, and she ordered the best from outside caterers. Nothing was too good for these ladies: even when they were touring India together, Jackie had white bread for her lunchtime cream cheese sandwiches.

At the White House there would be eight for dinner most evenings. The guest list was decided on late in the day, and the atmosphere was often casual, so much so that one friend took to calling the White House "the pizza palace on Pennsylvania Avenue." The first dinner party the Kennedys had at the White House, forty-eight hours after the inauguration, was fun, with a gold bucket containing ten pounds of coal black caviar, turtle soup, followed by filet mignon and profiteroles, all washed down with waves of champagne. They also held swish little finger-clicking dinner party dances, again with oceans of Cuba libre. Jackie might be smoking L&M cigarettes; JFK took a cigar after dinner. At one of these parties Lyndon Johnson drank so much that he collapsed on top of his dance partner: "He slid to the floor and lay like a lox," one guest remembered. The Kennedys deliberately chose as many beautiful guests as possible for the long, lovely evenings of dinner dances, a sort of human eye candy, playmates for JFK or the likes of the Aga Khan, to go with the temptations of the French menu on one evening in spring 1961 of *saumon mousseline a la normande, poulet a l'estragon*, mushrooms *aux fines herbs*, and casserole *marie-blanche*. Like the Clintons later, the Kennedys tried to make the White House table sumptuous—and often got it wrong. JFK and Jackie created a stomach-churning soup monstrosity called Boula (apparently named after a piece of collegiate whimsy, the Boula Boula song, but more likely to suggest what one might need to do after eating). It was . . . wait for it . . . *tinned* pea and turtle soup, a dash of sherry, finished with a garnish of whipped cream and cheese. Gulp. An experience perhaps akin to that undergone by the Queen Mum when FDR served her hot dogs in 1939—though George VI was so delighted by this quaintly described "Delightful Hot-Dog Sandwich" that he asked Mrs. Roosevelt for seconds.

As one aide described it, the "ping pong" of quick talk at Kennedy parties was invigorating and challenging, while Katherine Graham (the wife of the *Washington Post*'s editor) likened it to having your mind vacuum cleaned by Kennedy: she felt like a sick rabbit whenever JFK cornered her. At another White House lunch Grace Kelly was so nervous that she knocked back two Bloody Marys and then became mute, bombed.

Pre-Jackie, when Jack was growing up amongst the sprawl of his many other Kennedy siblings, the favorite beverage in the Kennedy family home was milk, and it was not uncommon to find the whole family each enjoying a glass en masse. Even as a child, precocious Jack was too skinny, like a "lively elf," an impression exacerbated by his jug ears, and Rose tried to give him extra gravy and tidbits. He wrote reassuring her that he intended to "build himself up" in the school tuck shop, in order to recover from swollen glands. He had even more brilliant ideas; once when he and Bobby spotted the sign "No dogs allowed in this restaurant," they scribbled on it "hot" and chortled at their great joke. The family loved to picnic on the rough, golden, windy sands of the Cape; they'd fill Thermos flasks with creamed chicken and run into a drugstore on their way to the beach for ice cream cones and a huge container of ice cream. Lollipops were also packed up and a big chocolate cake to slice up—if it survived the jostling. Best of all, though, was the luscious concoction, Boston cream pie, a light, fluffy cake with custard cream in the middle and a firm, semihard chocolate frosting on top. The Kennedy children held their breaths in anticipation when Rose cut into the Boston cream pie, and this awe passed on down through the generations. When John Jr. was asked if he liked having lunch with his grandmother Rose at Hyannis Port, he enthused, "Yeah, she has really good food! She has very good creamed chicken and Boston cream pie."

Hyannis Creamed Chicken

1 lb. roughly chopped, roast chicken, skinned
1 tbsp. butter
1 tbsp. all-purpose flour
¾ pint milk
1 tsp. Dijon mustard

¼ cup fresh, steamed green peas
2 scallions, finely chopped
1 tsp. finely chopped tarragon
sea salt
freshly ground black pepper
2 tsp. parsley, finely chopped

Dice the roasted, cooled chicken into 1-inch-size pieces. In a saucepan, melt the butter, then remove from the heat. Stirring, add the all-purpose flour and combine to make a roux. Now add the milk, a little at a time, stirring to incorporate it with the roux. When all the milk is combined, return the pan to the heat and, stirring constantly, bring to a boil. Once boiling, turn down the heat to a simmer and add the teaspoon of Dijon mustard. After about 8 minutes, remove the pan from the heat and leave the white sauce to cool.

In a bowl, combine the diced chicken, green peas, scallions, and tarragon. Now add the cooled white sauce. Taste and season with sea salt and black pepper, then serve with crumbled parsley on top.

Boston Cream Pie (. . . or the pie that is not a pie)

FOR THE CAKE
1½ cups all-purpose flour
generous pinch of sea salt
2 tsp. baking powder
2 tbsp. cornstarch
12 tbsp. or 180 g. butter

2 tsp. vanilla extract
1 cup granulated sugar
3 eggs
½ cup milk

FOR THE CREAMY CUSTARD FILLING
½ cup milk
½ cup double cream
1 vanilla bean, split, with its inky seeds scraped out

3 egg yolks
½ cup granulated sugar
pinch of sea salt
1 tbsp. all-purpose flour

FOR THE GOOEY CHOCOLATE FROSTING
5 oz. bittersweet chocolate, finely chopped
½ tsp. vanilla extract

1 tsp. butter
½ cup double cream
2 cups confectioner's sugar

Boston Cream Pie (*continued*)

Preheat the oven to 180 degrees centigrade. Take two identical cake tins and butter and flour them. Into a deep mixing bowl sieve the all-purpose flour, sea salt, baking powder, and cornstarch. In another bowl, using an electric beater, cream the butter, vanilla extract, and sugar together. When this has become fluffy, add the eggs, one at a time, incorporating thoroughly each time. Gradually, add the flour mixture and milk, a quarter of each at a time, alternating them. Now pour the smooth cake batter into the cake tins. Bake them in the oven for about 30 minutes, testing the cake with a skewer to see if it is done. Remove from the oven and cool.

Now it is time to make the delicious custard-cream filling. In a saucepan, heat the milk and cream with the vanilla bean and seeds. Bring to a boil and then take off the heat and let the vanilla infuse the milk for 15 minutes. Meanwhile, in a bowl, whisk together the egg yolks, sugar, and pinch of salt. When this becomes fluffy, add the all-purpose flour. Now remove the vanilla pod from the milk and cream mixture. Pour the milk-cream into the egg mixture, stirring rapidly. Return this cream-custard to the saucepan and heat gradually, stirring all the time until it thickens. When a thick custard has formed, remove from the heat and sprinkle with a little granulated sugar to prevent a skin from forming. Leave the custard to cool.

Place a glass bowl over a pan a third full of hot water. Put the broken chocolate, vanilla extract, butter, and cream in the bowl; stir constantly until this all melds together. When this happens, remove the pan from the heat, whisk the mixture thoroughly, and let the chocolate mixture cool. When it is lukewarm, add the confectioner's sugar, beating the mixture into a thick icing.

Now assemble the Boston cream pie with custard between the two airy cake rounds and the chocolate frosting on top.

2

Dining with the Rebels

From the shores of Cape Town to the menu at Charlestown Penitentiary, we follow the crumb trail of the world's leading revolutionaries. Ordering a Molotov are Nelson Mandela; Karl Marx; Vladimir Lenin; Fidel Castro; Che Guevara; Malcolm X; Osama bin Laden; and Yasser Arafat.

EATING A WAY OUT OF APARTHEID: NELSON MANDELA

Despite his love of traditional Xhosa African food, Nelson Mandela was open-minded and liked to give everything a try, to sample, explore, taste, and try to understand the other cultures of South Africa through food. In his eating history, you can see the path to the end of apartheid.

Primarily, it was to the traditional corn-based African dish of umngqusho and soured milk amasi that Mandela's food loyalties took him. They tasted of his childhood, where food memories are indelibly forged, among his own Xhosa people. The young Mandela suckled warm milk straight from the cow's udder, bit into cobs of corn toasted on the fire, and ate umngqusho, simmered and lightly seasoned. In *Long Walk to Freedom* Mandela remembers his mother preparing umngqusho in the village of Qunu. She had one hut for cooking, another for sleeping, and a third to store things in. The interior of the sleeping hut was unshaped by any Western-style furniture; the family sat on the ground and slept on mats (it wasn't until Nelson went to Mqhekezweni that he discovered the pillow).

His mother planted mealies (maize), watched them grow, and then snapped the swollen yellow cobs from the stem, sweet and fat with corn milk. The village women made bread from the mealies, grinding the hardened, dried corn between two stones. His mother boiled the mealies in milk; and made Mandela's beloved umngqusho, where the partially crushed corn (samp) was stewed with cowpeas. She prepared amasi, fermenting milk in a calabash until the thick, sour yogurt separated from the thin watery residue; the amasi was then drunk or poured over mealie pap. Years later, a fugitive, hunted revolutionary, Nelson was in close hiding in a friend's flat in a white residential neighborhood, when a desperate longing for amasi filled him; he decided to make his own. Putting a bottle of milk out on the thin window ledge, Nelson left it to thicken and sour (in hot weather this takes just a day or two). Then the voices of two men speaking Zulu wafted up from the pavements below; Mandela listened, his breath held, from behind the drawn curtains. "What is 'our milk' doing on that window ledge?" one asked the other. The implication was clear: only black Africans made amasi, and what was a black African doing staying in a white neighborhood? Nelson had to get out fast and find another secret hideout.

As a young, radical lawyer, Nelson Mandela developed a lifelong love of curry in his years in Johannesburg. He'd drop in on one of his Indian friends and spend the night drinking illicit booze, debating politics, exploring Indian culture, dancing, and eating a delicious multitude of curries. He had his first surprising taste of crab curry at his friend Naranswamy Naidoo's house; at first, Nelson stared nauseously at the river crab claws and curry-coated crab's armor, but then decided to venture a leg or two, only to find it delicious. Curries—sweet, vinegared, or hot—were served with sambals (diced and spiced vegetables), atjar (pickles), or blatjang (chutney) made with fruits cooked in garlic, plump chili peppers, onions, and spices and then pickled. Often as not, he'd settle down on the night on the floor for a night's sleep.

It was in December 1956 that Winnie first clapped eyes on the tall, handsome young lawyer at the Johannesburg Drill Hall; he didn't even seem aware of her existence. Winnie was staying with Oliver Tambo's girlfriend (and later wife), Adelaide Tsukudu. Nelson was representing a friend of Winnie's who had been assaulted by the police. Winnie thought he was awesome—older than her and very tall. Finally she was introduced to him as "Winnie from Bizana"—hardly the exotic introduction she might have hoped for—when he purportedly had to pay for her food in a delicatessen: Oliver had taken her and Adelaide there but forgotten his cash. "Winnie from Bizana" obviously caught Mandela's eye, and he followed up the delicatessen crisis with a phone call asking her to lunch. Desperately, Winnie riffled through her clothes; none of her knee-length, frilled schoolgirl dresses even came close to matching the sophistication required for her first date with Nelson Mandela. She borrowed an outfit and was driven to Mandela's papery, file-packed office where he worked seven days a week. Dinner was comic: Nelson took Winnie for her first taste of Indian food; a shock, she said, "for a little country bumpkin from Pondoland." Nelson chewed his way through the "hot, unbearable food," dishes of curried mutton and chicken with "this funny bread" called roti, while Winnie spluttered watery-eyed across the table from him. "If you find it too hot," Nelson advised, "it helps to take a glass of water." And even on their first date, after what felt like every mouthful Nelson took, there were comrades, friends, and associates coming up to consult with him—a sign that Winnie would have to share Nelson with an entire nation.

During the 1950s, when Winnie and Nelson were newly married and living at Number 8115, Orlando West, he'd be up at the crack of dawn and have a quick breakfast of toast and orange juice. When he returned home at night, he'd sometimes bring back as many as ten colleagues or friends and tease Winnie by saying he'd invited them back to sample her great cooking, knowing only a single lamb chop moldered in the fridge. When she burst into tears of embarrassment, he nipped off to the shop around the corner for a packet of tinned fish. This probably gave Winnie time to regret not dusting the picture of Lenin that dominated Nelson's study. Determined to please, the very first thing Winnie tried to learn to make in her kitchen was curry, but it went wrong, leaving behind a smoky mess; Nelson prodded it and helpfully suggested that perhaps it might help to add water to curry? Unlike Winnie, Nelson's first wife, Jehovah's Witness Evelyn Mase, was a calm, practiced cook who produced sensible staples such as a jelly and custard mold or tripe with dumplings—Evelyn had it easy, though; this was before Nelson had become hooked on curry. Even when Winnie made spaghetti, she layered it with curried mince and then topped it with cheese in a deep, heavy green casserole dish: Nelson always remembered the taste and longed for mouthfuls of Winnie's spaghetti from far away, imprisoned on Robben Island.

On nights out, he and Winnie listened to jazz music and then might round off the evening by climbing the creaking stairs up to white-and-red-checkered tables of the Indian restaurant Kapitan's on Kort Street, in order to assuage Nelson's hankering for rotis, samosas, and biryanis—he also enjoyed the beautiful, sour shock of drinking his first Campari at Kapitan's. Having had their first date there, they treated Kapitan's with joyful familiarity; plus it defied the urban racisms of Johannesburg. They might shake hands with the owner and chef at Kapitan's, Madanjit Ranchod, and then huddle up at a table with Oliver Tambo—he and Nelson had been running their fledgling law firm together since 1953, and it was only a block or two away—and roll up their sleeves over a crab curry, cracking the shell and sucking on the claws; or stuff fragments of naan with Nelson's favorite minced-meat curry with ginger pickle and rice (after his release from prison more than two decades later, he headed straight back to Kapitan's for the same meal there). Tandoori tasted different there—Ranchod always used an ancient iron stove in the kitchens, which had been forged by a Hungarian blacksmith at the cusp of World War I.

Blacks and whites ate together: Kapitan's was one of the few restaurants in Johannesburg that deliberately breached the gastro-political divide and had been operating since 1914. Ranchod, however, hadn't a clue that his regulars were political agitators; Mandela, he said, "was a quiet person. I didn't know he was a politician until they arrested him." A few months before Mandela was released from prison in 1989, Kapitan's was threatened with closure, and lo and behold, a letter arrived for Ranchod postmarked Robben Island: a letter of commiseration from prison, in which Mandela lamented the fact that citizens of the future would be unable to savor Ranchod's curries. "Dear Madanjit and Marjorie . . . I learn with sorrow that your famous Oriental Restaurant on Kort Street is closing down . . . There are many palates and tummies inside and out of the country which will justifiably be outraged at the disastrous news." With a sigh you can still hear, he signed off, "Sincerely, Nelson."

Mandela's tummy growled for past meals at Kapitan's when he was holed up for eighteen years on Robben Island in Cape Town's Table Bay. Flat as a dishcloth and nibbled into a near-desert by a massive rabbit population, Robben Island was enough to make any revolutionary's heart sink. Even the mountain tortoise, which had been introduced there as part of a "Noah's Ark" experiment in the 1950s, kept trying to leave the island, hopping off the rocks, making a beeline for the distant shores of Cape Town, only to be apprehended, fished out, and sent back.

The kitchens of Robben Island Prison were like men's prison kitchens every-where: those on cooking duty, always nonpolitical inmates, squirreled away the choicest morsels for themselves and, grinning, offered their fellow convicts platters of food thickened with sand and other gritty, sticky bits of dirt, all seasoned by the pellucid or polished black carapaces and legs of insects. It was most often black African prisoners who were served up this stomach-churning rubbish, slapped into metal bowls, the bowls often unwashed from the day before. The prison authorities decided, in a deliberately divisive move, that the food of Africans should be based on what they called the "F" diet, while "Coloreds and Indians" should receive the "D" diet. What they wanted to suggest was that the prisoners were not all equally "human." Mealie (maize) predominated in both eating plans, usually in the form of cornmeal porridge, mealie pap, in the morning. Mealies then reappeared at lunchtime; mealie rice was mixed with ground-up mealies to make samp. If you were given lunch at the quarry, though, van Rensburg, the officer in charge, always chose to urinate close to the food.

Those on the D diet had their diets enriched and bulked out with bread, topped with near-rancid butter and extra meat, vegetables, and coffee. Coffee was coffee only in name, constructed of blackened and baked ground-up maize. The bread, because of the way it looked when quartered, was called cat's head, "katkop." African prisoners finally got bread in 1971; it was assumed they wouldn't like bread, as it was too "European." All eating was done from a tray while squatting; anyone whose buttocks grazed the floor received a sharp rap to their bottoms. Any exchange of food between the two different diet groups was prohibited and punished, although food smuggling happened all the time, sometimes for sexual favors. African prisoners were allowed no jam but were the lucky recipients of a drink called phuzamandla—this means "drink of strength" and is made from mealies—powdered this time—and yeast, mixed with milk to form a frothy milkshake. Forbidden to pass the lips of nonblacks, it was a tasty concoction but was so smuggled about the prison and diluted multiple times in the process, that the drink that passed Mandela's lips was the thin, watery ghost of a milkshake. Then, for dinner? Mealie porridge again, purportedly enriched with meat and vegetables but, according to James Gregory (Mandela's prison officer, who became a loyal friend of Mandela's), what floated on its surface looked very much like burnt corn.

The first prisoner rebellion on Robben Island was the result of food shortages. Again, the African prisoners were the ones who went short, as they were always served last. The more politically radical prisoners from the ANC and PAC were determined to hunger strike; they also hunger struck to prevent the use of gang rape as a punishment for political prisoners. Sneakily, the prison authorities tried to break their fast by loading the plates they were offered with new scrumptious meals, packed with vegetables, hot and deliciously oozing with fat. The prisoners made their point, however, and food standards gradually began to improve in the jail. The protest did take its toll, though, and some prisoners who were accused of inciting the food rebellion had an extra six months added on to their sentences. Finally, the political prisoners managed to win some more control over their food supply when they began to garden. They were not allowed water for their seeds and plants, so they saved their own water; the plants needed feeding, so Nelson found ostrich dung. Eventually, the prisoners tried to hide the first sections of Mandela's biography in cocoa tins under the soil there.

A bit of culinary inventiveness could take you a long way on the island: on their working visits to Robben Island, beach prisoners were assigned seaweed duty, wading into the salty, shark-infested waters of Table Bay to harvest armfuls of seaweed, to be used for fertilizer. Apart from the sharks—or perhaps because of them—this was no pleasant duty: prisoners might gash themselves on the sharp rocks, their blood striping the water. When dragging the seaweed on the beach, they surreptitiously skirmished for seafood to collect the ingredients for a Robben Island seafood stew—cooked by themselves and, apparently, making a tasty foragers' lunch of fresh mussels, crayfish, small crabs, perhaps even abalone; this was oddly mirrored by the prison officers enjoying lobsters, abalone drizzled with butter, and white wine in their club. On the island were also rabbits for trapping, partridges and bony seagulls (their plump chicks were tastier), and once, on the shoreline, a sea lion that proved tasty and rich, like lamb.

Nelson's rehabilitation, the changing climate of South Africa's political culture, was signaled in food when, after seventeen years on Robben Island, Nelson was transferred with others, including Walter Sisulu, to Pollsmoor Prison, across the bay and close to Cape Town. A changed diet signaled the first improvements. Instead of an entirely mealie-based, wet and soft diet, Nelson got to taste fish again . . . except it was so overcooked it collapsed into a marshy fish porridge. Negotiations took place, and it was agreed that the ex–Robben Island ANC political prisoners should have their food cooked separately, and so their food was not thrown into the vast steel drums used to cook up the main prison population's food. Next came the right to have extra food brought for them; to great delight, a food and shopping wish list was compiled. Not only could biscuits and soap be requested, but also spices and extra condiments, which could make food more appetizing. Nelson's eyes glowed brightly when he heard this: "Ahhh, *biryani* . . ." he said immediately; the days of South African curry were upon him again, with the possibility of freedom.

But things remained complicated: James Gregory took the list down to the Pollsmoor prison shop, which was run by an ill-tempered officer called van Dyck. Furiously, van Dyck scratched out most of the items on the list, moaning bitterly: "I run this shop, and I don't have things in this shop for fucking terrorists. If they want it, they can get their whores to bring this stuff in."

Despite the promise of biryani, Mandela and Sisulu repeatedly asked to be returned to Robben Island; they missed their comrades. Pretoria, however, would never concede this. Thus, oddly, Pollsmoor seemed even more stifling. Until, that is, when one day, Mandela and Sisulu looked at the concrete waste surrounding them and decided that what was needed was a vegetable garden. Some beauty, growth, and green life could spring up amid the gray concrete of prison. They sliced in half oil drums, filled them with soil, and planted seeds donated by prison wardens. Even Monroe, the commanding officer at Pollsmoor, gave Mandela broccoli, beetroot, and carrot seeds. The white warden and the black prisoner discovered a shared interest in vegetable growing, and the prison allotment bloomed. Soon there were purple aubergine, dark green spinach, and heavy cropping tomatoes. The guards and Monroe gathered about Nelson's garden, and he, in his ancient straw hat, tended to the plants and vegetables every morning, whatever the weather. Incarcerated for so long, Mandela was on the lookout for vegetables to boost his health when he read about a terrific health drink he could make from the boiled leaves and stems of beetroot. Raymond Mhlaba yelled at him, "Hey, Nelson, perhaps this drink will reverse the aging process!" Nelson had no choice but to weather through, make the drink, and down it. He offered everyone a taste, and they all refused. By the end of the day, Mandela didn't look any younger, but he did spend a considerable amount of time in the toilet. Ever after, Raymond offered Nelson his socks for a brew.

Moments of liberty tasted of fish and chips, eaten with his fingers on a drive out in Cape Bay with James Gregory, although Nelson's health was soon to demand a low-cholesterol diet when he recuperated from an operation to drain his lungs of water. He discovered fish cakes with a poached egg on top in the hospital and liked this for breakfast, as often as possible. A further sign of a huge shift in the government's attitude toward Mandela was apparent when they had him recuperate in the Constantiaberg Clinic, a luxurious private clinic set in the suburbs of Cape Town. There, despite dietary instructions to the contrary, a breakfast was served to him of bacon, scrambled eggs, and buttered toast. The delicious, unfamiliar aroma wafted around Nelson's heart. The deputy commander from Pollsmoor tried to pull the tray out of the nurse's hands, until Mandela interjected: "Major, I am sorry. If this breakfast will kill me, then today I am prepared to die."

Finally Nelson was held, prerelease, in a farmhouse at Victor Vester Prison, surrounded by wild fig trees and custard apple trees, where he again set about fashioning a new vegetable plot. Nelson received the news that he was to have his own cook there, a figure well known to him, the prison warden Jack Swart, who used to drive the prisoners in the blistering heat of Robben Island to the lime pits, to quarry lime there. He drove so roughly that Mandela had yelled at him, "What the hell do you think we are, bags of mealie?" When they clapped eyes on each other again at the farmhouse, Nelson said, "I hope you're a better cook than a driver." Before you knew it, though, Swart was teaching Nelson how to make his own corn beer, and Nelson asked if he could show him how to do a braai; the Afrikaans word for a barbecue, braai symbolizes the culinary heart of white Afrikaans South Africa. Swart showed him how to season the meat with salt and garlic and which special woods rendered the most flavorsome smokes. Winnie flinched when she heard Nelson use the Afrikaans word. "What do you know about braaing?" she asked sharply. He replied, "This is one of my latest classes. Just like the corn beer I can now brew. I have become very domesticated." Nelson had never stopped challenging the food divisions of South Africa. The end of apartheid was at hand.

Aaah, Biryani

4 lb. lamb
1 medium-size onion, sliced
⅓ cup ghee
3 whole green chilies
½ tsp. turmeric
3 tsp. chopped garlic
1½ tsp. chopped ginger
1½ tsp. dried, ground cilantro
1½ tsp. cumin

9 cloves
9 peppercorns
4 cardamom pods
3 chunky pieces of cinnamon stick
1 large tomato
6 small potatoes (precooked)
1½ cups basmati rice
pinch of sea salt
3 hard-boiled eggs, quartered

Cube the lamb into medium-size pieces. Fry the sliced onion in ghee until it is pale gold. Now brown the lamb and then add the green chilies; turmeric; garlic; ginger; dried, ground cilantro; cumin; cloves; peppercorns; cardamom pods; and cinnamon stick. Cook the lamb slowly (for about 1 hour) until the meat is tender, adding water if necessary.

Add the tomato and the potatoes to the lamb and cook until the tomato is softened. Meanwhile, cook the rice. Get a medium-size deep pan (with a lid); put a little slick of oil in the base of the pan. Pour in a mug of rice and stir: the oil will coat each grain. Next add two mugs of water, sprinkle with sea salt, cover, and bring to a boil on a medium heat. Check after about 10 minutes: the rice is ready when the water has been absorbed. When this has happened, turn off the heat and leave the rice, covered, in its pan for 10 minutes.

Preheat the oven to 160 degrees centigrade. Now add the fresh cilantro and peas to the spicy lamb and its rich, dark, curried gravy. Stir well. Add the rice to the lamb stew and mix lightly. Embed the quartered eggs in the biryani. Cover the pot with a tinfoil lid and bake in the oven for half an hour. It will come out of the oven steaming, magnificent, and scented with cardamom, cinnamon, and cilantro. Serve with rotis, lemon atjar, ginger pickle, and cilantro-mint raita.

Cilantro-Mint Raita

1 bunch cilantro
1 bunch mint
1 green chili
1 clove garlic

8 peppercorns
1 tsp. sea salt
juice of 1 lemon

In a food processor, whizz up the cilantro, mint, chili, garlic, peppercorns, sea salt, and lemon juice. You will be left with a lovely, sharp-smelling green gloop. This paste will now keep in a sealed container in the fridge for about a week. When you want to use it, take a tablespoon of the zingy paste and mix it well with half a pint of runny yogurt. Serve this cooling yogurt alongside the biryani.

Lemon Atjar

2 lb. lemons
2 oz. coarse sea salt
500 ml. white wine vinegar
250 ml. oil
2 chilies, seeded and chopped

3 tsp. mustard seeds
3 tsp. cumin seeds
3 tsp. whole cilantro seeds, slightly
crushed
1½ oz. sugar

Cut the lemons into eighths and remove all the pips. Squash them down in a container and sprinkle with sea salt. Next, pour the white wine vinegar over. Cover and leave in the fridge for 36 hours. After this, drain the lemons and discard the fluid. Combine the oil, chilies, mustard seeds, cumin seeds, cilantro seeds, and sugar. Pour this over the lemons. Refrigerate.

Ginger Pickle

1 tbsp. ghee
1 cup fresh ginger, skinned and diced
1 oz. tamarind paste
2 cloves garlic, chopped
1 tsp. powdered fenugreek

1 tbsp. brown muscovado sugar
(or jaggery, if you can get it)
1 tsp. turmeric
½ tsp. chili powder
pinch of sea salt

FOR TEMPERING

1 tbsp. ghee
5 curry leaves
1 fresh red chili, split and seeds
removed

1 tsp. mustard seeds
1 tsp. black onion seeds

Warm 1 tablespoon of ghee in a large, heavy-based frying pan; add the ginger and cook gently until the ginger turns a little more golden. Now empty the ginger into a blender and process into a smooth paste. You may find some resistant "hairy" clots of ginger fiber remain—extract these and discard. Now stir in the tamarind paste, garlic, fenugreek, sugar, turmeric, chili powder, and sea salt. You are now going to temper the whole spices that complete the ginger pickle. Heat the second tablespoon of ghee in the frying pan and fry the curry leaves, chili, mustard seeds, and black onion seeds. Fry for 1 or 2 minutes—the curry leaves should not burn. Stir the ginger paste through this and then cool. This will keep in the fridge for a few days. Serve with the biryani.

Chapter 2

KARL MARX LIKED PICNICS

The *Memoirs* of Wilhelm Liebknecht reveal just what a fun-loving rogue Karl Marx really was. The Marx home was at Number 28 Dean Street, a court running off from Oxford Street in London, which among its residents counted a chiropodist dedicated to the study of yellowing Victorian feet, the chattering Western Jewish Girls' Free School, and seven tailors. The eccentric Marx family was crammed into noisy, cheap lodgings, along with an Italian confectioner, several language teachers, and one John Marengo, an Italian-born cook—the main occupant of the building and from whom Marx had rented two rooms: Marx himself is down on the census as one "Doctor (Philosophical Author)." Dean Street was an interesting street on which to live. Tantalizingly, a year or two earlier Karl might have bumped into young Charles Dickens hurrying along the pavement to act in an amateur theatrical production of Jonson's *Every Man in His Humour* (Dickens's acting was kindly described by a reviewer as of "debatable merit"). Fifty years earlier, Marx might have clapped eyes on Admiral Horatio Nelson, the day before the Battle of Trafalgar, being measured for a coffin.

Liebknecht vividly remembered all the merry times he spent with the Marxes at Number 28 in these early years of friendship: Dr. and Mrs. Marx always welcomed visitors with great camaraderie and delight, despite the fact that, according to one shocked "Prussian agent," they were living in chaotic poverty. All furniture was broken or lopsided—not one piece remained intact. Marx's manuscripts lay among the children's toys and tea cups with broken rims; on tables were dirty, sticky cutlery alongside seamy inkwells and Dutch clay pipes. A canopy of dust politely tried to draw a veil over all this. To sit down was to hazard an accident.

Liebknecht first met Marx at a picnic in the summer of 1850—roguishly, Marx insisted upon examining Liebknecht's head, an examination to which he patiently submitted. His skull was officially inspected, felt, and prodded; his head twisted at unusual, uncomfortable, and often unpleasant angles, Marx ruminating quietly all the time, his breathing a low, gentle grumble. But, phew, Liebknecht passed the phrenological test. Marx's examination was in jest, but many Victorians took it seriously: the captain of *The Beagle* was an admirer of phrenology and thought that Darwin had entirely the wrong sort of nose for a crew member and roundly refused to take him on any kind of voyage (till persuaded otherwise by Darwin's uncle).

A few days later, Liebknecht met up with Marx and his co-conspirator, Friedrich Engels, in a clubroom of the Communist Laborers' Educational Club on Great Windmill Street. All whiskery and cheery, Marx took him by the arm and led him through into a private parlor. Engels was already draining a huge pewter pot of toffee-brown stout, and another was quickly pushed into Liebknecht's hand. He sat down opposite Marx and Engels at a massive mahogany table, and the three men ordered English beefsteaks with every imaginable trimming of onion and gravy, which they ate while sipping their foaming stout, with the prospect of a good quiet smoke on long clay pipes ahead. It was, Liebknecht ventured, just like being living animations from the English illustrations of Charles Dickens.

Beefsteak, however, wasn't the only thing grilled that night. Liebknecht endured a tirade of questions. Both Marx and Engels good-humoredly believed him to be a little too susceptible to philistine ideas of "Democracy" and "South German senti-mental haziness." He ended up wishing he'd read more. The sun was already up by the time Liebknecht got to bed.

Liebknecht loved going to Hampstead Heath for a romp with the Marxes on Sundays. The heath seemed like a primeval wilderness of heather and tumble-me-down mountainous tufts. Their party set out at about 11 a.m., armed with a tasty, bulging picnic made by the Marxes' housekeeper, Helene Demuth, otherwise fondly called "Lenchen." She had been with Jenny Marx's family, the von Westphalens, since she was eight or nine years old and was the daughter of a Rhineland village baker. What was in Lenchen's basket was always the focal point for hungry curiosity, and there were always several famished volunteers ready to help her carry her basket across the heath.

That basket, Liebknecht claimed, would float forever before him in his dreams, crammed with delicacies of pastry, flesh, and cheese to satisfy not just the appetite of Marx but also all his fellow revolutionaries: the centerpiece of the basket was always a haunch of roast veal, with a crisp layer of golden fat and creamily pale, tender flesh. Then there was a flask of hot tea, steaming and sweetened with sugar, and often fruit—pink-cheeked apples and swell-bottomed pears, ready to eat. The revolutionaries also topped up with whatever noisome snacks were for sale on Hampstead Heath: there was no solitary Mr. Whippy van back in the nineteenth century, tinnily calling out the promise of bad ice cream by wasted duck ponds; no, Marx and Liebknecht could buy bread and cheese or hot water with milk on the heath. Even crockery was for sale; for small coin, delicate curls of local shrimp could be bought, with boiled or pickled periwinkles and dark green watercress.

After eating, they stretched out, read the Sunday papers, and discussed politics while the children played hide-and-seek. One Sunday, Liebknecht recalled a chestnut tree competition to see who could knock off the greatest number of chestnuts—competitive Marx couldn't move his right arm for eight days as a result of his efforts. Marx often lost at the competitive chess they played, and when he lost, he went into a deep, stormy huff. Understandably, Jenny often referred to Marx as "my big child." The happy group sang popular songs and, after a cigar or ten, Marx might recite Shakespeare—he loved Homer too—and passages from the *Divine Comedy*, all in a delightfully exaggerated manner. The day might be topped off with a helping of Lenchen's jam tarts; in her "Recollections of Karl Marx," Marian Comyn recalled Lenchen as a wonderful, awe-inspiring cook: "Her jam tarts are a sweet and abiding memory to this day."

But things weren't always rosy; the Marx family often faced penury and weeks of living on potatoes and bread. Marx was a martyr to carbuncles (including a few on his scrotum) and hemorrhoids, but here he was a bit of a drama king, complaining that his piles afflicted him more grievously than the French Revolution! In December 1867, carbuncles necessitated that Marx lie on one side on the sofa, groaning dramatically, while the rest of the family took refuge in the kitchen downstairs, described by Jenny as an area from which all "creature comforts" make their way up to the higher regions. Their respite was not to last long, because just as the Christmas pudding was being prepared, a statue of Zeus was delivered to the house! Jenny Marx wrote to thank the sender, a family friend named Ludwig Kugelmann, on Christmas Eve. Apparently they were in the middle of seeding raisins (a disagreeable and sticky task); chopping up almonds, orange, and lemon peel; minutely shredding suet; and kneading the whole lot together with eggs and flour when there was a ring at the door and a carriage was stopped outside. Mysterious footsteps followed, going up and down, and they could hear lots of whispering and rustling. Then a voice! "A great statue has arrived." Jenny claimed that if it had been, "Fire, fire, the house is on fire," the "Fenians have come," they could not have run upstairs more quickly. There was Zeus, standing in "colossal splendor, in its ideal purity, old Jupiter tonans himself, unscathed, undamaged (one small edge of the *pedestal is* slightly chipped) before our staring, delighted eyes!!"

Das Kapital Beefsteak with Fried Potatoes

¼ lb. butter	freshly ground black pepper
olive oil	3 large sirloin steaks, ½ inch thick
4 potatoes, peeled and sliced	2 tbsp. melted butter
3 onions, halved and sliced	a mess of herbs, finely chopped (thyme,
sea salt	oregano, chives, tarragon, parsley)

Put the butter in a large frying pan, add a splash of olive oil (this will stop the butter from burning), and place the potatoes and onions in the butter. Salt and pepper the fry and then cover the pan. Continue to fry the potato until it is a good brown color: shake the pan regularly to ensure the potatoes and onions are not sticking.

Heat a ridged griddle and rub it with olive oil. Pepper the steaks and, when the griddle is very hot, lay the steaks down on it. Do not move the steak for 4 minutes. Then, lift the steak, rub olive oil over the griddle tracks, turn, and let it sizzle for a further 4 minutes. Finally, baste the steak in 2 tablespoons of melted butter.

To serve, scatter the mess of herbs on the plate and crown with the delicious bronzed steak. Sprinkle with sea salt. Place a pile of crunchy fried potato and onion beside the steak.

Pour yourself a frothy glass of stout and hunt about for a clay pipe.

Jam Tarts for the Marxist Picnic Hamper

6 oz. all-purpose flour
pinch of salt
dessert spoon of granulated sugar
4 oz. butter, cold and cut into
   thin sticks

1 egg, the yolk separated from
   the white
2 tbsp. water

FOR THE JAM FILLING

mulberry jam
bramble jelly
raspberry jam

cherry jam
blackcurrant jam
marmalade

You'll also need a round pastry cutter (and the usual things like a rolling pin!).

The secret of really good short-crust pastry is to keep it as cool as possible. The Victorians didn't have mixers, so you might choose to be loyal to Lenchen and work the pastry with your fingertips—but this will add an extra half hour to your time, as you'll see . . .

Preheat the oven to 200 degrees centigrade. Sieve the flour into a mixing bowl with a pinch of salt. Either by hand or in a mixing bowl, do the following: add the sugar, stir through, and then mix the sticks of butter through the flour until it forms a soft, crumbly mixture. Do this by rubbing the flour, sugar, and butter quickly between your fingertips.

Whisk together the egg yolk and 2 tablespoons of water. Now, add the whisked egg and water to the butter-flour mixture and blend together. You should now have a pastry to be proud of.

If you have used your hands, then the pastry will be too warm and may be liable to separate. Wrap the ball of pastry in cling film and leave it in the fridge to chill for about 30 minutes (or speed this up by bunging it in the freezer for 20 minutes).

When the pastry is cool and slightly firm to touch, lightly flour the surface you will be working on; rub flour too over the length of your rolling pin. Roll out the pastry using light, gentle movements to the depth of about half a centimeter.

Next, using a round pastry cutter, cut out disks of raw pastry. Take a tart tin (the ones with indentations for about 12 tarts) and butter each pudding indentation. Place a disk of pastry into each indentation and touch it lightly into the shape of the mold. Next, place 2 teaspoons of one of your chosen jams in the base of the pastry. Continue to do this with all the pastry cases, varying the type of jam—or jelly—used in each.

Bake these in your preheated oven for 15 minutes. When done (the pastry crust becomes light gold), leave to cool (STAND AWAY from the tarts!). Later—but not *much* later—enjoy the slightly warm tarts with a hot cup of tea.

LONDON'S CALLING VLADIMIR LENIN

It is a bit bewildering trying to work out just how Vladimir Lenin and his wife-to-be, Comrade Nadezhda Krupskaya, ever got around to talking about marriage or love or swapping the odd kiss: small talk was not for them. Indeed, one friend made Nadezhda sound about as alluring as a lamppost: "a tall, quiet girl, who did not flirt with the boys, moved and thought with deliberation, and had already formed strong convictions." Sounds like fun? Wedded bliss continued in this lighthearted vein: at the point of their marriage in the summer of 1898, Lenin had just been sentenced to three years of internal exile in the village of Shushenskoye, Siberia.

Food wasn't up to much in Siberia; once a week some unfortunate sheep had its throat cut, and Lenin would systematically be fed mutton (in various forms and positions) until the carcass was picked clean and only a skull, a vertebra, and the odd tooth remained. This worked on a rolling program, alternating with a week's worth of meat cutlets that had been chopped up in a trough normally used for preparing cattle feed.

Mind you, in comparison to Trotsky's exile seven years later with the wild Ostyak nomads of northwest Siberia, Lenin was in the lap of luxury, albeit that it smelled of sheep. While Trotsky enjoyed the odd nip of brandy and morsel of roast veal, he was unprepared for the Ostyak tipple of hot, fish-scented tea, into which he had to pour two teaspoons of cranberry essence in order to be able to swallow it. And even that was tame by Ostyak standards: what they really liked was fish flesh eaten raw and quivering while the fish still floundered in its death throes.

All was not too bad, then: Lenin was soon to have Nadezhda *and* his future mother-in-law by his side. While he was out hunting one day with his Gordon setter, Zhenka, Nadezhda paid Lenin a surprise visit and, in his absence, settled into his cottage, where the whitewashed walls were festooned with green branches of Siberian fir. But she couldn't resist a practical joke: when Lenin returned, the landlord told him that an exiled Saint Petersburg worker, Oscar Engberg, had rolled into his cottage drunk and thrown all Lenin's books around. In a state of high alarm, Lenin charged the steps, ready no doubt to wrestle Oscar to the ground. But who stepped out? Comrade Nadezhda! Incidentally, Oscar later went on to prove himself a genuine loose cannon, shaking our happy couple to their core by declaring himself "against revolution."

So what did our revolutionaries get up to on their honeymoon? What honeymooners always do: worked through their ideas on party organization and translated Webb's writings on trade unionism from English into Russian. Oh, and Nadezhda found time to go through the Communist Manifesto in some detail with Oscar, which she simultaneously translated from German for him.

The local peasant who had been appointed to enforce their exile spent most of his time trying to flog them his veal, while Lenin's landlord partied, Siberian style. Wearied, Lenin and Nadezhda upped sticks and moved to another cottage, complete with vegetable patch and Russian stove. The vegetable patch was quickly planted out with beetroots, pumpkins, and carrots, and Nadezhda and her mother experimented with cooking on the cantankerous stove. It proved awkward at first, and Nadezhda's oven fork got tangled up with the dumpling soup, sending the dumplings flying onto the hot coals. A bony-elbowed thirteen-year-old girl called Pasha (whom Nadezhda taught to read and write) was conscripted to help at the cottage. Pasha took the household dictates of Lenin's mother-in-law very seriously and took to inscribing the cottage walls with phonetic versions of such homilies as: "Neva waste eny tee."

Comrade's Cabbage and Dumpling Soup (Shchi)

FOR THE BEEF STOCK

2 tbsp. beef dripping
1 lb. beef, preferably on the bone and in one whole piece (but not butchered in an animal feed trough!)
4 lb. beef marrow bones, split
2 large onions, skin left on, quartered

1 large carrot, roughly sliced
green, leafy tops of 1 bunch celery (retain the stalks for the soup)
1 bunch parsley (retain the stems for the soup)
3 bay leaves

FOR THE SOUP

2 tbsp. butter
2 tbsp. beef dripping
2 large onions, finely sliced
1½ lb. white cabbage, cored and shredded
1 bunch celery, shredded finely
parsley stems, finely chopped
1 tbsp. chopped dill

2 bay leaves
2 cloves garlic, roughly chopped
2 pints beef stock (made from above)
2 medium-size potatoes, diced
4 ripe tomatoes, peeled, seeds removed and then chopped
freshly ground black pepper
sea salt

AND FOR THE DUMPLINGS

½ cup milk
1 tablespoon butter
pinch of freshly grated nutmeg

pinch of sea salt
2½ oz. all-purpose flour
1 egg

TO GARNISH
sour cream

First, about 6 hours before you intend to make the soup, you need to make the beef stock. In a large, deep stock pot, melt the beef dripping on a high heat. Now add the beef brisket joint, the marrow bones, and the onion. Brown quickly. Pour

Comrade's Cabbage and Dumpling Soup *(continued)*

on about 6 pints of water—this will bubble wildly, so be careful! Establish a boil and then skim off any impurities. Reduce the heat to a simmer and add the carrot, celery tops, parsley, and bay leaves. Simmer for about an hour and a half until the meat is beautifully tender. Remove the meat at this point, lay it to the side, and let it cool, at which point you will dice the meat. Keep this until it is time to add it to the final soup. Let the stock bubble gently for a further 4 hours, partially covered. Eventually, strain the stock; remove the bones and vegetable matter. Leave the stock to cool, and strain off the surface fat—you want to be left with 2 pints of beef stock—if you find you have more, then return to the heat and reduce to 2 pints. Less, and you need to top up with water.

Now it is time to make the soup. In a large, thick-bottomed pan, melt the butter and beef dripping. Add the sliced onions and cook over a moderate heat until they are honey colored. Now add the cabbage, celery, parsley, dill, bay leaves, and garlic. Cover with lightly buttered, grease-proof paper and sweat gently on a low heat for about 15 minutes.

Meanwhile, begin to make the dumplings. Heat the milk with the butter, nutmeg, and salt, allowing the nutmeg to gradually infuse the milk. When it reaches boiling point, remove the pot from the heat. Sieve the flour into a bowl and make a well in the center. Pour the milk infusion into this well, add the egg, and stir vigorously. A smooth dough should have formed. Cool this in the fridge.

Pour the rich beef stock over the vegetables and add the diced beef. Simmer for a further 20 minutes. Now plop the diced potato in the shchi; cook for 20 more minutes. After 15 minutes, dip a teaspoon in very cold water, and spoon off dumplings. As you scoop up these dumpling gobbets, place them in the cabbage soup. Add the chopped tomatoes. Cook for some 10 minutes more; the stout little dumplings should have risen to the surface of the soup. Salt and pepper to taste.

Serve in deep bowls with a creamy blob of sour cream on top of each helping.

In the years preceding the First World War, Lenin encountered his mistress-to-be, the French-Russian Inessa Armand, in Paris 1909. Paris was glorious in the Belle Époque and a lure for discontented Russian émigré society. The Bolsheviks drank grenadine syrup topped with soda water in the Café des Manilleurs, while Lenin ordered mugs of beer, rolled his "*r*'s," tucked his hands under his armpits when talking about revolution, and tried not to look at pretty, vivacious Inessa; by 1913 she was living with Lenin and Nadezhda in Galicia. Lenin was magnetizing, not just because of his political ideals but for very personal reasons: he had a beaming smile, was unpretentious, and his laughter was infectious—so keen was his capacity to laugh at himself that he choked with laughter, till tears came; he said to his friend, Maxim Gorky, "Humor is a splendid, healthy quality. And really life is as funny as it is sad, just as much."

When Gorky was with Lenin in London in 1907, he noticed with approval the dining differences between Lenin and the German Social Democrats; the Germans were very bumptious in their eating style, while Lenin always opted to eat again and again in a small, cheap restaurant, eating little—just a slice of ham and couple of fried eggs, washed down with a mug of bitter, frothy brown beer. In disguise in London, Lenin and Nadezhda masqueraded as Mr. and Mrs. Jacob Richter, living at all sorts of demure, dowdy addresses to fox any sleuths from Tsarist Russia while Lenin studied in the British Library and produced the underground, polemical, Communist journal *Iskra*. Lenin loved London and hopping onto the top decker of the bus so that he could see all the unfolding panoply of Edwardian London beneath him; he was also brilliant at drawing maps for other Bolsheviks visiting London and was very good at bobbing into obscure, alleyway shortcuts that could magic him from Charing Cross to Piccadilly. Having translated Webb's writing from English into Russian with Nadezhda, Lenin thought speaking English would be a breeze—and it was for him later on. He could do a passable imitation of a Glaswegian accent, but at first English was pretty obscure; he hadn't reckoned with Cockney. Nor, at first, had the Lenin's first landlady in London, Mrs. Yeo, quite counted on letting her rooms to revolutionary insurgents. She thought "Mr. and Mrs. Richter" were Germans—an identity they cheerily adopted as part of their cover. She was never suspicious; as Lenin pointed out, to the English, all foreigners look the same. They, meanwhile, took to studying the innocent Mrs. Yeo as a prime, living, and housecoated version of "middle-class philistinism." Another surprise that London had in store for the Lenins was its expensive, terrible food. Why, Nadezhda wondered, would anyone want to eat skate fried in fat? What in hell's name was supposed to be appetizing about an ox's tail, and who would want one of the English's terrible, indigestible cakes? Mrs. Yeo, however, was equally perplexed by their weird habits: who were all these visitors who turned up? Why didn't Mrs. Richter wear a wedding ring or spend any time in the kitchen? Why didn't they hang curtains in their rooms, and when they did, why was it on a Sunday they chose to do so?

They were, however, nice to her cat, so it all worked out in the end.

London's Welcome: Skate Fried in Fat

2 skate wings

FOR THE BATTER

1½ cups all-purpose flour   ½ cup water
pinch of sea salt   1 egg white
1 tbsp. oil

London's Welcome: Skate Fried in Fat (*continued*)

FOR DEEP-FRYING
5 packets lard—the fat should be
  about 4 inches deep—add more
  lard if necessary

Sieve the all-purpose flour into a mixing bowl and add a pinch of salt. Pour the tablespoon of oil into the flour and mix until the flour and oil have a crumbly consistency. Now add the water, whisking it in a little at a time to form a loose batter—discard any remaining water. Separately, whisk the egg white and then fold it into the batter. The batter should now be light and bubbly.

Put the fat on a high heat in a large, deep pan. The fat will make bubbling and crackling noises at first but then fall silent. It is when it is silent that it is ready to cook in. Test a drop of batter in the hot oil; it should fall momentarily to the bottom of the oil and then rise in a cloud of bubbles. When it responds this way, it is time to dip the skate wings in the batter and then drop them, one at a time, into the hot oil. Cook for about 8 to 10 minutes, until golden brown. Drain the skate wings on a kitchen towel and then eat immediately with sea salt and a sprinkling of vinegar.

But it was in Kraków that Lenin spent time with the man who was to become his terrible, monstrous successor: Stalin, whom Lenin cheerily described in a letter as "a wonderful Georgian." One evening, while a red cell of Lenin, Stalin, and other comrades heatedly discussed the national question and the future of *Pravda*, Nadezhda, feeling peckish, dusted down her mother's cookery book and treated Lenin, Stalin, and other comrades to a "blini party," using caviar, salmon, and a cured filet of sturgeon, which had just arrived in a parcel. Indeed, parcels from well-wishers were to plague Lenin throughout his revolutionary life. During the cruel famine of 1919 parcels of flour, butter, and sugar were delivered to his flat, which he'd redistribute among others; once, he winced with embarrassment when he offered a visitor smoked sturgeon sent to him from Astrakan.

Thyroid trouble took Nadezhda and Lenin to the mountains of the canton of Saint Gallen in Switzerland in 1916. They were incarcerated for six weeks in the Tschudiwiese nursing home, where a "dairy diet" of milk meals, including milk soup and curd cheese, was religiously enforced. Escape was impossible, unless you wanted to risk a bare-backed donkey ride down precarious mountain trails. The Lenins were, at first, nauseated by the strange diet but then managed to gather wild raspberries and bilberries to supplement it. Nor was the "milk cure" the only oddity the Lenins encountered; in the mornings the local inhabitants chose to make their way by foot to a train station that lay some eight kilometers distant. Why? So they could serenade train commuters. At sleepy 6 a.m. a bell chimed, summoning locals to the long march. They'd rally their spirits by singing a song about a cuckoo, each verse of which was completed by the refrain: "Good-bye, cuckoo!" Lenin groaned and pulled the blankets over his head.

The year 1916 and the beginning of 1917 found the Lenins living in Zurich, next to a sausage factory, the smell from which was so eye-wateringly bad that they risked opening their window only at night. Lenin was absorbed in his political work, but on Thursday afternoons, when the library was closed, he and Nadezhda climbed the Zurichberg. For those Thursday walks Lenin always bought two bars of chocolate with nuts for fifteen centimes that they ate as they lay and read deep in the grass, in their favorite spot in the woods. These were perhaps the last months of anything resembling peace that the Lenins were to enjoy before they moved into the Kremlin in the spring of 1918.

Ahead lay the overthrow of Czar Nicholas, the attempted assassination by zealous Dora Kaplan, the Red Terror, and Lenin's mute, paralytic death in 1924. All would change: even food in future years would be different. Postrevolution, Lenin and Trotsky shared the same dining room in the Kremlin. When Gorky called on Lenin in Moscow, Lenin commiserated with Gorky about dining in the Kremlin: "I heard the dinners are not good there," Lenin stated, angling for an answer.

"Not bad, but could be better."

Lenin was bamboozled: "Why can't they get an expert cook there? People work literally until they faint; they must be fed with good food so that they will eat more. I know there is little food to be got, and that bad; they must get a good cook there."

The dining room churned out peaky-looking, worthy, hard-times food: there were reams of fat-curdled corned beef; sand was mixed into the barley and flour. Dinners of rheumy soup and unpolished buckwheat were served on plates adorned with the Tsar's crest of double-headed eagles. Ironically, they had to eat shedloads of red caviar because they could no longer export it from Russia.

Red Cell Party Blini

½ cup lukewarm water
2 tsp. active dry yeast
½ cup buckwheat flour
2 cups all-purpose flour
2 cups milk, warmed
½ lb. butter, melted

generous pinch of sea salt
1 tsp. white sugar
3 egg yolks, beaten
2 cups sour cream
3 egg whites

Red Cell Party Blini (*continued*)

TOPPINGS

black and red caviar

red onion, finely chopped

strips of smoked salmon

finely chopped fresh dill

lemon, sliced into very thin semicircles

minced, hard-boiled eggs

moist and buttery slices of cold-smoked
   sturgeon

herring fillets

Pour the warm water into a bowl, add the yeast, stir, and leave in a warm place for 15 minutes, until a froth forms on the yeast.

In a large mixing combine *half* of the buckwheat flour with *all* of the white flour. Add the water-yeast mixture with *1* cup of lukewarm milk. Stir vigorously with a wooden spoon until the mixture is smooth. Cover it with a clean, dry tea towel, put somewhere warm, and let this batter rise until it doubles in size and bubbles a little, like the head on a beer—this will take about 3 hours.

After this, stir the batter and add the remaining buckwheat flour. Return to the warm spot and leave to rise for 2 more hours. When the 2 hours are up, stir the batter again and slowly incorporate another cup of lukewarm milk, 3 tablespoons of melted butter, sea salt, sugar, 3 egg yolks, and 3 tablespoons of the sour cream.

Now, using an electric whisk, whisk the egg white until it forms stiff, glossy peaks (but it should not appear dry). Granted, the Comrades wouldn't have electric whisks, but let's not be pedantic. Fold this into the batter gently, using a metal spoon. Cover the mixture again and leave in a warm spot for 30 minutes.

Heat the oven to 110 degrees centigrade and put a baking sheet into it. Using a nonstick brush, coat the base of a nonstick skillet with melted butter; you'll need to dip into the butter regularly when you think the skillet is drying out, so keep it alongside. Place the skillet over high heat ready to cook your blini; test that it's hot enough by scattering a drop or two of water on it; this will evaporate immediately when the skillet is at the optimum heat. Each blini takes about 3 tablespoons of batter. Drop this onto the skillet, fry for 2 to 3 minutes, brush the top of the blini with butter, and flip over for 2 to 3 minutes on the other side. Put each blini on the baking tray in the oven to keep warm.

Serve the blini while they are warm with a bowl of the remaining melted butter and a bowl of sour cream. Spread a little melted butter on each blini and then top with whatever takes your fancy. Round this off with a little dollop of sour cream.

THE MANLY MEALS OF FIDEL CASTRO

Fidel Castro stopped smoking in 1985; old age held the smoke-free pleasures of night fishing with Gabriel García Márquez. Gone are the days of El Presidentes, rumored to be a favorite cocktail of Castro's, made with Cuban rum and sugar and topped with a maraschino cherry. Red wine was Castro's choice tipple in his dotage at supper—purely for its antioxidant properties, you understand.

And no doubt he could do with a break. Apart from running postrevolution Cuba, he's had to weather plots, subterfuges, and scandals—such as the CIA-generated rumor about the Cuban-Russian pact that Cuban children were going to be sent to Russia to then be processed and returned to Cuba as tinned meat. Fidel has survived exploding cigarette packets, plots to set fire to his beard, guns inside TV cameras, and even cyanide capsules in his chocolate milkshake. In fact, rather than sounding like CIA trickery, these plots read like the sort of vendetta someone very bad-tempered who worked in a joke shop might wage against you.

Ever since December 1956, when he sailed forth from Mexico in the company of a further eighty-one revolutionaries, all jammed onto the sixty-two-foot yacht the *Granma* (am I the only person for whom the vessel's name conjures up someone with a silver perm, knitting?), and launched the Cuban Revolution, Fidel hadn't stopped. Remarkable for his energy and garrulousness, Fidel cultivated an aura of revolutionary machismo that is also found in his food. Before old age set in, the Jefe was often to be found eating meat of some form or another—although he matched this with a tenacious ability to fast for protracted periods of time. Even during his days of exile in Mexico, Fidel was generally found chewing on cooked oxtail.

No doubt the ability to starve well, fast, *and* enjoy oxtails stood Castro in good stead after he landed on the eastern edges of Cuban soil at Oriente. The revolution began with the stomach as well, for Castro and the Cuban guerrilla forces had to survive for six months in the inhospitable landscape of the Sierra Maestra Mountains, evading capture by Batista's army. Not much was to be had by way of grub, unless you happened to be one of the hungry mountain horseflies that gnawed at the revolutionaries. The guerrillas dined on a lot of fou-fou, which Castro claimed he everlastingly adored. Originating in Africa, fou-fou is made from starchy staples like corn, manioc, or plantain, mixed with water. Fou-fou can seem, at first glance, to be masquerading as mashed potato, but this charming exterior masks its true force. It has a strangely gluey texture that goes beyond the starchiness of the humble potato. A hollowed out calabash, slippery and buttered on the inside, can be used to shape fou-fou, a scoop of which is rolled about inside the calabash until a smooth ball forms. The butter helps to stop the fou-fou from forming an unwelcoming, crusty overcoat. What the guerrillas found most appealing about it was that fou-fou filled you up, akin to swallowing a modest fist of wet cement.

When he was in prison from 1953 to 1955, Castro reinvented himself as a chef, and he couldn't resist showing off. His brother had sent him a small ham, he wrote to a friend, and he rustled up some juicy ham steaks with guava jelly. This was pretty effortless, he claimed; that very day he'd received pineapple slices preserved in syrup and had already begun to conjure new dishes with these, though he immediately disappointed by writing that he liked to cook, erm, ham with pineapple. His cheese tortillas, though, were guaranteed to melt the heart, he reassured his correspondent, and then there were all his spaghettis to consider. . . . And so he went on and on and on . . .

Indeed, when he reflected on the years of exile in Mexico City with Che Guevara for company, Castro was very sure that he was the better cook, only conceding a little jealously that Che had a bit of a knack when it came to making Argentine roasts, but these were only good for cooking in the middle of the countryside. In Mexico Fidel had recruited Che as his revolutionary guerrilla army's doctor. By way of celebrating this alliance and Che's marriage to his first wife, Hilda, Castro and his fellow revolutionaries turned up for Che and Hilda's wedding feast in August (Hilda was pregnant). Ernesto prepared an asado, a traditional Argentinian barbecue, to celebrate, and Fidel and Cubans tucked in. Then, on Christmas Eve in 1955 the Cuban exiles invited the newlyweds to tuck into Cuban Christmas dinner of roasted pork with yucca with mojo and moros y cristianos on the side. Even as they picked their teeth, Castro set out his plans for nationalization and agrarian reform once the revolution was won. Che's "knack" for roasts was, Fidel thought, far outweighed by his own mastery: he was the expert cook in the Mexican prison they shared. Che could only be the junior chef; spaghetti, rice, and beans were the expert cook, Fidel's, affair. Fidel's bitchiness aside, Che recorded cooking a monkey for the Yaguas, an Amazonian tribe. They'd slain the luckless primate with a curare-tipped blowpipe in the jungle in the early 1950s to celebrate their white visitors' arrival. By way of thanks, Che set up an Argentine pampas-style barbecue, much to the excitement of the Yaguas—and the piquantly sharp monkey meat was sweetened by the barbecue, thus proving the point that barbecue à la Che must have been a treat.

Yucca with Mojo Sauce

FOR THE YUCCA

2 lb. yucca	2 tsp. sea salt

FOR THE MOJO SAUCE (make this a couple of days before you are going to serve it)

7 cloves garlic, minced	½ tsp. oregano
generous pinch of sea salt	½ tsp. paprika
½ tsp. cumin seeds	freshly ground black pepper

Yucca with Mojo Sauce (*continued*)

3 tbsp. olive oil
⅔ cup freshly squeezed blood
   orange juice

⅓ cup freshly squeezed lime juice

Using a mortar and pestle, make a paste of garlic, salt, cumin, oregano, paprika, and black pepper. Heat the olive oil in a frying pan and add the sticky garlic paste. Fry for a minute. Now add the orange and lime juices. Cook for a further minute, remove from the heat, and cool.

Peel the yucca, cut into chunks, and boil in salted water for about 20 minutes — test it is tender with a fork. Turn off the heat but let the yucca steam-dry on the warmth. Now serve with the Mojo Sauce drizzled over.

Moros y Cristianos (Moors and Christians)

FOR THE BEANS
½ lb. dried black beans
3 bay leaves
2 tsp. oregano

1 sprig thyme
½ lb. smoked ham hock

FOR THE SOFRITO
1 onion, finely chopped
1 bell pepper, finely chopped
5 cloves garlic, peeled and chopped
3 large, ripe tomatoes, chopped

pinch of saffron strands
1 tsp. cumin
1 tsp. oregano
1 tsp. paprika

FOR THE RICE
½ cup long-grain white rice

pinch of sea salt

Soak the beans overnight in just enough cold water to cover them by an inch. The next day, begin by making the sofrito. In a large frying pan, sauté the onion until golden; add the bell pepper and the garlic. Fry over a moderate heat for 5 minutes. Now add the tomatoes, saffron, cumin, oregano, and paprika. Lower the heat, cover, and cook for 20 minutes. Now, place the beans (still in their overnight water), bay leaves, oregano, thyme, and the ham hock in a deep pan. Top up with enough cold water to ensure an inch remains above the beans. Stir in the delicious sofrito. Bring to a boil, cover, then reduce the heat to a low simmer and cook for an hour and a half. Remove the ham hock bones from the stew and keep to the side. Once the ham has cooled, remove the bone and roughly dice up. Continue to cook the beans, covered, for another hour. Stir regularly to ensure the beans aren't sticking to the pot. Wash the rice in some cold water until the water becomes clear. Return the diced ham to the beans. Finally, cook the rice in water and a pinch of sea salt and serve mixed through with the beans.

Having Fidel pop by your house when you're cooking must be joyless, like being descended on by a bossy and humorless aunt. With strong opinions about every aspect of cooking and a strong conviction that only his opinions count, Fidel can hold forth, for instance, on the subject of shrimps and lobsters at great length: boiling them, according to Castro, is a fatal mistake, turning them into tough pellets. Broiling over hot coals is a far better approach, accompanied by basting with butter, crushed garlic, and lemon juice. This is the only way to even look at a shrimp. You can understand why he's made for one-man government. Bossy-boots Castro scolded his university supervisor's wife for not cooking bananas the right way—when her patience frayed and she asked if there was anything he *didn't* know, he quipped, "Not much." He is recorded as sulking when a friend's wife refused to bread crumb her lamb chops—in keeping with *his* advice—and went her merry way barbecuing them instead. Fond also of foie gras, he's tried in the past to dragoon the Cuban goose (and the odd hapless duck) into eating huge quantities of grain; in fact, he supplied experimental Cuban foie gras to the Nicaraguan Sandinistas to celebrate the victory anniversary of fellow revolutionary Daniel Ortega. Castro went so far as to tell the secretary-general of the French Communist Party, Georges Marchais, to ensure that when the Communists seized power in France, they were on no account to nationalize agriculture, or the French would have to say good-bye to foie gras!

In his book *Castro's Cuba, Cuba's Fidel,* journalist Lee Lockwood gives a colorful account of dining with Fidel. Lockwood was visiting Cuba in the mid-sixties to conduct a series of interviews with Castro and spent time with him at his old haunt, Uvero. He listened to Castro speak before local campesinos and sugar cane cutters; they watched him as if he were magical. Afterward, Castro retired to eat in a huge mess tent at an army base in the woods; the assembled company included the son of a former president of the Soviet Union and Fidel's lookalike brother, Raúl Castro. Instead of the customary waiters and waitresses, serving them dinner was a muscular unit of Cuban GIs.

The centerpiece of dinner was lechón asado, roast suckling pig, delicately fleshed, with crisp butter-yellow skin, washed down with Spanish white wine and Cuban beer. The booming voice of Fidel dominated all other voices at the table. Plates of food were passed from man to man; every eater seemed possessed of a fierce "macho" appetite. Lockwood watched Fidel carefully: in this testosterone-fueled environment, Fidel's appetite had to surpass all others. He began with yogurt—no, it's *not* a sissy way to start; he probably ate it using a bayonet, *and* he said that he's learned to use yogurt as a digestive in Russia, no less. "It prepares the stomach," he growled, making the whole eating experience sound more like a wrestling match. Then Fidel went on to eat a full plate of roast pork, fou-fou, a plate of fried chicken, rice, ham and cracker sandwiches, tomato slices, malanga (a hefty tuber, like taro), and a salad of lettuce. Enough? Hell no! José María, Castro's personal army chef, staggered into the tent with an enormous filet mignon speared on a stick. It was a challenge. Castro looked at it, paused, squinted—the way one might if looking down the sights of a gun—and raised his knife to cut down into the dense, juicy beef. He ate half and then pushed the plate away, like an unwanted mistress. The signal for the meal to end.

Not much has changed since. Indeed, things have gone on from strength to strength for Castro—he has been variously serenaded at dinner by Westerners singing "Popeye the Sailor Man" and Carole King crooning "You've Got a Friend." American playwright Arthur Miller had dinner with Castro in 2000 and recorded that, while Miller and company—including Gabriel García Márquez, who was so short that Miller said he looked up at all his fellow eaters like a schoolboy in adult company—dined out on "pork, dream pork" and shrimps, Fidel ate only vegetables, "intending to live forever." Castro, Miller noted, glimmered with Hollywood potential: he was stagey and slick. Miller was stumped by a nearly mute writers' group he met on the evening, and one man in particular who kept asking Miller: "What is your message?" Miller realized he had none. Castro further supplemented his diet on the evening with special vitamin pills; a sign of his liking for Miller can be read in Castro later gifting the American playwright a bag of such pills. The after-dinner conversation consisted of Castro imitating the Russians in a deep bass voice and delivering a series of set pieces on his deepest Thoughts and Observations. This went on for hours, by which time Castro's retinue were sitting glaze-eyed, and Miller noticed that Gabriel García Márquez had fallen fast asleep bolt-upright in his chair, his posture suggesting an air of serious concentration.

Lechón Asado

The traditional dressing drizzled over lechón asado is ajilimojili, a wickedly delicious sauce of garlic, chilies, vinegar, lime juice, salt and olive oil. Lechón asado is served with arroz congri (red beans with rice).

FIRST CAME THE PIG . . .

1 whole suckling pig, about 20 lb. in weight, emptied, cleaned, and opened in half through the belly	¾ cup salt
	achiote coloring
	10 sour oranges—Seville oranges will do
8 chipotle chilies, crushed	1 bottle brown rum
24 cloves garlic, crushed	3 cups muscovado sugar
1 tbsp. whole black peppercorns	banana leaves
3 tablespoons oregano	

Lechón Asado (continued)

Two days before you intend to cook the pig, begin to marinate it. (Beware: you must have *somewhere* to marinate it. I had to put the pig in a black plastic bag and keep it in my bath.) Firstly, place the pig in a large basin. Crush together the chipotle chilies, garlic, peppercorns, oregano, and salt. Make deep scores over the pig and rub the marinade into the gashes and inside of the pig.

Baste with achiote and squeeze enough sour oranges to allow the pig to "bathe" in the juice. Pour in the bottle of rum. Add the sugar. Cover with foil and refrigerate. Every few hours, baste the pig again.

Decide whether you want to cook the pig by the "burial" method in an underground oven or whether you would like to spit roast it. If you opt to spit roast the pig, then you will need to invest in a motor for turning the carcass—or some weary, half-drunk soul will have to spend about 9 hours laboriously trying to turn a pig which will invariably roll back to its favored position (my preferred method).

THE "BURIAL" METHOD

After the 2 days have passed, dig a pit large enough to accommodate the pig (hope that some neighbor doesn't report you to the police). Line the base of the pit with piles of banana leaves (these protect the pig from acquiring any earthy residue). Remove the pig from the marinade and discard the marinade. Place the pig on top of the banana skins. Assemble another layer of banana leaves over the pig and place on top several large aluminum sheets big enough to completely cover the hole. Build a wood fire over this. Light it and keep it going. The pig will slowly cook over 9 to 10 hours. You can test the meat by pricking it with a fork. When the juice runs clear, the pig is ready to eat.

After 9 hours, the skin becomes very crisp, and the pig is covered in a thin caramel layer of crackling. Test it is cooked by pricking the thigh with the point of a knife: if the liquid runs clear, the meat is done.

THE SPIT-ROAST METHOD

Drain the marinade from the pig and keep to one side: in an act of obeisance, you can brush the pig with the marinade every 20 minutes or so once it starts cooking. Next, pass a metal pole through the pig. Cut a slit just under the tail and thread the pole through this and out of the pig's mouth. Tie the front legs very tightly and securely around the pole. Do the same with the hind legs, stretching them out as far as possible.

Place the pig over an open fire of hot charcoal placed over layers of stone, resting both ends of the pole on Y-posts. Rotate the pole slowly and constantly in order to roast the pig evenly, and baste frequently with the marinade.

Cook for about 7 hours, or until the meat is well done. Test in the same way as is suggested for the buried pig.

Ajilimójili

6 Scotch bonnet chilies, seeded
6 bell peppers, 4 red and 2 green, seeded
8 garlic cloves, peeled
1 small bunch fresh cilantro

1 cup lime juice
1 cup olive oil
8 black peppercorns
3 tsp. sea salt
½ cup malt vinegar

Puree all the ingredients in a food processor, other than the olive oil, black peppercorns, sea salt, and vinegar. Now add the olive oil, black peppercorns, sea salt, and vinegar. Process the ajilimójili once more. It is now ready to drizzle over the roasted pork.

Arroz Congrí

12 oz. red beans
¼ lb. smoked ham
¼ lb. chorizo sausage
3 tbsp. olive oil
4 garlic cloves, peeled and roughly chopped
2 medium onions, chopped

2 red bell peppers, finely chopped
1 tsp. ground cumin
1 tsp. dried oregano
½ tsp. brown sugar
2 tsp. sea salt
1 tsp. freshly ground black pepper
2 cups long-grain rice

Soak the beans in a large pot with water for at least 8 hours or overnight.

Next, bring the beans to a boil, reduce the heat, and let cook for up to an hour and a half or until tender, adding water if necessary. Cut the smoked ham into medium-size pieces and add to the bean pot. Cook for a further 10 minutes.

Dice the chorizo. Heat the 3 tablespoons of olive oil in a deep pan. Add the garlic, onion, and bell peppers and fry over a medium heat until they are tender. Now add the chorizo pieces and fry these for 5 minutes.

Drain the beans and smoked ham, reserving the cooking liquid and add the beans and ham to the deep pan. Now add 5 cups of the cooking liquid to the pan: you can discard the remaining liquid. Increase the heat and add the cumin, oregano, sugar, sea salt, black pepper, and rice. Do not cover. Cook for 15 to 20 minutes until the liquid has been absorbed. Next, break the rice up with a fork, cover, turn the heat down to very low, and cook for another 10 minutes.

MOSTLY MONKEYS: CHE GUEVARA

Che Guevara's first youthful journey through South America was full of food camaraderie: he ate empanadas with the bowler-hatted peasants or "cholos"—the name given to native South Americans by the white Spaniards—in the second-class carriage of a train, swapping empanadas for chocolate bonbons (incidentally, the bowler hats are a legacy from 1920s British railway workers in Bolivia). Che loved to eat whatever came to hand with whoever offered it to him, in exchange with whatever he had on his person. Food, he understood, allowed us to connect. And, to connect, he was always prepared to be adventurous: the time was past for familiar dishes like the Argentinian locro he loved so much—roasted baby monkey might be on the menu.

Empanadas

FOR THE DOUGH

3 tbsp. lard	2 small eggs
½ cup water	1 egg white
3 cups all-purpose flour	1 tsp. vinegar
generous pinch of sea salt	

FOR THE FILLING

1 tbsp. olive oil	1 tsp. chili flakes
1 onion, finely chopped	1 tsp. cumin
½ lb. roughly minced beef (traditionally, this would be very finely diced steak)	4 scallions, very finely chopped pinch of sea salt
2 cloves garlic, chopped	freshly ground black pepper
2 tbsp. raisins (these should have been soaked in boiling water and drained)	2 tbsp. finely chopped cilantro 1 egg yolk, beaten 2 hard-boiled eggs, cut into eighths lengthwise
1 tsp. paprika	olives, stoned and diced

An hour before you intend to make the empanadas, prepare the dough. In a saucepan, melt the lard in the water. Remove from the heat. Into a large mixing bowl, sieve the flour and sea salt. Whisk the eggs, egg white, vinegar, and lard water together. Add the wet mixture slowly to the flour, working it through with your hands until a smooth dough forms. Now wrap this in grease-proof paper and chill in the fridge to stiffen—this will take 1 hour.

Empanadas (*continued*)

Meanwhile, prepare the enchilada filling. Heat the olive oil in a frying pan and add the onion. Fry until it has softened and turned golden. Now add the chopped beef and brown in the oil. Turn down the heat and cook for 10 minutes. Now add the garlic, raisins, paprika, chili flakes, cumin, scallions, sea salt, black pepper, and cilantro. Cook for 1 more minute. Set aside and leave to cool, then add the beaten egg yolk and mix through.

Preheat the oven to 200 degrees centigrade. Lightly flour a surface for rolling the pastry. Roll the pastry out to a thickness of about ⅛ inch. Using a 5-inch pastry cutter, cut out circles. In the center of each circle, place 1 to 2 tablespoons of the spiced meat mixture. Be generous: too little filling will make the empanada dry. Top each mound of meat with a slice of egg and a sprinkle of olive. Now wet the edge of the circle and fold in half. Pinch the edges closed and make into a crescent shape.

Now bake the empanadas on a baking tray in the oven for about 30 minutes, or until they are brown. If you don't want to bake them, then you can deep-fry them . . .

Serve hot or cold—or barter on a bus with your empanadas.

No sooner had Che and his companion Carlos "Calica" Ferrer reached the city of Cuzco, wandered into the local police station to register their presence as aliens and show their passports, they were accused of theft by the less-than-sober Peruvian police. When they finally managed to establish their innocence, however, their ordeal was far from over. By way of apology, one policeman slurred, "Have you ever eaten in a picanteria?" Turns out, they hadn't, and their new friend decided that a tour of local picanterias was in order. Carlos and Che followed the policeman's robustly alcoholic wake into a picanteria, a type of Peruvian eating joint which serves late afternoon "picante" food; while "picante" does not necessarily mean spicy in all picanterias, in this one, spice was the name of the game. Plate after plate of Peruvian food appeared, adorned, stuffed, spiced, and fragranced with chilies. Roaring, machismo contests were held to see who could stomach the hottest dish. Che's drunken host kept scattering more chilies onto their communal plates; the chilies, he explained over his black corn beer, were introduced to sedate your taste buds when you were forced to eat old, semirancid meat. The tears running down their faces, Che signaled to Calica that they should escape through the kitchen door. They sidled in that direction, only to see the waiters emptying the half-consumed leftovers back into the cooking pots. Che put on a gloomy "professional" scientific voice and whispered to Calica: "Don't worry, just carry on eating—all the chilies will have killed the bacteria. It's like sterilizing the food."

The bus to Lima held even less promise for the hygienically minded: although rice and chilies was offered free to passengers, this was conditional on Che and Calica waiting in line to use the *only* plate and spoon about. The two eventually struck up a deal whereby they helped load the bus in exchange for tamales. Passengers slept under the bus at night, and the bus floor was splattered with hen shit and heavy with the permanent stink of dirty feet—Che often climbed onto the roof tarpaulin to gulp in fresh air. Fortunately, back in Cuzco, Che had bought some World War II rucksacks—still containing army provisions—from a crafty local antiques saleswoman. Seated next to an Indian, Che and he both broke out in ironic laughter when he told Che that all he'd brought to eat for the four-day journey was a tiny pouch of cooked chickpeas. Nevertheless, he still offered Che some of his chickpeas. Delighted by this generous companionship, Che dug into his rucksack and pulled out a tin of sardines—circa the 1940s—and some similarly ancient crackers. The fishy, darkened oil jetted out of the can when Che opened it. Together, they made sardine canapés. Calica screeched at Che: "You son of a bitch, listen to me. Your mother asked me to look after you. And you're going to eat from that tin from 1940, you're going to fall ill in the middle of the jungle and we're not even going to find a witch doctor for you. You're going to die, you idiot. What am I going to do with you dead?"

No matter how bad those sardines were, *nothing* could prepare the taste buds of Che for what he was going savor in the final months of guerrilla warfare in Bolivia. In 1965, following the burst of the Cuban Revolution and a four-year stretch in the new Castro Cuban government as minister of industry, Che Guevara decided to don his beret again to fight for revolution in other countries. He resurfaced in Bolivia in 1966, directing the guerrilla movement there and traveling unrelentingly toward his execution by anti-Communist, CIA-backed Bolivian militia.

Guevara's *Bolivian Diary* provides an account of the rebels' desperate attempts to feed themselves in hostile jungle. Che and his comrades cooked from the jungle; at its best this involved jolly times when provisions and jungle fare combined in meals full of camaraderie; at worst, we're talking underdone tapir eaten half-raw in the rain. Guevara's concern for his fellow men and the permanent growl of his stomach add piquancy to his constant references to food. You can hear him slowly starve. The jungle is no paradise: plants aren't helpfully labeled "Poisonous: don't touch!" or "I taste great!"; fish have a habit of darting off when you're poised to harpoon them; and the hairy little face peeking out of some wild game—like a monkey or boar—isn't easy to spot between split branches, foliage, and the patterning of light and dark.

Scouring the forest for deer or turkey, the guerrillas set traps . . . they bagged sparrow hawks, caught tatú, a giant armadillo about three feet in length, and sometimes pulled catfish out of the streaming rivers. Guevara watched his men's behavior toward food, using this as a sort of litmus test for their loyalty to the cause they'd said they were prepared to die for! So next time you are planning a martyrdom, make sure you are very good at missing meals. All of them. The sneaky scoffing of rations Che took as a bad sign, worrying that Polo had illicitly gulped down his can of condensed milk, wiping the splashes guiltily from his beard, or that Eusebio had already scarfed his ration of sardines; each man had to stick to a ration of one-third of a can of tinned food each day. If they sneaked on this, Che guessed it might mean that their courage had crumbled. Mostly they held out, though, surviving the long, lean days by eating only "totai," hearts of palm. But the lucky catch of wild game allowed them to liven things up with a side dish of dove, two small monkeys, and a bundle of parrots. Sometimes *choclos*, large, starchy ears of young corn, were smuggled to them by Bolivians. From this, the rebels made humitas.

As-Good-As-It-Gets-in-the-Jungle Humitas

1½ lb. fresh corn kernels
4 tbsp. full-fat milk
2 large eggs
2 tsp. paprika
pinch of sea salt
freshly ground black pepper

2 tbsp. butter
1 tbsp. scallions, chopped
1 tbsp. green bell pepper, chopped
1 oz. mozzarella, chopped
1 oz. Parmesan cheese, grated

In blender, combine the corn and milk. Now add the eggs, paprika, salt, and black pepper. Melt the butter in a deep pan and sauté the scallions and bell pepper for about 5 minutes. Now add the corn pulp and cook for a further 6 minutes, or until the humitas thickens a little. Finally, throw in the mozzarella and Parmesan; this will melt deliciously through the humitas. Adjust seasoning and serve.

Despite such moments of food prosperity, their meager, protein-empty diet took its toll. By March, Che's legs began to swell into solid logs; Miguel's feet became loaves of puffed, tight flesh. Drastic action had to be taken: "We decided to eat the horse." Fortunately, but too late for the horse, Urbano turned up at the camp carrying a urina, a deer-like jungle animal that had been shot by Ricardo. Soon, the heady aroma of grilled urina, beans, and rice rose from the foliage, and the guerrillas could preserve their supply of horse ribs.

The guerrillas had to be divided into groups, some traveling ahead, path clearing, while a small, edgy knot of men, Moro, Inti, and Chinchu, were the hunters. They had planted stores of pork, bread, sugar, coffee, canned food, and ripe corn along their route, and the arrival at one of these secret deposits always triggered a surge in optimism: condensed milk spelled well-being. The sweetened milk made them sigh with delight. In celebration, at one such camp, they made mote, a white corn hominy, with meat using some of their newly acquired provisions. Sometimes, the entire troop delayed their journey in the hope that food might arrive from the outside; Guevara records one such wait for "the temptation of bread" which never turned up.

In May 1967 they found a supply of lard in a cave; on the eighth of May some prisoners were captured with "sacks of roasted and raw corn, four cans of onions, plus sugar and coffee. This solved our food problems for the day, with the help of the lard, which we ate in large amounts. Some of the men got sick from this." By the next day, their only remaining food was lard, from which they made turgid lard soup, the melted animal fat swimming in pools on the surface.

Relief was found on May 12 when the guerrillas happened on a huge cornfield, fringed with calabash trees; unfortunately there was no water to drink, though. The men toasted corn and cooked up roasted and salted jocos, with the ubiquitous lard and corn kernels. A scouting party brought back news of a house nearby, belonging to an individual named Chicho, who, according to Guevara's intelligence sources, was counted as a staunch pro-Government supporter. The guerrillas took great delight in catching a particularly large pig of Chicho's, which they cooked along with rice, fritters, and calabash. When they withdrew from the farm, they left an inventory of damages and expenses for Chicho and paid the farm workers ten pesos each for their help.

But their elation was short-lived: they fell sick after the meal, their digestive systems barely able to cope with the sudden introduction of rich food. The next day was given over to a concert of wind and human gasses as the rebels struggled to digest Chicho's pig. But it would have its revenge. The men were unable to move from the clearing they lay in, its various corners slippery with vomit and diarrhea. Dinner was a regretful one of fried corn and calabash.

Discontent and poor morale continued to be expressed through food. Two days after the incident with Chicho's pig, Che accused Urbano of eating extra charqui; Benigno of opening and eating a can of food, then on top of that lying and denying he'd done so; and Aniceto of being slow to do any duty unless it was connected to food. The ominous, distant rumble of approaching trucks cut short this food inquisition; although the rebels' desperate appetites still drove them onward to pick beans. They did take the precaution, however, of stashing jocos and corn in a hiding place. Explosions could be heard. They watched in amusement as planes bombed them—several kilometers from where they stood. The guerrillas took this opportunity to reconnoiter and spied a lake in the distance. Eventually, they came across an abandoned house where they cooked up a scrumptious chicken fricassee, all food crimes forgotten.

Chicken Fricassee

olive oil
2 lb. chicken, thighs, legs, some
    breast, cut into 2-inch pieces
2 onions, cut into fine strips
1 green pepper, finely diced
1 red pepper, finely diced
1 tsp. ground cumin
½ tsp. ground black pepper
1 tsp. crumbled, fresh oregano

4 cloves garlic, minced
½ cup cayenne pepper
sea salt
6 spring onions, cut into thin strips
2 pints chicken stock
½ cup bread crumbs, to thicken
4 cups cooked white corn
8 peeled and quartered potatoes
    (cooked separately)

Heat about 2 tablespoons of olive oil in a deep, large frying pan. Add the chicken and fry until it becomes golden. Next, add the onions, green and red peppers, cumin, black pepper, oregano, minced garlic, cayenne pepper, sea salt, and strips of spring onion. Stir and pour on 2 pints of golden brown chicken stock.

Bring to a boil and then reduce the heat, letting the fricassee simmer gently for at least 2 hours. Before serving, add the bread crumbs to thicken the fricassee. Serve in deep bowls with the white corn and potatoes.

By October, Guevara was dead, and no, it wasn't the fricassee. Guevara had no real idea of the forces ranged against him: the Bolivia Communist Party looked to Moscow for its allies; Guevara's radio transmitters for contacting Havana were to fail; the Bolivian peasants turned into informers; and, not only was the CIA controlling and supplying Bolivian forces but it is rumored that the Nazi war criminal Klaus Barbie, the terrible Butcher of Lyon, advised the Bolivians on how to capture Che Guevara, based on his counterterrorism experience of fighting the French Resistance (Barbie had plans for a Fourth Reich in the Andes). As he faced his half-drunk executioner, Guevara demanded, "Shoot, coward! You are only going to kill a man!"

THE PORKY PREDICAMENT OF MALCOLM X

"Coffee is the only thing I like integrated," Malcolm X told Alex Haley, staring levelly at him as he poured cream into one of his innumerable coffees. And Malcolm X wasn't joking. In tandem with all the seismic political changes Malcolm X went through in the course of his short and eventful life, this revolutionary's approach to food was as radical as his politics. The black soul food he grew up on in his early years he came to associate with slavery, with what could be begged from the leftovers of the white slave owner's table. He saw it as no surprise that pork, the meat he came to view as unclean, was at the very heart of "soul food," the definitive term for black food of the southern states and first coined in Harlem. The way forward for brothers in Islam was with a diet swept clear of the trotter and the snout.

Malcolm was often dizzy with hunger in childhood, as his mother, Louise, desperately tried to pad out every meal that came their way. She had firm ideas about what her children should eat; pork was already in danger of being struck off the menu (as was rabbit). She often argued with their father, lamenting his fondness for Georgia-style soul food. Common ground was found in eating the chickens raised by the family.

Malcolm's mother had a premonition of his father's death. They had been quarrelling about . . . yes . . . cooking a rabbit. His father left the house, and his body was later found neatly sliced in two, lying across some streetcar tracks. His skull had been crushed. The black community of Lansing was alarmed and fearful: either the Ku Klux Klan or the Black Legion (another cheerful, far-right group of night riders) had killed him. In a further tragic twist, the insurance company refused to pay out any policy money.

Further poverty followed: life on diminishing credit and dependence on welfare and charity was brutal. All the welfare food that came to the house was officiously stamped; "Not To Be Sold," like some type of brand name. Louise, determined and feisty, took any kind of work. Fortunately, a Lansing bakery sold tall flour sacks of day-old bread and cookies for a nickel. The children carried a sack two miles to their home. Louise immediately embarked on a series of bread-based recipes; bread with stewed tomatoes, bread pudding with the occasional splattering of raisins, bread burgers laced with ground meat, French toast if their chickens laid any eggs . . .

Sometimes there wasn't as much as a nickel. Malcolm and his brother, Philbert, dug out their father's .22-caliber rifle and took to shooting rabbits that their white neighbors would buy. They trapped muskrats at the creek and learned how to spear bullfrogs, cut off their legs, and sell them on, a nickel a pair. Cornmeal or oatmeal mush was eaten for breakfast, lunch, and supper. Not to be beaten, Louise baked corn bread or stewed a big pot of dandelion greens, but the children were teased for eating "fried grass."

But there is, again, a tragic twist to this tale. Poor as she was, Louise finally made the decision that she wasn't going to have pork in her house. She had joined the Seventh-Day Adventists, and it was the sect's dedication to Mosaic dietary laws that had the greatest pull on her. Yes, guess what was off the Seventh-Day Adventists' menu? Rabbit *and* pork. The welfare workers decided she was losing her mind when a black farmer offered her a whole pig, even two, butchered by him and she turned him down. This refusal of food meant she was "crazy," with all the repercussions that would have for the care of her children. It was the final blow; Louise couldn't cope with the hatred, the gossip, the lack of solace, the pressure that the welfare workers placed on her. She had a nervous breakdown. The authorities came and took her to the State Mental Hospital at Kalamazoo, where she was to remain for the next twenty-six years. And the children? They became "state children," wards of the court.

When Malcolm was a teenager, he was adopted by his half-sister Ella and moved in with her and his Little relatives, Aunt Sas and Aunt Gracie. Both aunts were staunch spinsters: Aunt Gracie because her fiancé was lynched by the Ku Klux Klan for being too "uppity." Since then, she'd refused to think romantically about any fine black man; she didn't want to lose another sweetheart, and the aunts told Malcolm tales of the fearsome KKK night riders who terrorized blacks in the South. Better than these horror stories were the parcels of fresh, delicious pecans which arrived annually, sent by relatives in Georgia: Aunt Sas baked smolderingly good, honey-dark pecan pies, which Malcolm and his brother Rodnell ate huge slices of until they were full to bursting.

Pecan Pie

FOR THE PASTRY

6 oz. butter, chilled and diced into sticks
2 tbsp. lard, chilled and diced into sticks

12 oz. all-purpose flour
2 oz. demerara sugar
pinch of sea salt
3 tbsp. chilled water

FOR THE PECAN FILLING

4 large eggs
1 tsp. vanilla extract
2 cups maple syrup

2 tbsp. melted and cooled butter
170 g. pecan halves

Pecan Pie (*continued*)

First, make the crust. Put all the ingredients other than the chilled water into a large mixing dish and rub the flour and fat between your fingertips, till you have a coarse, grainy texture. Now add the chilled water and combine to make a dough. If it looks a little too dry, add a further tablespoon of water. Wrap the pastry in grease-proof paper and leave to chill in the fridge for an hour.

Butter a 9-inch pie dish and preheat the oven to 200 degrees centigrade. Flour a board for rolling out the pastry and then shape the dough into a roughly circular shape. Roll out until it is about ⅛ inch thick. Drape over the pie dish and press down gently to fit the pastry to the contours of the dish. Trim the crust. Now prick the pastry base with a fork, taking care not to pierce the base. Cover in grease-proof paper and baking beans. Bake blind in the oven for 10 minutes. Remove the beans and paper and bake for a further 3 minutes. Take the piecrust out of the oven—but leave the oven on as you'll need it again soon. Let the piecrust cool.

Now make the pecan filling. Whisk the eggs, add the vanilla, and then whisk in the maple syrup; let it trickle into the eggs. Add the butter and whisk well. Pour this mixture into the pastry case and then shake the pecans over the top; they'll naturally rise to the surface. Return to the oven and bake for a further 30 to 40 minutes.

Let's fast-forward now to 1940 and Malcolm's first trip by Greyhound bus to Roxbury, the Harlem of Boston. Malcolm was reinventing himself with red "conked" hair and light-green zoot suits. He hadn't known there were as many black people in the world as those who filled the thronging downtown pool halls, nightclubs, and bars. Beneath the neon lights, driving spunked-up cars, with Cootie Williams and Duke Ellington singing on the jukeboxes, black brothers and sisters were everywhere. The smell of their rich, downtown black food wound its way about the streets—especially Ella's home cooking. Her outspoken style was matched by her culinary skill, and the tall, gangling, six-foot Malcolm ate her food with all the enthusiasm a hungry sixteen-year-old can muster. She heaped Malcolm's plate with glories of ham hock, tender on the bone, smothered greens, steaming sweet potatoes, black-eyed peas, gravy-soaked grits, and hunks of warm corn bread.

From Ella's pots and Boston, Malcolm migrated to the real Harlem, in New York. Pearl Harbor had just been bombed by the Japanese (but Malcolm was too young to enlist), and Malcolm got a job on the coach aisles of the "Yankee Clipper" railroad, selling cheese and ham sandwiches and "Uncle Tomming." He found Harlem as seductive and exciting as a narcotic; this was the city of Dizzy Gillespie and Billie Holiday (he made friends with Dinah Washington); a bohemian city, full of grotesque, harmless eccentrics. One famous singer smoked reefers through a chicken thigh bone, and Malcolm could make a tidy profit from supplying marijuana. Gone was the light-green suit of the Roxbury days; now he donned a wolfish shark-skin-gray zoot suit (à la Cab Calloway), complemented by knob-toed shoes. On "layover" nights he'd leave his small room in the YMCA, walk past the tiny, clattering, underground dance halls, and head off to Lindy Hop at rent-raising parties, held in scruffy, hot apartments packed with up to forty blacks, some gambling, some dancing, others passing between them plates of fried chitlins with potato salad sides, sold for a dollar a plate and knocked back with fifty cents' worth of eye-popping liquor, chased up by iced cans of beer.

New York Fried Chicken

sea salt	2 tsp. dried oregano
freshly ground black pepper	1 tsp. dried chili flakes
2 tbsp. paprika	1 cup finely chopped green onions
2 tbsp. garlic powder	3 lb. chicken, legs, thighs, and breasts
2 tsp. cayenne pepper	7 cups whole-meal flour
2 tsp. ground cloves	3 eggs
2 tsp. dried thyme	sunflower oil

In a large bowl, mix together the sea salt, black pepper, paprika, garlic powder, cayenne, cloves, thyme, oregano, chili flakes, and green onions. Place the chicken in a tray and empty a third of the seasoning mix onto the chicken. Massage this into the chicken, cover with cling film, refrigerate, and leave to marinate for 4 hours.

When the 4 hours are up, whisk the eggs in a bowl, add a further third of the spice seasoning, and mix thoroughly. Mix the last third of the seasoning with the flour and incorporate well.

Preheat the oven to 170 degrees centigrade and get out a baking tray. Empty the sunflower oil into a deep pan; it should fill a third of the pan. Place on a high heat: at first you will hear the oil crackle. When this dies down and it becomes silent, it is ready for the chicken.

While the oil heats, dip each piece of chicken into the egg, then dip into the seasoned flour. Do this twice over for each piece of chicken. When the oil is ready, place your first piece of chicken in the oil: it will drop momentarily to the base of the pan and then rise, covered in a "bubble wrap" of boiling oil. Cook the chicken in batches for 6 to 8 minutes until each piece becomes golden. Remove with a slotted spoon (this will help the fat drain off) and place on the baking tray in the oven to finish off.

Homemade Potato Salad

6 medium-size potatoes	sea salt
2 eggs	black pepper
4 green onions, very finely chopped	3 tbsp. mayonnaise
1 small bunch fresh lovage, chopped	paprika

Boil the potatoes until they are cooked; test them with a fork. Drain immediately and then return the potatoes to the pan. Although you must turn off the heat, leave the potatoes, uncovered, sitting on the warm ring, as this will dry them. Boil the eggs until hard-boiled, then peel them and chop. Cut the potatoes into uneven quarters.

Now, while the potatoes are still warm, place them in a bowl, stir through the egg, add the green onions and lovage, crumble sea salt over, and grind about a teaspoon of black pepper over. Next, gently fold the generous dollop of mayonnaise into the potatoes and egg. Sprinkle paprika over the top.

Malcolm X was in love with New York in 1942 and was "one of the most depraved parasitical hustlers among New York's eight million people—four million of whom work, and the other four million of whom live off them." Our precocious seventeen-year-old drank bourbon and was called "Detroit Red" on account of his bright red conk. You could see it coming; his new lifestyle was way too cool for the Yankee Clipper and its sandwiches. Malcolm landed a job as a waiter (and hustler) at Small's Paradise, a Harlem bar. Malcolm was testing out his newfound masculinity, testing out urban blackness. His job was exciting, and his tips could be gambled. He had a new girlfriend, a white girl called Sophia. Together, they would go down to Creole Bill's speakeasy. Alright, the speakeasy was in Bill's apartment, but the atmosphere and the food made it a Harlem soul spot. The drinks were gutsy and unlimited; soft, moody, smoochy music played; and Brown Sugar—Bill's gorgeous girlfriend—spooned out jambalaya onto plates, the spicy tang of great Creole home cooking working the room.

But "soul food" wasn't destined to stay on Malcolm's menu. His involvement in petty crime and harder drugs than marijuana was deepening; he was snorting coke, chain-smoking four packs of cigarettes daily, and trading in stolen goods, moonshine, and bootleg whisky. Allah and Islam were on their way—albeit by a circuitous route. Picture Malcolm four years on, still young—he was only twenty-one and hadn't even started shaving—when he was caught trying to sell stolen goods that he'd burgled with his partner in crime, Shorty. A sentence of ten years was accorded, courtesy of the Charlestown State Prison. It was the best thing that ever

Brown Sugar Jambalaya (. . . Nation of Islam style)

1 large onion, chopped	3 tbsp. chopped parsley
3 tbsp. oil	2 bay leaves
½ lb. halal chicken thighs, unskinned and on the bone	2 tsp. dried oregano
	1 tsp. Tabasco
1 lb. halal chicken breast, unskinned	2 tsp. creole seasoning
	½ tsp. dried thyme
1 cup rich chicken stock	6 cloves garlic, chopped
5 ripe tomatoes, chopped	sea salt and freshly ground black pepper
2 celery ribs, chopped	
3 shallots, chopped	2 cups cooked rice
1 bell pepper, chopped	1 lb. shrimp, cleaned and shelled

In a thick-based pan, sauté the onion in the oil over a gentle heat until it becomes golden brown. Add the chicken thighs and breast and brown; you may need to do this in batches. Now add all the remaining ingredients—with the exception of the 2 cups of cooked rice and the shrimp—and cook, covered, on a low heat for an hour and a half. Stir occasionally to make sure the jambalaya isn't becoming too dry. When the 3 hours are up, add the shrimp. Cook for 4 minutes, then add the cooked rice and stir through to heat the rice. Put on some Ella Fitzgerald and serve on paper plates.

happened to him, but it took him some time to recognize this. In the "dry" environment of Charlestown Penitentiary, Malcolm tried desperately to get high smoking grated and powdered nutmeg. Seven years of his sentence passed, and Malcolm was so irreligious as to be dubbed "Satan" by his fellow inmates.

Then in 1948, after his transfer to Concord Prison, his brother Philbert wrote to him. "I have discovered," wrote Philbert, the "natural religion for the black man." It was the militantly black organization, the Nation of Islam, run by the Honorable Elijah Muhammad. Their role was to deliver Allah's message to black people in the "wilderness" of North America. That devil, the white man, had brainwashed the black man. Brother Reginald had the Nation of Islam bug too, and a letter from him followed close on the heels of Philbert's. The unsuspecting Malcolm never dreamed of associating the two letters. Reginald's letter was deceptively gossipy but also contained the curious instruction "Malcolm, don't eat any more pork, and don't smoke any more cigarettes. I'll show you how to get out of prison."

It could have been the voice of his mother.

So not eating pork was a way out of prison, was it? Or did Reginald mean the prison of the mind? Malcolm hadn't a moment's hesitation; he opted for the former interpretation—Reginald was hinting at some prison-breaking ruse. After all, he and Reginald had been fellow hustlers and in quite a few scrapes together. And yet perhaps something more spiritual was at work within Malcolm. A couple of days later, when hungry Malcolm was lined up in what he called the "sit-grab-gobble-stand-file out" noon meal queue, he noticed that pork was on the menu. As if from nowhere came Reginald's advice, and Malcolm found himself uttering what can be understood as his first act of Islamic submission: "I don't eat pork."

Malcolm X was born.

OSAMA BIN LADEN AND THE SWEDISH SECRET WEAPON

What a cliché: bejeweled, lonely, little rich boy grows up to renounce his wealth and overthrow the empire.

A youth of hedonistic luxury was blighted by the isolation of being one among about fifty siblings. Not only that, but Osama bin Laden's Syrian mother, Hamida Alia Ghanoum, was ostracized by the bin Ladens for her refusal to wear a burka; Hamida favored more dashing, modern fashions, and they named her "the slave"—Osama's loving siblings dubbed him "the son of the slave." It is little wonder that Osama went on to rebel against Daddy, who had made his millions in construction.

Born in 1957, Osama grew up in Riyadh, Saudi Arabia, although his family is Yemeni. His food origins were Middle Eastern, but by all accounts, Osama was no foodie: at his old school stomping ground of the Al Thagher Model School, Osama, a shy and "gracious" student, was remarkable in his lack of greediness. At school, sandwich theft was rife, with pupils stealing each other's sandwiches in jest or even eating each other's sandwiches when they were left lying around on desks. But Osama would never dream of stealing a sandwich and became a sort of walking safety deposit box, carting other boys' sandwiches around to fox the thieves. Eventually, this service escalated into his guarding a whole number of valuables.

Nor did rich and spicy foods tempt his appetite: rather, the reverse. He preferred the monasticism of gentler, blander flavors. A defecting al-Qaida member described Osama's near hermetic, chaste relationship to food. Black tea, yogurt, Afghan flat bread, and dates were for breakfast. In 2001, *Observer* reporter Jason Burke detailed a meal shared in Pakistan between Osama and Mullah Omar of rice, grilled mutton, and vegetables as they discussed the action that would be taken post–September 11.

In part, Osama acquired his food tastes in the school of stomach bugs. Teenager Osama went on a family trip to Falun, famous for its copper mines, in central Sweden, with a scattering of what was just short of two dozen of his siblings. There is a photo of the bin Laden children on this trip, tumbled together like the Partridge family. Gangly Osama, or "Sammy" as he liked to be called at that time, grins out of the photograph, flared jeans, arms crossed, and hair folded into a side part in an attempt to curb adolescent curls. Stories gather about their stay at the Astoria Hotel, the children's wealth gleaming through the smoke of rumor; a glint of seventies decadence is suggested in tales of the older boys going "disco dancing" in the evening (though they liked to eat in the privacy of their own rooms). The hotel owner claimed she found trash bags of jewels when cleaning their rooms and white, beautiful Christian Dior shirts cast into the rubbish, having been worn only once.

Even in the photograph Osama's wealth shines through: the gawky "Sammy" leans against a pink Cadillac, framed by the headless dummies in the windows of Büréns clothes store.

On this trip "Sammy" risked trying a toothsome Swedish specialty called "Stekt Falukorv med Senap och Potatis"—consisting of smoked bologna beef sausage baked with potatoes and mustard. Perhaps he was trying to impress a girl? But the mustard proved too much for him, and he was violently ill, vomiting and despairing of recovery. This was the same year that Osama purportedly visited a language school in Oxford in the summer, befriended some Spanish girls, and punted on the Thames. Over twenty years later, Osama can be glimpsed in London watching his first competitive football match at Arsenal's Highbury Road, touring Edinburgh Castle, and dropping in at the British Natural History Museum.

But all through the summers and the trooping of the color, Osama the political animal was emerging. On the Hajj pilgrimage to Mecca in 1977 the twenty-year-old Osama shed "Sammy" and experienced personal revelation. Had, however, the CIA known of Osama's horror of the Swedish dish Stekt Falukorv med Senap och Potatis, a powerful psychological tool would have been at their disposal. In fact, herein lay the answer to the question that Osama posed to George Bush in 2004: "Contrary to what Bush says and claims—that we hate freedom—let him tell us then, 'Why did we not attack Sweden?'"

Stekt Falukorv med Senap och Potatis

LET ME DECODE THIS FOR YOU . . .

Stekt: fried	Falukorv sausage
Falukorv: type of Swedish sausage	apple
Med: with	½ an onion
Senap: mustard	tomato
Och: and	mustard
Potatis: potatoes	grated cheese
Equals: Fried Sausages with Mustard and Potatoes	

Preheat the oven to 170 degrees centigrade. Remove the skin of the Falukorv sausage and cut deep incisions along the length of the sausage. Fill the gaps with alternating slices of apple, onion, and tomato. Spread a layer of Swedish mustard over the top of the sausage. Place a blanket of grated cheese over the top. Cook for 30 minutes.

Swedish Mashed Potatoes

The secret ingredient of really good Swedish mashed potato is swede.

1 yellow swede, peeled and cut
  into chunks
1½ lb. potatoes, peeled and
  quartered

sea salt
¼ tsp. allspice
¼ lb. butter

Place the swede and the potatoes in a large pan of cold water, with a generous pinch of sea salt. Bring to a boil and cook till ready: test regularly with a fork. When the potato and swede yield to the fork, drain them, return them to the pot, and, even though you have turned off the ring, place the pot back on the hot stove without its lid. This will allow the potato and onion to dry.

    Sprinkle with allspice and begin to mash. Add the wedge of butter and work it through the mash thoroughly. If the mash seems too dry, add a splash of milk.

IT'S NEVER TOO LATE FOR BREAKFAST: YASSER ARAFAT

It was 1968. While you and I were trying on cat suits, he was in hiding from Israeli forces, a hunted man, moving by stealth from camp to camp under darkening Palestinian skies. Occasionally, he broke cover. But for what? Arms? Secret communiqués? No, Yasser Arafat took to dropping round unexpectedly at the house of Omar al-Khatib, a Fatah official resident in Amman, where he pointedly expressed a hankering for stuffed squash.

Never one to skip a meal during revolutionary agitation, Arafat liked to breakfast on cornflakes and honey while he conducted early morning meetings. In fact, breakfast played a crucial part in almost destroying the popular revolutionary mythology about Arafat. On the morning of March 21, 1968, Arafat's kudos hinged upon whether or not he was tucking into breakfast. Israeli forces had swarmed into Palestinian refugee camps in the Jordan valley, and the maelstrom of the battle centered on the town of Al-Karameh. Among the thick of the fighting PLO Fedayeen forces was Yasser, leading his troops in hand-to-hand combat.

Or was he?

Although Yasser made good political mileage out of this version of events, the Jordanian forces were less than convinced. Yasser had been spotted enjoying breakfast in the city of Salt at the very same moment when he was supposed to be rallying freedom fighters in Al-Karameh.

But then who can blame him for trying to enjoy a safe meal? Osama bin Laden's run-in with Swedish sausage was not an early assassination attempt, but revolutionaries must be circumspect. Take Yasser. A trusted aide had to inspect his victuals; at certain low points in his existence he had to have all his food tasted. Think for instance of the Mossad plot of 1971, when a treacherous associate in the Lebanon tried to poison Arafat's rice by slipping rice-shaped pellets of poison among the grains. The fact Yasser managed to stay alive for so long until his dubious and sudden end is no doubt the result of such caution . . . but perhaps it also has something to do with honey. Johnnie Walker whiskey held no allure for him, but instead that jezebel, honey, had him in her sugared clutches. Long could he digress on the subject of where the best honey came from, but his softest spot was reserved for smoky Yemeni honey. Late at night, Yasser snacked on jars of this drizzled over sliced apples and crumbling, nutty halva. A sweet-toothed revolutionary, Arafat also liked to sneak the odd marron glacé or Tunisian date into his daily diet. He took a childlike delight in Baci chocolates. Kenafas were also a favorite—small haystacks of shredded filo layered with unsalted, fresh cream cheese and sugar—though he worked these off with a jog first thing in the morning, just prior to his first meeting with advisors and staff.

One of Arafat's biographers, John Wallach, enjoyed a bizarre, very-early-in-the-morning repast with "easy-going" Yasser that typified Yasser's hearty, indulgent approach to food. Wallach was involved with Arafat and others in a debate about Zionism. It was the hour when appetites are really keen: 3 a.m., and Arafat's male secretary announced that breakfast was ready. The group staggered through to a table spilling over with every conceivable snack and delicacy the Middle East could offer: honey, halva, and ful medames were there—no cornflakes, though. Wasting no time, Arafat seized upon a pita bread and cheese. Then, sucking on watermelon, of which he ate slice after slice, Arafat reopened the thorny topic of Zionism.

Bless him.

Dolma (Stuffed Squash) (A word of caution—you may hear your doorbell go . . .)

10 squash

FOR THE STUFFING

1½ lb. lean minced lamb
½ cup rice
½ cup parsley, finely chopped
1 tsp. cayenne pepper
¼ cup lemon juice
1 tsp. black pepper

½ tsp. allspice
½ tsp. cinnamon
½ tsp. nutmeg
1 tbsp. dill, chopped
2 tsp. sea salt
2 oz. butter, melted

FOR THE SAUCE

8 oz. crushed tomatoes or
   tomato sauce
1 tbsp. dill
2 garlic cloves, crushed

½ tsp. honey
1 cup water or enough to cover
   the squash

Core the squashes, removing the soft interior with their seeds—use a corer, but whatever you do, keep the outer shell of the squash intact! Discard the squash filling (or keep for another purpose). Rinse the squash. Preheat the oven to 180 degrees centigrade.

Mix all the stuffing ingredients together. If it looks too dry, add more melted butter.

Put a "lid" of tinfoil over the open end of each squash and secure with kitchen string. Place the squash in a large baking tray. In a bowl, mix together the tomatoes, dill, garlic, and honey. Pour this over the squash, plus 1 cup of water (or enough to cover the squash). Cover the baking tray in a "hood" of tinfoil.

Place the squash in the oven for 1½ hours.

Ful Medames

2 cups dried fava beans   black pepper
  (*ful medames*)   1 tsp. dried flaked chili
sea salt   2 tsp. cumin
6 cloves garlic, crushed   ¼ cup olive oil

IN SMALL BOWLS, TO SERVE
4 green onions, minced   1 green pepper, diced
2 tomatoes, chopped   2 eggs, coarsely chopped
2 tbsp. tahini   3 lemons, quartered
1 cup parsley, minced

Soak the fava beans overnight. Cook the drained beans in a large pan of cold water, bring it to a boil, add a good pinch of sea salt, and let the beans simmer for 2 to 2½ hours—until the beans are tender. When the beans are soft, add the garlic, black pepper, chili, and cumin. Let the liquid reduce. Help the sauce to thicken by removing a ladle or two of the beans. Roughly mash them with some of the cooking liquid and return them to the beans, to help to thicken the sauce. When it is thick, add the ¼ cup of olive oil.

Serve ful medames with the side dishes of onions, tomatoes, tahini, and so on, which each diner can use to customize their beans.

Halva (Sesame Seed Fudge)

1½ cups mixed pistachios,   1½ cups tahini
  hazelnuts, and almonds   1 tsp. natural vanilla essence
2 cups runny honey (preferably
  Yemeni)

Preheat the oven to 180 degrees centigrade. If your cake tin has a press-out center, then butter it. If not, line the cake tin with buttered grease-proof paper. Once the oven is hot, place the nuts on a baking tray and put in the oven to brown. Keep an eye on them—they can burn easily. You will know they are ready when they bronze slightly and exude a scrumptious, buttery, baked-nut scent.

Heat the honey in a pan, stirring it regularly, until it reaches a "soft-ball" stage (this means that if you drop some of the honey into very cold water, it will form a ball shape). Remove your nuts from the oven and add to the honey. Quickly warm the tahini to about 50 degrees centigrade and then fold the warmed tahini into the hot honey. Add the teaspoon of vanilla essence.

Pour the warm mixture into the buttered cake tin and cool. After it has cooled, seal the cake tin with aluminum foil—or place a plate on top of it—and store it in the fridge for 24 hours. Cut immediately into squares.

3

Dining with the Heroes

Serving up supper with heroes, geniuses, and explorers. On a pedestal are Lawrence of Arabia; Sigmund Freud; Scott of the Antarctic; Mahatma Gandhi; Martin Luther King Jr.; Charles Darwin; Albert Einstein; and Men on the Moon.

THE EATING ADVENTURES OF LAWRENCE OF ARABIA

Trudging across Turkey in July 1911, on his way to Harran, an ancient Meso-potamian city of honey-colored adobe beehive houses, the young archaeologist T. E. Lawrence walked through searingly hot days and slept beneath a bright, cold moon at night. He ate on the road and expected to pay for his food, but when he came across Kurdish tents at Tell Ahmar, the kind-hearted Kurds greeted him with warmth and fed him creamily cool and sour leben and toothsome barley bread, refusing any payment. He limped on for another three hours, a sore wisdom tooth troubling him, and when he finally got to the village Khan, he tried to douse the pain with iced, distilled rose-petal sherbet. Lawrence thought it delicious, but it didn't shake his damned toothache. At least his appetite was stilled by a plate of rice with bahmia, lamb and okra braised in a thin tomato sauce, and he watched a local woman, dressed in traditional Bedouin clothes, using a hand mill to make barley pottage, which Lawrence later enjoyed. In another village the local women had great fun teaching Lawrence how to make bread.

Bahmia

3 tbsp. olive oil
2 onions, chopped
2 cloves garlic, chopped
2 lb. lamb, diced
1 tsp. cumin
1 tsp. ground cilantro powder
sea salt

freshly ground black pepper
1 tbsp. tomato puree
1 lb. tomatoes, peeled and finely
   chopped
½ kg. very small okra
2 tbsp. fresh, chopped cilantro
1 lemon

Heat the oil in a deep stew pot and add the chopped onions; sauté the onions until they are softened and light gold. Add the garlic, cook gently, and then add the lamb, browning it in the oniony, buttery base. Now add all the dried spices and stir through thoroughly. Add the tomato puree and chopped tomatoes. Top with enough water to cover and stew it for about 1½ hours. Meanwhile, prepare the okra by cutting off their stems. After the stewing time is up, add the okra and cook it for 20 minutes. In the last few minutes, add the chopped cilantro and the juice of 1 lemon.

Rose-Petal Sherbet

2 cups water
4 oz. granulated sugar
pinch of cardamom powder

4 cups cleaned, fresh petals from
   large-headed pink or red roses
¼ cup lime juice
¼ cup fresh pomegranate juice

Warm the water in a pan. Add the sugar and cardamom. Stir until the sugar dissolves in the water. Put the rose petals in a mixing bowl and crush them using a pestle. Add the warm sugar water, the lime juice, and the pomegranate to the mixing bowl. Leave to infuse and blend for 12 hours. When you want to serve the rose-petal sherbet, strain the juice and pour over ice cubes—yes, Lawrence had none, but time has moved on!

Soon, the strange, insectile mounds of Harran wobbled into view through the hazy heat; Lawrence found the sheikh there ensconced in his castle. Grandly, the sheikh made various fraternal inquiries after the health and appearance of the "Sheikh of London" before, in a generous and courteous act, using his own hands to serve Lawrence delicious white bread, cucumbers, and hard-boiled eggs. Close by, the sheikh's men dined on boiled mulberries and bread. Lawrence woke one morning with an ancient cockerel by his head, looking down its beak at him. He stayed with the sheikh for several days and was surprised into tenderness when the sheikh fell asleep with his head on Lawrence's knee.

But there was all of Arabia to see, and Lawrence could not linger in Harran. He set off with the sun rising over the hills of Mesopotamia, and delicious local food and hospitality sustained him all the way; in a later village he ate burghul and meat, with stewed apricots and beans, and in one village, Lawrence was greeted with such excitement and elation that the women started to clean and sweep the village as soon as they saw the tiny figure of Lawrence approaching over the hills. Finally, he reencountered an old friend he had first met in Syria, Ahmed Effendi, and was received with open arms into Ahmed's village. Ahmed helped him heal his blisters and treat his festering hand, and he fed him a welcome sweetmeat of a paste of burghul wheat, spices, and onions, with a bowl of leben alongside—though Lawrence complained he smelled of the onions ever afterward. Then, together, Ahmed telling his beads and smoking, they studied a history of Turkey together, and, sitting in the garden near a spring, they drank arrack all afternoon.

Such experiences prepared Lawrence for the two years between 1916 and 1918 when he worked covertly, at the command of General Allenby and the British Empire, to foster the Arab uprising against the Ottoman Empire. He crossed the Al-Hejaz desert region, searching for the Arab sheikh Feisal al Husayn, with Tafas, his guide, to lead him through the vast reaches of the desert. Waking in the chill of dawn, Tafas would hand Lawrence a glass of fire-brewed, hot, sweetened coffee. This was followed by a breakfast of meltingly sweet dates and bread. It is easy to envy Lawrence his breakfasts, till we discover that, at one point on his desert journey, he welcomed the dawn on a plateful of suckling camel calf, boiled in sour camel's milk.

The desert was not the unmarked, nameless wilderness Lawrence may have expected, coming from Oxford, via Cairo: each dune was the possession of an owner. "That one there belongs to Fakhir," Tafas explained, "and the one on the right to Ahmed." The two men cantered on camel back for long dusty hours, the salt of the sand jumping on the camels' backs: the jaunty movement, as Lawrence put it, shaking "down our bellies far enough for us to hold more food." In the night, when velvety darkness fell, the fire Tafas built flamed up, sending shooting sparks to meet the stars as the sweat of the day dried on the men's backs and shoulders. Tafas was ever-inventive and kept Lawrence's belly full with true desert fare: when they stopped at the watering hole of Bir el Sheikh, Tafas begged flour from a hut and plastered this together into a cake of dough, about two inches thick, which he tucked into the ashes of the aromatic fire to cook. When the cake was ready, he brushed off the ashes, and they ate it together. These cakes could then be carried across the desert for eating, although any Arab who took a snack like this with him on a journey of a couple of hundred miles by camel would be seen as a bit of a sissy. To revive the cakes, they were moistened with liquid butter till the dough fell apart and then sweetened with ground sugar, at which point the damp, buttery, sweet pellets could be eaten.

When Lawrence found Feisal in Wadi Safra, he knew he had discovered a leader born to be king and lead the anti-Ottoman revolt. They watched each other over the smoking bowls of rice and meat that had been set on the carpet by slaves. Almost like a sketch in a Tin-Tin adventure, Feisal had hooded eyes, a black beard, and a masklike face—but his body seemed to listen and watch, even when it was still. Lawrence's heart leaped. Feisal, meanwhile, realized that the young Captain Lawrence, and the British forces he represented, was an endlessly rich source of money and guns.

Lawrence learned much about Feisal from watching him eat. Conspiring for the Arab insurrection began each morning in the depths of Feisal's tent: the latest developments, guerrilla tactics to attack and undermine the Ottoman lines, plots, tricks, and schemes hung in the air. Emissaries from across the desert would sit beneath the folded curtains of the tent, and a tray of breakfast was brought in by slaves. This was a box of Feisal's Circassian grandmother's famous spiced cakes, all the way from Mecca, plus cereals and biscuits invented by Hejris, the body slave. These slaves sound pretty useful, wouldn't you say? Feisal had a very small appetite, so he made only some small gesture of eating. His poor appetite can perhaps be accounted for by his incessant, heavy smoking—a fug of tobacco followed him wherever he moved.

At lunchtimes, with fingers or a spoon, Feisal would make believe he was eating from dishes of beans, lentils, spinach, rice, and sweet cakes—out of courtesy to his cortege, who otherwise would go hungry without the cue from him: etiquette demanded that they eat only when their leader did. Feisal's portly follower, Mohammed Ibn Shefia, would watch him desperately for the cue to eat and comically grieved Feisal's small appetite and the hold it exerted. But Mohammed made up for this forced starvation by secretly tucking into a stash of tasty grub in his own tent. When they had all finished, servants at the door would pour water over the hands of the eaters. In those meals, many things were revealed to Lawrence: familial loyalty (granny's cakes); feudalism (Mohammed's obeisance); and Feisal's intensity (tobacco and lack of gluttony).

Traveling through the desert, engaging in skirmishes and guerrilla warfare against the Ottoman forces, the interdependence between man and camel became comically apparent. Camels have to be kept happy—a full-body massage was in order. The Arab forces had to rub down the camels with butter to try and relieve their mange. Not only was a camel a means of transport, but it represented two hundred pounds of meat on which you rode *and* camel milk had some wonderful uses: Lawrence was given bowl after bowl of camel milk as a diuretic.

Superstitions abounded between Arab tribes about what other tribes considered edible: one popular food misconception, held by the upland Arabs, was that certain "mean" foods damaged the character of men . . . these being chicken, eggs of all kinds, and fish (fish could make your brain puff up and lead to extreme foolhardiness). *Some* tribes would go far for lizard and jerboa meat, *others* would do anything for camel meat, but *most* tribes liked hare. This was bad news for hares. The best hunting catch, however, was commonly agreed to be gazelle, because no matter how arid the land, the gazelle remained fat and juicy. Lawrence loved the Arab style of preparing gazelle: they pulled the meat over a skewer and roasted the gobbets of gazelle till they were coal black on the outside, juicily sweet on the inside.

But all of life could not be gazelle kebab. Lawrence had smellier adventures with food. Around breakfast time one day the men saw "puffs of dust scurrying into the wind": ostrich! They searched the ground and found two ostrich eggs. There was no fuel to cook them, though, so they ingeniously shredded up sticks of gelignite, whose official use was for blasting rocks and detonating enemies, and placed both the eggs to roast on a fire ignited by the gelignite. Each egg was propped up by stones. Breakfast at last, they thought. . . . When the eggs had been fully roasted, they approached the first with a knife to knock its top off, like opening a huge boiled egg, but as soon as the top was sliced off, a stinking, flatulent blast hit the air. The men all screeched and scattered, kicking the second egg before them. When calm was restored, the second egg turned out to be nice and fresh, and each chipped away at his share of ostrich egg with a knife. The head of one Arab hung particularly low, though, never before having stooped so low as to eat a "mean" food like an egg. He was clearly an upland Arab.

The Arabs could tell if an English party had camped in any desert spot by telltale signs such as empty sardine tins near a fire. Ah, it was ever thus. It was as if the sardine stood between the British and the foreign hordes. Indeed, most Europeans in the desert had a habit of lugging along all sorts of ludicrous national delicacies with them. The Brits were also keen on bully beef and biscuits, perhaps because they were pretty ignorant about how to find food in the desert.

Meanwhile, the Arabs distrusted tins and bottles: later in the conflict, Lawrence came across some Arab forces who had managed to waylay a truck packed with delicacies that had been intended for an enemy German canteen. To his dismay, Lawrence found that the Arab captors had spoiled many of the provisions, uncertain of their use or purpose. There was a great deal of bottled asparagus there and one Arab, prizing open a case of these, wailed, "Pigs' bones!!!" in horror.

There was also considerable curiosity (and alarm) in the way the Arabs and the Brits perceived each other physically. In one village Lawrence politely ate a bowl of saffron rice with torn lamb over it while the mother of one of the Arabs marveled over his appearance; his dreadful blue eyes looking, as she described them, "like the sky shining through the eye-sockets of an empty skull."

Lawrence, for his part, was equally intrigued by the physicality of the Arabs, as in the fine horseman, Abdullah's, hair with its several nits. Abdullah styled his hair in black plaits, which he washed with camel urine and kept glossy with butter. They hung down on either side of his face, and he told Lawrence that the lice which crawled in his braids were a very good thing, in homage to the Bedouin proverb that "a deserted head showed an ungenerous mind."

Other eccentricities and prejudices abounded. One fierce Arab warrior, Auda, joined forces with the Brits and Feisal as they prepared to stand against the Turks, particularly one fiendish Turkish archenemy, Jemel Pasha, known as "Jemel the Butcher" on account of his bloodthirsty execution of Arab nationalist leaders. Auda was a physically powerful, majestic man, with a beard and moustache and coal black eyes—but, curiously, fitted with a set of false teeth. As they ate supper after Auda's arrival, he suddenly leaped to his feet wildly with a roar of, "God forbid!" and sprang from the tent. His fellow diners looked on in consternation at this abrupt departure, which was followed by the sound of hammering outside. Lawrence went after him and found Auda bent over a rock outside, smashing his false teeth into fragments with a rock. "I had forgotten," he lamented, "Jemel Pasha gave me these. I was eating my Lord's bread with Turkish teeth!"

Lawrence experienced legendary Arab hospitality when he stayed with the chiefs of Fitenna, who, as a point of honor, insisted on feasting with Lawrence's party no less than *twice* a day. A different tent was selected each time, with families squabbling to be their hosts. So even as the fifty visitors waited for their supper and supped coffee patiently, they heard sharply exchanged whispers from behind the scenes over wild and frantic cookery, with delicious puffs of roasted meat scent and the smell of broiling fat wafting past, while various mangled pets were paraded in front of the guests, from baffled sea birds to a dusty-looking ibex. At each different feast, a "special" food bowl (for want of a better word) kept reappearing, the common property of the tribe, and fondly cherished. To Lawrence this seemed, for all intents and purposes, to be "a shallow bath, five feet across, set like a great brazier on a foot." It was emblazoned about with curlicues of Arabic: "To the Glory of God, and in trust of mercy at the last, the property of his poor suppliant, Auda abu Tayi."

The bath was packed to the brim with rice like a white earthworks, a foot wide, with legs and ribs of mutton striking out in all directions, as if someone had buried a dismembered sheep there, covering up some woolly crime. In the center of the bath towered a pyramid of meat . . . but the true centerpiece were the "victims" who had made the dish possible: the heads of the sheep, upside down, staring at the eaters, each head topped with a section of severed neck, brown ears still attached, the edges flopping over the surface of the rice. The jaw of each was manipulated to give a good throat view and vision of rows of incisors and each pink tongue, as if about to speak from the blackened lips. They could have almost breathed down their bristled nostrils.

Small cauldrons arrived simmering with "the inside and the outside" of the skin and some wreaths of intestine, and the tails of each sheep were ladled out, lifted from pools of butter. Finally, to gasps of joy and astonishment, pools of gravy were poured to fill the moat made by the rice, until, eventually, the gravy in its abundance poured in a slow waterfall trickle out of the bath and into the dust.

Using his right hand, Lawrence dipped his fingers into the liquid fat, cautious not to scorch himself—often his hands could be smarting from the burn of hot grease after such a meal. He kneaded the food between his fingertips, cementing the rice, gravy, and meat into a ball, which could easily be popped into his mouth: any remaining butter or rice on Lawrence's fingers he licked off. An experienced eater would *never* grub up the palm of his hand with food. But no one truly cared about the rice: "flesh was the luxury." A Howeitat leader would draw his silver-hilted dagger, its turquoise stone winking, and cut from the bone a long diamond shard of meat. As a joke a man handed Lawrence a large meatless bone, suppressing his laughter; Lawrence returned his gift in the form of a handful of poached sheep's guts.

Wiping the grease from his hands on a tent pole, Lawrence then held his hands out to a slave, who washed and lathered his hands with the tribal soap cake. After he and his comrades had departed, the next wave of eaters would come, and the next, till finally the children would scavenge the meat and, at very last, the master of the tent fed the remaining offal to his greyhound.

When Lawrence was finally reunited with General Allenby and the British forces, the contrast between the two cultures could be seen in stark clarity, simply in the food on our hero's table. Lawrence and Allenby sat down, napkins on their laps, to a tidy salad, chicken mayonnaise, and foie gras sandwiches, beautifully cut like little white flags; and for breakfast there were the certainties of sausages and tea.

FREUDIAN SUPPERS WITH SIGMUND FREUD

Contrary to what one might expect, the father of psychoanalysis, Sigmund Freud, did not get his greatest kicks from the female hysterics on his couch or a ripe set of spooky dreams about teeth or penises to interpret. To the contrary, Freud affirms what *anyone* who has spent some decent time on an analyst's couch suspects: your analyst is watching the clock. They are even mildly bored by your psychosis. Although Freud seemed to be staring abjectly at the carpet while he puzzled over your relationship with your mother, he was secretly watching his dog, a chow called Jofi. Why? Because every time an hour was up, Jofi felt an irresistible need for a stretch, scratch, and shakedown—a cue for Freud to plan his exit and escape (unlike you) from your mother fixation.

Among other things, Freud got his kicks from food foraging: he could think of few things he'd rather do with his time than go for a long walk in the countryside and hunt around for free, wild food; if he was still with us now, he'd probably be a freegan. It delighted him to scrabble about the fields and hedgerows collecting wild berries. In the early summer Freud loved picking pinkly sweet wild strawberries, while the early autumn offered up purple blackberries and winey bilberries, the bloom rubbing off on Freud's fingers.

But most of all, Freud was a sucker for mushrooms in every conceivable form— fungi hunting in the mountains and pine forests of favorite foraging places like Altaussee was one of his grand passions—and his foraging style was impressive. Donning his adored sea-green velour forager's hat (tied about and adorned with a generous swath of dashing green silken ribbon), Freud gathered his team of six children together (they jovially referred to themselves as a "platoon") and encouraged them to scoop up all the wild fungi they could find. He then declared each specimen edible or inedible. Freud had armed himself with a little flat silver tin whistle, which he'd blow on sharply whenever he found a perfect fungus. He also always made sure he flung his hat over the fungi before he blew his whistle. The flying hat and the toot of his whistle alerted the platoon to the discovery, and the magical unveiling could begin.

They'd then take their mushroomy harvest back to Mrs. Martha Freud's kitchen, where Mrs. F. ably assisted by her spinster sister, Minna, a permanent resident with Martha and Sigmund following the death of her fiancé, picked through the dun and violet fungi, cleaning and skinning them. Mrs. F. then told the cook exactly how to prepare each different type: at the right time of the year, with the right kind of conditions, there'd be scrumptious mushrooms at every meal.

When they weren't tucking into the spoils of Freud's foraging, the family still loved their mealtimes in the sedate domesticity of their flat (which also doubled as Freud's office) at Berggasse 19, Vienna, where Sigmund set up home for forty-seven years, from 1891 to 1938, at which point they emigrated to Britain; four of Freud's sisters were to die in concentration camps. But in those happier, earlier years, before the nightmare called, the Freuds gathered at Freud's mother, Amalia's, house for key festivities—though not necessarily the expected Jewish ones. It may have been something to do with her being a Galician Jew, but Amalia was, with brilliant perversity, very keen on Christmas. Amalia was a little stick of dynamite right into her dotage; for instance, taken to buy a hat in her nineties, she rejected the one she tried on in the mirror, shouting deafly, "I won't take this one, it makes me look old." Amalia's culinary homage to Christmas was a real treat with goose roasted to deep honey-gold perfection, frosted indulgent cakes, homemade punch, and sticky candied fruit. Freud always turned up late, causing Amalia to scurry about in a panic, imagining him dead or vanished.

Freud got away with being late for Amalia's Christmas dinner but was never let off the hook by Mrs. F. who was a stickler for mealtimes: at 1 p.m. on the dot every day the Freuds had to show up for lunch, the *mittagessen*, their main meal of the day, with the tastiest food the Austrian table could offer. The maid sailed in with the soup, and Freud's study door was flung open to ensure his arrival at the table, where he was to sit at the head, while Mrs. F. sat at the foot.

Their eating choices were always seasonal, and the Freuds stuck to a three-course menu of soup, meat and vegetable, and a dessert. In springtime, though, as if in homage to the verdant freshness of that season, there was always an additional course of snappily green asparagus. The warmth of the summer was signaled by plump, buttercup-gold cobs of fresh corn or scrumptious Italian-style artichokes, stuffed with a delicate combination of bread crumbs, Parmesan, garlic, lemon zest, and mint, much adored by Freud, who had his eye on a second helping.

Coming forth from the Freud family kitchen was the other juicy and tasty food-stuff Freud couldn't get enough of: *rindfleisch*, known to you and me as beef, but which in German sounds like a type of flagellation. Freud liked to eat it at least three times a week, often more, with lots of different sauces and cooked in as many as seven different ways by Mrs. F. who was privy to the best secret Viennese cookery recipes. To round off lunch, there might be a beautifully crafted and executed *mehlspeise* such as a buttery and complex *apfelstrudel*—apple strudel!

Even Sigmund Freud's food hate list makes one pause for thought: what was his aversion to cauliflowers about? Their pellucid whiteness? Their resemblance to peeled brains? And why did he refuse to eat chickens—was it because they were female? Or reproducers of eggs? Did he see eggs as sacred? All he tells us gruffly is, "One should not kill chickens; let them stay alive and lay eggs." Sensible? But *why*? And in a brilliant little familial piece of reverse psychology, the entire platoon of Freud children secretly longed for chicken . . . were their actions Oedipal when they ate it in spite of his rule?

Indeed, every single one of his aversions offers psychoanalytic fun: where did Freud's hatred of bicycles come from? Or love of corn on the cob—were they golden phalluses . . .? Sometimes, though, a corn on the cob is just a corn on the cob.

Altaussee Wild Mushrooms

1 tbsp. olive oil
3 tbsp. butter
1 clove garlic, pulped
2 shallots, very finely chopped
1 lb. wild mushrooms, cleaned (very roughly chop the large mushrooms; keep the smaller mushrooms intact)
sea salt

freshly ground black pepper
1 tbsp. fresh, green chives, finely chopped (don't hesitate to use the bushy, purple chive flowers too)
1 tbsp. fresh flat-leaf parsley
1 tsp. finely chopped lovage leaf (optional)
dash of sour cream (optional)

In a large, wide frying pan, heat the olive oil and melt the butter at a high heat until they foam. Add the garlic, shallot, and mushrooms. Sprinkle on the sea salt and black pepper. Fry for 3 minutes, stirring every 30 seconds with a spurtle or wooden spoon. By now, the mushrooms should have softened and become bright with a glossy, confident sheen, and you should add the chives, parsley, and lovage. Stir through for a further minute. Now add a dash of sour cream.

Sigmund's Summer Italian Artichokes

1 cup freshly made bread crumbs (try to use really good bread, such as stale sourdough—it will give more texture to your stuffing)
¾ cup finely grated Parmesan cheese
½ tbsp. fresh parsley, finely chopped
½ tbsp. fresh mint, finely chopped (you can alternate this with the same amount of fresh oregano)

zest of half a lemon
1 clove minced garlic
4 tbsp. olive oil
pinch of sea salt
freshly ground pepper
4 large artichokes
2 cloves garlic, sliced finely

In a bowl, combine the bread crumbs, Parmesan, parsley, mint/oregano, lemon zest, minced garlic, 2 tablespoons of olive oil, sea salt, and pepper. Get a pot just large enough to fit the artichokes and which will help you to pack them in tightly.

   Wash the beautifully sculptural artichokes—Pliny had the cheek to call them one of "earth's monstrosities" back in 77 BC, but what did he know?

Sigmund's Summer Italian Artichokes (*continued*)

Rub some lemon juice into your hands before handling the artichokes—this will stop them from staining your hands. Chop off their stems at exactly that point where the stem meets the base of the artichoke—this will give each choke a flat base on which to stand in the pot they'll cook in, though packing them tightly together will also keep them upright. Clip off the sharp, pointed leaves from the top of the chokes. Gently spread and tease out the leaves of each choke and, using your fingers still, push and pack the stuffing in between each of the leaves.

Keeping the chokes upright, line them up in the pot—handling them carefully so that the stuffing doesn't spill. Pop the slices of garlic between the chokes and drizzle the remaining 2 tablespoons of olive oil over the chokes. Put the kettle on.

Under the pot, turn the heat up to medium. When you hear the artichokes start to sizzle, maintain the heat for 2 minutes. Now, without pouring water over the artichokes, by running it down the side of the pot, add enough hot water (from the kettle) to reach halfway up the pot. Put a lid on the pot and cook until the artichokes are tender . . . you know the artichokes are tender when a single leaf can be pulled easily away from the choke. Take the time to reflect on the fact that California nominated Marilyn Monroe the "Artichoke Queen" in 1947, leading to more people eating artichokes than ever before or since. But don't forget to take a peek in the pot every so often—you don't want the liquid to evaporate, so add a little more water if necessary—the whole cooking process shouldn't take much more than 45 minutes.

After 45 minutes are up and the chokes are tender, they are ready to serve. They are so delicious, and each choke really is a little bowl of heaven: you will be ready afterward to lie back on the sofa and think of Freud fondly . . .

Viennese Rindfleisch Goulash

3 tbsp. beef dripping
2 lb. stewing beef (it should have some fat marbling, to break up in the stewing process)
2 lb. shallots
1 tbsp. all-purpose flour
2 tbsp. tomato puree
2 tbsp. wine-red Hungarian paprika
grated zest of ¼ unwaxed lemon
2 tsp. roughly ground caraway seeds
2 pulped cloves garlic, pounded in a mortar and pestle with the caraway seeds

1 tbsp. freshly chopped marjoram
3 green bay leaves
4 pressed and cracked juniper berries
sea salt and freshly ground black pepper
2 large tomatoes, roughly chopped
1 pint beef stock (many recipes call for chicken stock, but in deference to Freud's esteem for this splendid bird, I think we'll leave that out)

Viennese Rindfleisch Goulash (continued)

TO GARNISH

3 tbsp. sheep's milk yogurt or   2 tbsp. finely chopped flat-leaf parsley
  3 tbsp. sour cream

Warm the beef dripping in a deep pot. Brown the chunks of beef in the dripping, a couple at a time, and remove with a slotted spoon; keep aside. Add the shallots and cook them gently until they turn dark gold. Return the beef to the pot. Sprinkle on the tablespoon of all-purpose flour and coat the beef with it. Add the tomato puree, paprika, grated lemon zest, caraway seed/garlic mush, marjoram, bay leaves, juniper berries, sea salt, and black pepper. Add the roughly chopped tomatoes. Pour in the beef stock and bring the goulash to a boil. Turn the heat to low-medium and simmer gently for 2½ hours, till the meat is really tender.

Ladle the goulash onto a serving platter, spoon over dollops of the sheep's milk yogurt/sour cream, and sprinkle with parsley. Serve with buttered noodles.

A LAST BIRTHDAY WITH SCOTT OF THE ANTARCTIC

Polar explorations usually involve a diet of over-slim seal as one dodges ice floes and tries to live through what resembles a frozen prequel to *The Rime of the Ancient Mariner*. But before the frozen horror begins and toes drop off, there are always moments in the accounts given by the likes of Shackleton and Scott which seem to bloom and are warm with joy—when plum puddings, birthdays, juicy plump emperor penguins, and Christmases were had beneath a bunting of bright stars. When there wasn't so much as a thought spared for a last will and testament.

Exploring frozen wastes is not easy, and Robert Falcon Scott of the Antarctic tried his hardest to take the best care of his men. Some who went before him were less thoughtful. Canadian Vilhjalmur Stefansson, for example, was hailed as a conquering hero for mapping the Arctic between 1913 and 1918 (he also discovered *blond* Eskimos), but while he trotted offstage to polish the Hubbard medal, his surviving crew brooded; fourteen survived out of twenty-four. Stefansson had abandoned his ship, *The Karluk*, leaving them to chew on their belts and seal flippers, drink blood soup, and nibble on the occasional guillemot egg, while he sauntered off to trap caribou. The caribou tale was one his former buddies believed he spun when he realized the ship was going to be pulverized by moving ice—which it was. Scott would never have been such a rat, but, as you will see, he made some tragic foodie mistakes as he busied himself for his last, doomed expedition to the South Pole.

His shopping list for the voyage was very long and groaned with food to fill the bellies of countless hungry young men. This was crucial—sledging gobbles up 6,500 calories a day! There were crates of kidneys and sweetbreads to supplement the Antarctic game they would kill, a substantial flock of sheep, 162 carcasses of mutton—a number which dwarfed the three carcasses of beef Scott recorded—all to be kept in the icehouse of the expedition boat, the *Terra Nova*. Yes, there was an icehouse, and, irony of ironies, it didn't work properly: a pong began to creep its way up from below deck, and a faint pollen of mold was found on the mutton.

Despite a full larder, Scott always watched with trepidation the vast amounts the crew consumed in the freezing weather; and he was right to. Supplies were diminished by unavoidable delays, as when the boat was swallowed by rigid pack ice for twenty days, captured in what Scott called an "ice prison" on the journey from New Zealand to Antarctica. This was bad news, not the least so because the race was already on to beat the Norwegian explorer, Amundsen, to the South Pole. Amundsen's challenge had surprised Scott—Amundsen had originally planned to take the North Pole, only to be beaten by others: he turned his sights to the South Pole. Scott, expecting no contender or race, had taken ponies as well as dogs with him, to test their worth in a polar landscape; plus, he stuck faithfully to his promise to undertake scientific experiments. In contrast, Amundsen, aware of the fierce competition, had a lean team of dogs and no intention to whittle away his time with science. Even worse, he planned to set off for the Pole from a point 60 kilometers closer than Scott.

From the outset, as soon as game was to be found on the "great sheets of open water," the crew began to take their pick of what they could: birds, some edible like skuas—their eggs were delicious, freshly buttered; some inedible, too sour, too oily, too fishy, like fulmars, whale birds, and what Scott calls "Cape chickens." On the ice floes, seals were always good game, and the men ate the livers of the crab-eater seals that filled the seas. There were creatures that were firmly on the "uneatable" list: hourglass dolphins and albatrosses with their quizzical sooty brows. Penguins, though, offered a tasty snack. Daydreaming as they roosted on the ice floes, they were a sort of slow-witted packed lunch—and were lamentably easy to catch. Little, tubby Adélie penguins were so kindly that they'd hurry toward a predator, like a starving, slavering, barking dog, becoming short of breath in their rush to say hello, rather than head in the more sensible, opposite, direction.

Scott was struck by the teeming life that existed among the barren stretches of pack ice, as well as the Adélie penguin, comic and wrong-footed on land, agile and swift in the water; underwater drapery of shoals of small shrimp; white seals; the near-transparent snowy petrel; and skuas. Scott saw the "long lithe sea leopard," one of whom was found to have eighteen penguins in its belly; grinning, hungry killer whales; and the vast sofas of browsing whales.

Scott's expeditionary team was trapped again on the ice on Christmas Day in 1910. But the crew of the *Terra Nova* was not downhearted. Tom Crean's rabbit gave birth to no less than seventeen little ones and, to follow this furry Nativity, the men dined, courtesy of Clissold, the cook, on a Christmas dinner offering such delectables as tomato soup, stewed penguin breast, beef, roasted to perfection, and stout little mince pies and puddings. On the table stood anchovy and cod roe kickshaws, and they toasted absent friends, something they often loved to do. Recording the meal in his diary at midnight, Scott's inky hand tells us: "A merry evening has just concluded." Although the meal lasted just one hour from 6 till 7 p.m., the men then sat around the table, singing lustily into the night, talentless as singers but happy nevertheless. Perhaps the food was less cheesy than Scott remembered. On his previously successful *Discovery* expedition to Antarctica with Shackleton in 1901, they scarfed a Christmas pudding that Shackleton had kept hidden among his socks.

Apart from proving a dab hand with penguin cookery, Clissold could also rustle up a terrific, deboned, stuffed galantine of seal; seal liver contains relatively high quantities of ascorbic acid and is a good defense against scurvy. Therein lies a story: the cook's choices, preferences, and understanding of the properties of different foods could make all the difference to the success or otherwise of a polar expedition. Clissold trained as a chef only to qualify for the Scott expedition; he was, by trade, an artificer, otherwise known as a mechanic, in the Royal Navy. He was a bit of a wiz at invention and could construct a sled out of packing cases and cure the ailing motor of any car. And while Clissold was undoubtedly adventurous and produced a good, tasty spread, the problem was that he lacked an understanding of the type of diet that worked best in polar conditions—a shortcoming that distinguished him from Lindström, the cook for rival Amundsen's Norwegian team, who had clocked up some seven years on different expeditions. Clissold's wonderful bread was white; Lindström made buckwheat pancakes, thickly spread with whortleberry or cloudberry jam, and his wholemeal bread was dark brown and rich with wheat germ and fresh yeast. There was, crucially, much more vitamin B coming out of the Norwegian cook's oven. The seal that both rival expeditions ate was high in vitamin C, but the Norwegians ate it daily, and not stewed but lightly cooked, a procedure which tended not to destroy the vitamin! Scott hadn't fully realized that scurvy was caused by vitamin C deficiency; he attributed it to contaminated tinned meat.

By early January, the *Terra Nova* was trying unsuccessfully to land at Cape Crozier. Tantalizingly, Scott could see the old wooden post office pole from his earlier, successful *Discovery* expedition poking up erect from the snow and ice. Eventually, they managed to hole up west of Cape Crozier at "Cape Evans," named after Scott's second-in-command. The men unloaded dogs and some supplies onto the packed frozen ice, which was no mean feat. They had to give one pony a medicinal whiskey after swimming it ashore in the icy water, and skua would swoop down on the heads of the men, bombing them and thumping the men's heads with their wings. The immense cunning of killer whales was also a threat. When the whales saw the moving shadows of the dogs through the ice pack, they arched and bridled their backs, cracking and splitting the ice, then would shoot their long-snouted tawny heads up vertically through the broken ice, eyes gleaming with blood lust, full sets of teeth glistening like a set of saws, ready for a noisome canine snack. Later, they were to snap up several of the ponies Scott had brought with him: Amundsen had opted solely for dogs, a wise move as it turned out because dogs can eat the plentiful seal and penguin caught en route, while ponies' feed had to be transported from the *Terra Nova*—although one pony, called Snippet, started to eat blubber.

The men built a hut in Cape Evans, complete with a cooking range, stove, and chimney—it even had a porch. Fuel blocks they had brought on the *Terra Nova* substituted for coal; Cherry-Garrard hoped eventually to use blubber to fuel the stove. Clissold baked his bread in the oven, which was rigged so that when the bread rose, its crust completed an electric circuit, causing a bell to ring and a red lamp to light up. He was always on hand to make really lovely "welcome home" meals for the explorers, who ventured out to lay depots and supplies for the polar journey and the final push to the South Pole in the spring. One expeditionary team came home to find he'd made a big basin of figgy rice pudding, with a bucket of Fry's cocoa on the side. Even marmalade and toast was a possibility. Others had to fend for themselves: the night watchman who was stationed to look out for aurora australis had to make his own cocoa on a Bunsen burner, to accompany the sardines and bread he snacked on. The aurora australis wasn't the only eerie nighttime phenomenon—mock moons were even seen in the sky. The moon vision may have been brought on, though, by too many of Clissold's seal rissoles—as good, Scott claimed, as any common beef rissole. Clissold's seal steak and kidney pie was moreish, as was a thick seal soup, which, Scott mused, was rather like thick hare soup.

The dining was never as good, understandably, away from Clissold and Cape Evans. Despite that, every camp seemed luxurious after the privations of a trek; there were coffee, tea, bags of sugar, and a stash of chocolate, raisins, sardines, and jam. An endless supply of Huntly and Palmers captain's biscuits at Hut Point in early March seemed to be food heaven, but this was also another "food mistake" made by Scott. Amundsen's team ate oatmeal-based biscuits, another source of vitamin B. When the team discovered a colony of seals at Pram Point, this guaranteed a supply of seal meat. In cooking, they'd spice this up with curry powder and a handful of raisins. There was nothing like hard work and polar ice to sharpen the appetite. The polar explorer Frederick Cook claimed that a deficient diet led to "polar anemia," characterized by very pale, greenish skin.

They set up a blubber stove, which filled the hut with black, acrid smoke, turning their faces soot black, and ate biscuits fried in blubber, with a steaming, hot pannikin of tea. They experimented with purifying penguin blubber, to rid it of its odor: thinking they had been successful, they fried up seal in the fat, only to find their seal supper again steeped in eau-de-penguin. Even the water sometimes had a faint, suspicious taste of penguin, quarried as the water was from ice slopes. . . . Some men left their pannikins of seal meat uneaten, a fact Scott lamented, aware as he was of the necessity of a high fat content in their diets. This was a lesson Shackleton knew well. His polar exploration mission survived on half rations. Starving, they fantasized about the fat content of a dish invented by explorer Frank Wild, which they called "the Wild roll," made as follows: "Take a supply of well-seasoned minced meat, wrap it in rashers of fat bacon, and place around the whole an outer covering of rich pastry so that it takes the form of a big sausage roll. Now fry it in plenty of fat." Shackleton gave Wild his own ration of biscuit to keep him alive, and Wild recollected: "All the money that was ever minted would not have bought that biscuit and the remembrance of that sacrifice will never leave me."

On June 6, 1911, Scott's forty-third (and LAST!) birthday fell—an occasion Scott may well have forgotten, but which his friends did not. Laughing, they photographed themselves around the huge birthday cake that Clissold had baked and then decorated with chocolate, flags, crystallized fruit, and photographs of Scott himself. They hung the banner from their sledge about the room, Saint George's flags, and sat about the table with their now emblematic roll-neck gray sweaters on, hot-faced and blithe. They quaffed a cider cup and dished up in tin crockery simmering hot seal soup, roasted mutton with ruby red currant jelly, asparagus, and tinned fruit salad. They might have played Snapdragon that night—an eating game they also played later at their midwinter feast. Plump raisins were sprinkled on a shallow, wide bowl of brandy. The brandy was then lit and the lights dimmed so that the blue flame illuminated the table; the raisins looked like tiny burning wicks, and the faces of the men were bright, hanging like lanterns above the dish. Each contestant had to snatch hot, brandied, flaming raisins from the bowl and pop them in their mouths. The winner was he who could snatch the greatest number of raisins. Finally, miraculously, from some secret store of Clissold's, appeared golden sherry and a liqueur. Twenty-one days later Cherry-Garrard had set off to find emperor penguin eggs destined for the Natural History Museum into temperatures of minus 60 degrees Fahrenheit and a pitch-dark landscape of roaring winds—it was only faintly light at noon—and on a seven-day journey so terrible he said, "Sometimes it was difficult not to howl"—especially when his teeth chattered so much that they shattered.

The final, terrible journey to the South Pole began in September: the team experienced terrible thirst trudging over the Beardmore Glacier, chipping at the ice to suck it for water. The exhausted ponies that Oates had tended were shot at various intervals, supplying the men with meat—Christmas Day 1911 saw the last eight men eating a dinner of pemmican with horsemeat steaks dusted with onion and curry powder, topped up with a sweetened arrowroot, cocoa, and biscuit hoosh. "Hoosh" was a term invented first on Scott's *Discovery* expedition and was mushed biscuits, plus, usually, pemmican, a cake of animal fat, and dried powdered meat—a must-have for any of you thinking of going on a polar expedition. Despite his care, Scott's polar rations fell 2,000 calories short of the recommended 6,500. And even worse, Scott had bought his tinned pemmican from the mainstream suppliers, J. D. Beauvais of Denmark, while his shrewder rival Amundsen had made his own pemmican, upping its nutritional value. In a Conan Doyle-ish manner, he had developed his special top-secret pemmican mix under the watchful gaze of physiologist Professor Sophus Torup from Christiania University.

The hoosh, then, wasn't going to save Scott's men; their health already taking a blow from the onset of scurvy and the poor calorific count of their rations. You could, Cherry-Garrard claimed, make a great "fat hoosh" out of pony meat and biscuit, or a pony-free, lovely sludge of chocolate hoosh with raisins thrown in. Back this up with a slice or two of plum duff, some caramels, and crystallized ginger and, said Cherry-Garrard, you'd want someone to put you to bed. On no account, Scott insisted, were the men to eat the dogs; not a bad piece of advice, given than Douglas Mawson, on his terrible Aurora expedition of 1910, decided to lunch on dog livers, only to find that they caused hypervitaminosis, a grim condition which leads to human skin coming off in sloughs: Mawson lost the soles of his feet this way. Ouch.

Finally, the team wearily arrived at the South Pole on Thursday, January 18, 1912, only to find that victory had been plucked from their grasp: Amundsen had got there more than thirty days before. All that was left was to turn back defeated, dressed in their damp British woolens (again in contrast to Amundsen's Eskimo wear), and drag themselves home, their lost victory weighing down every step. Evans began to lose his nails; a war wound from the Boer War reopened and gaped wide on Oates's leg—the reopening of healed wounds is a side effect of scurvy. Oates wanted the others to have his rations and said famously, "I am just going outside and may be some time," to be swallowed by the blizzard. On Monday, March 19, supper was cold pemmican and biscuit with a half-measure of cocoa. By Thursday all was lost, and Scott died eleven miles from his food and rations, his arm cast across his friend, Bill Wilson, the instigator of the Snapdragon game and of whom Scott wrote in his diary: "Words must always fail me when I talk of Bill Wilson. I believe he really is the finest character I ever met."

Pemmican

1 lb. beef, with no marbling, cut into very fine, paper thin strips
½ lb. beef suet

¾ cup dried cranberries, raisins, or blueberries

Preheat the oven to 160 degrees centigrade. Place the strips of beef in a single layer on several baking sheets and dry in the oven for 8 hours; they should eventually appear dry and crispy. In the meantime, render the beef fat. Cook and melt the fat in a wide frying pan at a low heat, gradually removing all moisture from the fat—it will turn rancid if its moisture is not fully evaporated. When the beef strips are dry, use a food processor to grind them as finely as possible. Add the dried fruit and combine. Strain the warm beef tallow and add to the meat-fruit mixture, until the tallow has coated all the dried ingredients. Shape into cakes and allow to harden—the tallow should appear white and waxy when dry.

A BIRTHDAY FEAST FOR CAPTAIN SCOTT

Seal Soup

3 tbsp. olive oil
2 onions, finely chopped
1 lb. seal (if you can't get this,
   replace with reindeer or
   venison)
2 carrots, chopped
½ turnip, chopped
1 large potato, diced

2 bay leaves
1 pint stock, beef or venison (it must
   be possible to make stock from seal
   bones, though!)
sea salt
freshly ground black pepper
½ cup barley, soaked overnight and
   drained

Warm the olive oil in a deep, heavy-based pan. Add the chopped onion and very gently brown it. Next, add the dark chunks of seal meat and brown them in the oil. Now add all the chopped vegetables and the bay leaves. Cover with the stock, salt, and pepper and cook on a medium heat for 1½ hours. After this time, add the barley and cook for a further 20 minutes. Serve with freshly baked bread.

Roast Mutton and Red-Currant Jelly

1 shoulder of mutton
6 parsnips, peeled and split
5 branches rosemary

4 cloves garlic, sliced
¾ bottle white wine

Preheat the oven to 150 degrees centigrade. Put the shoulder of mutton on top of a bed of parsnips and 3 whole branches of rosemary in a deep roasting tin. Using a small, sharp-pointed knife, pierce the shoulder, slipping shards of garlic and rosemary spears into the incisions. Do this all over the shoulder. Now drizzle with a little olive oil and salt and pepper. Pour the white wine into the base of the roasting tin, so that it drenches the parsnips. Now cover the shoulder with foil and put it in the oven. Allow 40 minutes in the oven per 450 grams of weight. In the last half hour of cooking, remove the foil and give the shoulder's fat and skin a chance to brown and caramelize.

Serve with a generous dollop of tart red-currant jelly.

Snapdragon

½ bottle brandy
2 cups raisins
1 box of matches!

Heat the brandy in a saucepan until it is hot. Meanwhile, sprinkle the raisins into a heat-proof, large shallow dish. Make sure they are widely distributed. Dim the lights . . . pour the hot brandy over the raisins and immediately set the brandy on fire. Now try to snatch the raisins from the burning brandy and eat them while they are still alight: he or she who manages to do this wins the game!

FINDING VEGETARIAN LONDON: MAHATMA GANDHI

In 1888, vegetarian trials lay ahead of Gandhi: he was on his way from Bombay to Britain on the SS *Clyde*. He was destined to study law in London, and his gentle Hindu parents were aware that the flesh pots of England held considerable temptation. Before leaving India, Gandhi had vowed to his father that he wouldn't eat meat during his time in London, and he was determined to collect certificates along his way attesting to the fact that he had never been seen eating meat (I wonder what the Victorians made of that).

For two long days on board the *Clyde*, Gandhi ignored the bell calling the passengers to dinner; he was too shy to mingle and lent his black dinner jacket to an Indian companion, one Mr. Mazmudar. Instead, Gandhi lived on Gujerati sweetmeats, Indian fruit, and handfuls of ganthias, which are delectable, crunchy threads of deep-fried, spiced gram flour, often further enriched with a spoonful of mango chutney or some onion seeds. Many of the other travelers were seasick, and Gandhi was later to attest to the powerful properties of fruit and boiled peanuts to combat motion sickness. He was further bewildered by the lack of water in the WC to clean himself and the British predilection for instead using "pieces of paper" to do the same job.

After forty-eight hours Gandhi and his Indian companions had managed to find a native sailor who was happy to make them dal and rice. The flour was "provided free of charge by the steamer authorities," so they could have rotis too. But Gandhi noticed the man's hands were grubby, so he demurred and decided to use white European loaf for dipping into his dal. Soon, Gandhi was doing well on three meals a day, ordering special foods from the chief steward—breakfast was porridge and stewed fruit, plus cocoa. Dinner was curried vegetables, rice, and perhaps the odd jam pastry or two. Finally, the maritime day was finished off with more cocoa, bread and butter, cheese, and peppered lettuce. Twice a week, nuts and fresh fruit appeared on the steamer.

Seaman's Roti

8 oz. chapati flour
pinch of sea salt

1 tbsp. ghee, melted
water

Pour the flour into a large mixing bowl and add the salt and ghee. Mix together into a crumbly state. Now add cold water a little at a time until the dough is soft and elastic. Divide the dough into balls, then roll out on a floured surface to form a circle of dough roughly 6 inches in diameter. Heat up a dry frying pan. Dry cook one disk of roti at a time, allowing it to brown and blister, then turning and repeating this process. Press down on the bread with a fish slice, as this will make the dough puff and blister more. Keep the rotis warm under a clean dishcloth and serve with dal.

Dal Fit for the SS *Clyde*

2 cups green or brown lentils
1 tsp. sea salt
2 tbsp. ghee or butter
1 onion, thinly sliced
½ cup tomatoes, roughly chopped
1 tsp. fresh ginger, finely chopped
1 tsp. garlic, pulped
1 tsp. cumin

1 tsp. dried, ground cilantro
two 2-inch cinnamon sticks
2 cardamom pods
6 cloves
1 tsp. turmeric
1 green or red chili, chopped
¼ cup fresh green cilantro, chopped
¾ tsp. garam masala

Put the lentils and sea salt into a saucepan and cover with boiling water. Simmer until the lentils are cooked and tender. Drain. Heat the ghee or butter in a large, wide frying pan and then cook the onion very gently until it is dark gold. Add the tomatoes and all the other spices, with the exception of the fresh cilantro and the garam masala. Cook for 2 minutes and then add the strained dal. Cover the frying pan and let the dal simmer gently for 15 minutes. Stir occasionally to prevent it from sticking. Two minutes before serving, add the fresh cilantro and the garam masala. Eat with rotis.

But the closer the *Clyde* nosed its way toward European waters, the more dire predictions were made by fellow passengers. Gandhi was warned he'd catch consumption if he didn't eat meat in Britain (later, onshore, a doctor tried unsuccessfully to force him to drink beef tea as a cure for bronchitis); he would be numbed completely by the cold if he didn't drink wine or alcohol of another form in regular doses. One worried-looking chap predicted, "The weather has not been severe, but in the Bay of Biscay you will have to choose between death, and meat and wine." This news horrified Gandhi: his caste, the Banias of Gujurat, was a vegetarian one, with a huge respect for other creatures; they must have no association with food at all—even a stray fly in your soup polluted it. An egg was an offense. Banias were mocked by other castes as "dhili dal," which translates as "as mushy as lentils." But there was no mush to Gandhi's vegetarianism: he was a determined pioneer.

Finally, the SS *Clyde* made it through the Bay of Biscay and docked at the Tilbury Docks in Southampton on a Saturday. It was three weeks since Gandhi had waved farewell to Bombay. Stepping ashore in the spanking white flannels which he'd hoarded to make an entrance, Gandhi immediately regretted the decision: his body felt the physical shock of late September in Southampton. Plus everyone was dressed in the modest, cozy duns, grays, browns, and blacks of Britishness. Gandhi traveled in a flurry of mortification to the Victoria Hotel in London. There, to get to his room, he had to step into a strange metal cage which turned out to be an elevator. He had no change of clothes, having left everything to be delivered by an agent, so he had to spend his first twenty-four hours in London in his Persil-white summer suit. This was a far cry, of course, from the basic, homespun *dhoti* he was to wear to London in 1931. Dr. Pranjivan Mehta, one of Gandhi's contacts in the United Kingdom, arrived at the Victoria Hotel in a top hat and smiled with street-wise indulgence at Gandhi's flannels. His mood turned sour, though, when Gandhi picked up his hat and ran his fingers over its fur, disturbing its gloss. "Do not touch other people's things," Dr. Mehta instructed stiffly, "and do not ask questions all the time the way we do in India."

Shocked by the extortionate £3 cost of the Victoria Hotel, given that Gandhi was also still eating the makeshift food he had brought from Bombay, he moved across London to lodgings recommended by his fellow traveler and student, Sjt. Mazmudar. Gandhi watched every farthing he spent in Britain and settled down with nothing more than cocoa and bread for his supper most nights—he was also learning how to use a fork and spoon, British-style. What Gandhi hadn't reckoned on was his Anglo-Indian London landlady's interpretation of vegetarian cooking; despite her familiarity with India, she had learned nothing of its cuisine. Oatmeal porridge for breakfast was a safe bet (he was to introduce his family in India to oatmeal porridge and cocoa on his return from London), but, other than that, she offered up unsalted boiled vegetables, gluey potatoes, and disconsolate cabbage, without condiments. Gandhi's heart sank. For lunch and dinner there was bread, jam, and spinach, but Gandhi was too polite to ask for more than a slice or two of bread. Milk was unheard of as an accompaniment to meals. But even the landladies of London couldn't drive Gandhi away from vegetarianism. And all because of a murdered goat . . .

Right from the start, Gandhi's personal notion of wickedness had been pretty narrow: as a boy, Gandhi's hobby was playing the concertina (not usually considered a first step on the path to vice), and although he was married off young at thirteen, it was in all innocence. Indeed, the occasion meant little more to him than the chance for a slap-up meal and the discovery of a great new friend to play with. Unfortunately, beyond his tiny new wife, Gandhi also had a naughtier friend, a boy called Sheikh Mehtab, who convinced Gandhi that meat eaters were always stronger. Take a look at the Brits, urged Sheikh; they are very big, and they have colonial control over India. Why? Because they eat meat. Sheikh chanted the well-known school rhyme:

Behold the mighty Englishman
He rules the Indian small,
Because being a meat-eater
He is five cubits tall.

Sheikh ate meat and was very good at the long jump, so Gandhi reckoned there might be some truth in this. Gandhi fell for Sheikh's reasoning: he would try goat meat. He took a first bite, but it was tasteless and leathery, yielding none of the promised deliciousness and not increasing his height by so much as an inch. Gandhi doesn't say whether he tried jumping. Worse was to come: Gandhi spent a troubled, sleepless, restless night, waking intermittently, convinced that he could hear the goat bleating inside him, calling out its injustices. Sheikh continued to get Gandhi into a lot of hot water later on by dragging him to a brothel and, when Gandhi sat looking gormless next to the prostitute he'd been assigned, she lost patience with him and threw him out.

The bleat of the goat pretty much drowned out any hankering for meat Gandhi might have in the future.

By the summer of 1890, Gandhi had moved into his own room at Tavistock Street and was cooking for himself. Invariably, breakfast was a staunch bowl of porridge with a splattering of stewed fruit, followed by bread and butter. Dinner might be taken in a vegetarian restaurant, and supper would be bread again with milk, stewed fruit, or radishes. In total, Gandhi spent two years and eight months in London as a student. Eventually, in Pretoria, he wrote a "Guide to London," essentially a survival guide for Indians who wished to visit London (which he recommended). In a way, Gandhi's travels in London essentially equipped him with an understanding of the British "character," making him a much more effective conduit for India's independence. Naturally, he didn't want his fellow countrymen to turn up smelling strongly of spirits, with meat between their teeth since the Bay of Biscay, and dressed in white linen. Hence his "Guide to London" suggests that the Indian visitor pack a pair of woolen drawers and indeed as many woolly garments as can fit in a trunk case. English white bread should be avoided at all costs; only wholemeal is truly digestible. His readers should keep their eyes peeled for green pea soup and lentil cutlets in London. On Sundays, be prepared to eat at home, as that's what all the Londoners do. Indian students visiting England should not hesitate to try certain, choice English foods but should also try to cook for themselves: they required no smoke, cow dung cakes, or wood in Britain but could instead use a stove, which was rather like an Indian chulas. "Moreover," Gandhi adds, on an English stove "the cooking does not take much time. Twenty minutes would be found quite sufficient. Ten minutes are required for boiling milk" and while you wait, he suggests, you could pass the time in reading a newspaper.

Porridge comes highly recommended on the grounds that thousands of Scots do very well on it, and Gandhi explains this exotic dish further: it "tastes like wheat and is sweeter." Then he continues with a recipe: "You can stir one ounce of oatmeal into a sufficient quantity of water and put it on the oil stove. If it is fine oatmeal, the porridge would be ready in 20 minutes. If it is coarse, it would take

30 minutes. It can be eaten with sugar and milk or stewed fruit." Then, just in case his reader is in any doubt, Gandhi thoughtfully adds, "Stewed fruit is fruit cooked in water with a little sugar."

While Gandhi very much wanted to qualify as a barrister and had enrolled in the Inner Temple, until he sat his exams it was obligatory that he make an appearance for dinner in the Inner Temple every ten days. This was Gandhi's idea of hell; his fellow diners were stuffy and very posh, drawn from the English upper classes. On top of that, the food was the sort of meaty, artery-hardening fare that seems to typify English snobbishness. Two bottles of heavy wine were plonked down on the table, alongside fatty, roasting slabs of mutton and beef, which had his colleagues sharpening their knives in carnivorous glee. Gandhi asked for a vegetarian option, and it might as well have been his landlady working in the kitchens: out came cabbage and boiled potatoes. To give some relief to this, Gandhi swapped his share of wine for his fellow diners' fresh fruit. And so, in London, after a month of near starvation, Gandhi took it upon himself to hunt out a vegetarian restaurant, which was no mean feat in the London of the 1880s. Then, as luck would have it (or God, as Gandhi put it), one day on Farringdon Street he spotted a vegetarian restaurant: the dully named "The Central" restaurant. His pulse raced. "The sight of it filled me with the same joy a child feels on getting a thing after its own heart," Gandhi enthused. Even better, it stood hard by the evangelical London Vegetarian Society. On sale inside The Central were rows of wise books, and in the window, a copy of Henry Salt's *Plea for Vegetarianism*. Gandhi immediately bought a copy, tucked it under his arm, and headed for the nearest table, assured at last that he wouldn't die of starvation in London. Curried eggs, Scotch broth, and a noisome tomato and macaroni pudding beckoned to him from that October 1888 menu, but Gandhi's fancy was taken by porridge for a starter, followed by a very agreeable vegetarian pie.

Gandhi also bought a copy of *The Vegetarian Messenger* and, leafing through its pages, picked out the addresses of the ten or so vegetarian restaurants in London; he was to go on to write several articles for the journal, explaining the ways of Indian vegetarianism to the readership and promoting Salt's teachings. Doses of Percy Bysshe Shelley's transformative "A Vindication of Natural Diet" further spurred Gandhi on. When he finally met Henry Salt, he introduced himself, "My name is Gandhi. You have, of course, never heard of it." Then, one damp London day, he stood before an audience of concerned Victorian vegetarians and lectured them on "The Foods of India," wishing perhaps that his first landlady had been in the audience to make notes on the proper treatment of a potato. "I have known," he said, with an air of enlightenment, "peas spiced with salt, peppers, turmeric, cloves, cinnamon, and the like. . . . Simply boiled vegetables are never eaten. I never saw a boiled potato in India." Eventually, Gandhi's path to food enlightenment meant that he abjured spices, eggs, milk, and raw onions—which could titillate the passions. But for the moment, his approach was more indulgent, as he tipped off his audience about the use of the rather mysterious, hairy coconut: "I will just point out one of the various ways in which we use the cocoanut [sic]. It is first ground and then mixed with clarified butter and sugar. It tastes very nice. I hope some of you will try at home these cocoanut sweet balls as they are called."

Eventually, Gandhi teamed up in London with the Gujerati writer Narayan Hemchandra, a fellow vegetarian, and someone who seemed at the time to Gandhi to remain almost obstinately Indian in his dress and manner: he knew no English, wore no necktie, dressed in the Parsi fashion, and sported a long beard. Gandhi volunteered to teach him English, and they ate together daily while Gandhi cooked in "the English style" such dishes as a "soup of carrots"; Narayan insisted on dal and even managed to hunt down mung in London, cooking it and bringing it to share with Gandhi. The taste of mung was the taste of home in Gandhi's mouth, and the two often swapped dishes ever afterward on those chilly London evenings.

Soup of Carrots

2 tbsp. ghee or butter	sea salt
1 onion, finely chopped	freshly ground black pepper
1 lb. carrots, peeled and finely chopped	1 tbsp. all-purpose flour
2 cloves garlic, pulped	1 tbsp. curry powder
2-inch piece ginger, peeled and very finely chopped	1 potato, diced

In a deep saucepan, melt the ghee and fry the onion, carrot, garlic, and ginger gently. After 5 minutes, salt and pepper and cover the vegetables with buttered grease-proof paper and sweat over a low heat for a further 10 minutes. Next, stir in the tablespoon of flour and the curry powder. Combine well. Remove from the heat and slowly add hot water, stirring all the time. Add the diced potato, bring to a boil—still stirring—and then simmer for 20 minutes. At the end of this, either blend the soup to make it creamy or be true to Gandhi's late-nineteenth-century style and mash it, producing a lumpier but no less satisfying version.

THE ULTIMATE WIFE TEST: MARTIN LUTHER KING JR.

Martin Luther King Jr. was to learn a thing or two about food in his teenage years: coming from Atlanta, Georgia, he was very familiar with the segregation of black and white: parks were for white Georgians only; a drinking fountain declared itself for "coloreds"; restaurants shrugged off one race or the other. Senator Lester Maddox's restaurant, the imaginatively named Lester's Grill, served skillet-style fried chicken— a cartoon chicken was his jolly logo—but the chicken was only for white plates. African Americans were not welcome. Maddox defended his restaurant from civil rights activists who wanted to eat there with an axe handle, and—according to Maddox—his own customers even armed themselves to fight off black would-be diners.

In 1945, instead of taking a white-collar job in Atlanta over the summer, student Martin wanted to touch the real experiences of impoverished blacks, and so, aged eighteen, he took a summer job working in the heavy-leafed tobacco fields of Connecticut. Hard though the labor was, King loved the heady, exhilarating liberty of the northern states, of blacks and whites worshipping in the same church, sitting alongside each other, and the freedom of being able to eat in any restaurant he chose. After a trip to Hartford, he wrote home: "I never thought that a person of my race could eat anywhere but we ate in one of the finest restaurants in Hartford." Everything changed on his return train journey to the south: after Washington he was sharply reminded of the Jim Crow laws. King strolled in to eat in the dining car. The waiter intercepted him, ushering him to sit away from the white diners. He was hustled into a rear seat and a curtain pulled down in front of him. He said, "I felt as though that curtain had dropped on my selfhood." Separate, King understood, spelled unequal.

As an eligible bachelor, King was much sought after . . . he could have had any number of a flock of starry-eyed young ladies, but there were two serious contenders for the role of minister's wife. First in the queue was a young lady from Atlanta who was, apparently, the very model of perfection. Next was one Coretta Scott, a fellow student in Boston. Quite frankly, he was lucky that Coretta tolerated him on their first date in Sharaf's Restaurant. Very deliberately, King asked Coretta a question that required some grasp of the capitalist versus communist debate. Would she even know what communism was? On finding her response an intelligent one, he said, "Oh, I see you know something other than music." Coretta listened in mild amazement as King schoolboyishly cited the four main criteria he wanted in a wife: (1) Character, (2) Intelligence, (3) Personality, and (4) Beauty. Coretta, he announced, as if conferring a rosette on her, had met the criteria.

What King didn't make any mention of was that the perfect minister's wife had to be a good cook too. So when he asked Coretta, half-seriously, "Coretta, how good a cook are you?" she rose to the challenge. Rolling up her sleeves, she cooked her "specialty," a soft, custard-rich banana pudding; her sister Edythe made

Creole pork chops (well, so what? Coretta was cheating a bit here . . .); and Coretta served the chops with King's favorite cabbage smothered in bacon, alongside corn bread and tossed salad. King ate every last crumb and sat back, patting his belly: grinning, he told Coretta she had "passed the test." Her sassy response, showing Character, again fulfilling criteria number one, was, "Though I didn't like the idea of a 'test,' I felt pretty good."

A WIFE-TEST LUNCH

Creole Pork Chops

4 pork chops, still on the bone

FOR THE CREOLE SAUCE

2 tbsp. butter	1 tbsp. Creole seasoning
1 lb. fresh tomatoes, diced	1 tsp. fresh tarragon, finely chopped
1 onion, finely chopped	1 tsp. fresh thyme, crumbled
2 cloves garlic, minced	½ tsp. dried basil
1 red bell pepper, finely chopped	2 tsp. Tabasco
1 green bell pepper, finely chopped	sea salt
½ tsp. dried oregano	freshly ground black pepper

Warm the butter in a large frying pan. Brown the pork chops in the butter for about 3 minutes each side; remove them and keep to one side. Now put all the other ingredients into the same frying pan. Sauté the vegetables, herbs, and spices for 2 to 3 minutes. Nestle the pork chops into the Creole sauce. Bring to a boil; turn down to a low simmer until the Creole sauce has reduced to a third of its original volume. Serve accompanied by white rice and the smothered cabbage.

Cabbage Smothered in Bacon

1 lb. smoked bacon	1 whole small loose green cabbage, shredded
2 onions, halved and sliced	sea salt
3 cloves garlic, chopped	freshly ground black pepper

Fry the bacon up so that it is very crisp and plenty of bacon fat has dripped off. Lift the bacon, cool it, and then chop, crumble, and break it up. Meanwhile, using the same frying pan, add the onions to the bacon fat and cook for a few minutes until the onion is golden. Now add the garlic, shredded cabbage, and the bacon bits; put a lid on the pan and sauté all together for 8 minutes. Season to taste with sea salt and black pepper.

Banana Pudding

FOR THE CUSTARD

2 cups milk
1 vanilla pod, split open and
   seed-pulp scraped into the milk

3 egg yolks
½ cup granulated sugar
3 tbsp. all-purpose flour

FOR THE OTHER LAYERS

4 ripe bananas

vanilla wafers

FOR THE MERINGUE

3 egg whites (kept at room
   temperature)

pinch of sea salt
¼ cup granulated sugar

Begin by making vanilla custard. Warm the milk with the split vanilla pod and its seeds in a saucepan; meanwhile, cream the egg yolks with the granulated sugar and flour. When the milk is hot, add it to the egg yolk mix in a thin stream, whisking all the time. Return this mixture to the saucepan and, still stirring constantly, heat over a low heat until the mixture forms a thick custard. Remove from the heat and let this cool completely. Take out the vanilla pod and wash it. When dried, you can store it and use it again.

Preheat the oven to 220 degrees centigrade. Now begin to assemble the banana pudding. Slice the bananas. Using a large, heat-proof Pyrex bowl, place a layer of custard in the base, followed by a layer of vanilla wafers and then a layer of bananas Repeat, finishing with a layer of custard. In a large mixing bowl, begin whisking the egg whites with the sea salt until they are stiff. Gradually, beat in the granulated sugar until the meringue is very solid. Scoop the meringue onto the pudding to form a deep, foamy head. Now bake the pudding in the oven for 5 to 10 minutes, until the meringue has a delicious, deep gold sheen.

As any hotel owned by white people banned blacks, the couple spent their first night in a funeral parlor owned by black relatives. Once they settled into domesticity, the couple shared housework—King was sure enough of his manhood to use a duster without facing a crisis of masculinity. Thursday night was Martin Luther's night to cook, as Coretta had a lecture at that time. He adored cooking pig's ears—"They're good, and they're cheap." Coretta was less keen, though both wouldn't turn down a pig's snout or ear if it was offered. Good southern soul cooking was central to their table, although they cheated on the corn bread, opting for the packeted version. One of the best dishes King cooked up was turnip greens with ham hocks and bacon dripping. King tried to watch his waistline, but often when Coretta dropped into his pastor's office in Ebenezer, she'd catch him tucking into a pig's trotter, watched by the joyful parishioner who'd brought it as a gift.

How to Make a Pig's Ear of It

2 pig's ears	2 branches thyme
2 onions, quartered	8 peppercorns
2 carrots, roughly chopped	pinch of sea salt
2 bay leaves	1 tbsp. all-purpose flour, salted
1 bunch parsley	and peppered

Begin by singeing the ears over an open flame to remove any residual hairs. Bring water to a boil in a deep saucepan. Add the ears, with the onion, carrot, bay leaves, parsley, thyme, peppercorns, and sea salt. Allow to simmer for about 2½ hours. Drain and then dry the ears with a kitchen towel. Put a pan of sunflower oil on to heat. On a plate, put seasoned all-purpose flour, drop the ears into the flour, and pluck them out again, dredged in flour. When the cooking fat is silent and very hot, drop the ears into it and fry until they are crisp and golden. Drain and eat while hot and crispy with a shake of hot sauce.

As much as he was hated by white supremacists, King was adored by many pro–civil rights whites: Joan Baez thought he looked like a "big chocolate angel"; when she sang, he thought he could hear the angels choiring from the clouds. Not afraid to show her unequivocal support for King, touring the south in 1962, Baez had it written into her contract that she would refuse to sing unless blacks were admitted into any hall where she performed. She stayed with King and his entourage at the Gaston Motel in Birmingham; blacks and whites could stay there, but at a later date it was to have its front façade blown off in a bomb attack on King.

Meanwhile, the FBI was protecting King and Baez to stop the Ku Klux Klan from lynching them, but King never let that get between him and a good meal. When they entered a soul food restaurant, King's presence was transformative. Some diners brushed away tears with embarrassment, and others repeatedly thanked him for all he'd done. King laughed and smiled and ate apple pie and ice cream. A day later, Baez and King led a protest group of black elementary school students up to the gates of a school that refused blacks. Their way was thick with Klansmen, using switchblades to pare their nails and peel apples.

When a blue-eyed boy of eight bounced up to Baez and said, "Nigguh-lovuh," curling his lip, she could only reply, "Well, yes, I suppose so . . ."

EVOLUTIONARY EATING WITH CHARLES DARWIN

It was on the *Beagle* voyage, after an extended bout of sickness in Chile in 1834, that Crohn's disease first appeared; flatulence, upper abdominal pain, and vomiting troubled him for the next forty years and puzzled physicians. After his adventures, Darwin was to follow a restricted, circumscribed diet. The "inductive phase" of Crohn's began in Valparaiso, Chile, when he sank, groaning, into his bed for a month. At first he blamed his condition on some local hooch "chicha" he had drunk on a visit to a gold mine. Chicha is a lightly fermented corn juice and can be made also from grapes, apples, and amaranth and must have tasted great at the time, but no doubt Darwin wished he had stuck to his favored, nonalcoholic cup of maté and a cigarette.

With the return of the *Beagle*, Darwin thought he had the eggs and bacon of London to look forward to and married life with his cousin Emma Wedgewood. At their new home at 11 Gower Street—which was so garishly painted Darwin re-named it "Macaw House," the Darwins had had Thomas Carlyle and his wife over for their first-ever dinner party of turkey. But back in England, Darwin was unwell for two years, becoming very thin and shadowy, suffering from spasms and farting through the night. His mouth was ulcerated, and he frequently vomited. He put it down to salad and spices and was convinced that puddings containing milk eased his discomfort, so Emma Darwin tried to feed him "plain puddings." Gradually, Darwin was to give up eating dinner for the solace of a safe boiled egg.

Twenty-two-year-old Charles Darwin's famous, elephantine, five-year wander across South America and beyond—as recorded in the *Voyage of the Beagle*—began in 1831, but it wasn't solely a journey toward a theory of evolution—it was also a journey through food. Darwin's eating experiences waver between the nasty, the barely digestible, the acceptably odd (but tasty), and the delicious or, indeed, revelatory.

First there was *the nasty*, and this was superbly illustrated by what was on the menu at the Tierra del Fuego peninsula. The weather was dire. Through the moil of sleet that fell about him on the deck of the *Beagle*, Darwin could just make out the outlines of wild, naked women, one breast-feeding through her tangled hair; while the hearts of many would leap at such a sight, Darwin wasn't in the mood. All of them looked as though they'd had a bad time at the hairdresser's. And this wasn't the worst Fuego offered: every day the locals scraped up whatever sandy, hunched shellfish clung to the wind-beaten rocks: sea eggs, even some gobbet of rotten whale, represented a feast. Darwin found this grimy, fishy diet tough, the worst part being the local penchant for doughnuts of whale blubber that the Fuegians buried in the sand till they felt peckish. These fishy treats would be broiled and served up with a side of fungi and berries. Worst of all was the ghastly rumor Darwin heard that, in the long, harrowing winters, Fuegians reverted to cannibalism. Scandalized, Darwin gossips in his diary that Fuegians would rather polish off the old women of the tribe for supper in hard times than one of their numerous dogs—the logic being, as one traveler put it, "Doggies catch otters, old women no."

Accounts of how Fuegians chose to dispose of Granny should be taken with a pinch of salt (boom boom): the said pensioner was apparently held, kicking feebly, over fire smoke until she choked to death, like some terrible on-the-spot kipper. Perhaps less surprisingly, when the nights drew in, it was rumored that old women fled to the mountains, and that these pensioners would dart about the murky mountainside, only to be hounded by their menfolk back to the fireside where they would be barbecued . . . well, Darwin fell for it . . .

In a beautifully ironic cultural about-turn, Darwin's distaste for Fuegian dining customs was mirrored by one Fuegian: he accidentally touched the meat that Darwin carted about preserved in a "tin case," (we're talking early corned beef here) and, finding it horribly soft and cold, recoiled in disgust. Perhaps if it had been tinned grandmother he might have been keener . . .

Then on Darwin's journey came the *barely digestible*—no longer in Tierra del Fuego but in Uruguay. At a stopping-off point on the Rio Tapalguen, Darwin hungrily ate a bowl of meat. One diner asked whether this scrumptious meal was indeed a popular Uruguayan dish. Now Darwin knew what that meant and had been hoping to avoid such Uruguayan delicacies. In this case he suspected he might be eating the half-formed embryo of a calf. The veal-like taste and bridal-white flesh of what was in his bowl suggested the worst. He listened, fork poised, as the conversation developed. But no! It was alright! What rested in his bowl was puma, prized for its tenderness and delicacy, more uniformly popular even than jaguar. Thankful, Darwin popped another forkful of the wildcat into his mouth.

Next comes the *acceptably odd*. In Argentina Darwin enjoyed baked armadillo, tucked up in its own shell, but found that roasted kid made him thirsty. In Chile, Darwin loved charqui, dried strips of beef, also a favorite, some hundred years later, of Che Guevara. On the edge of the Sierra Tapalguen, giant musket balls of hail plummeted from the sky, felling wild deer and ostriches—the travelers had a tasty dinner of ostrich. Not only did Darwin find himself eating peculiar meat most of the time, but he also found it peculiar to eat nothing *but* meat and was always glad of the opportunity to buy some biscuits. Mendoza held relief from carnivorous fare, and they bought pinkly fragrant watermelon and half a wheelbarrow of peaches, with scents of Darwin's own English childhood.

Tortoise was the name of the game in the Galapagos: the *Beagle* voyagers roasted the breast plate of the tortoise, copying the gauchos' carne con cuero (beef roasted with its skin still on, protecting the succulent meat from the heat, unglamorously translated as "leather meat"), and they made lip-smacking tortoise soups.

White-meated lizard was reliably delicious: in intertropical South America, lizards living in dry regions were the tastiest.

When the *Beagle* holed up at Tahiti, Darwin's dining opportunities really began to look up: the glassy lagoons, long reefs under white-hot heat, and dazzlingly green mountains all promised good food. And Tahiti delivered. One afternoon, after Darwin had climbed in the mountains under a burning sun, a Tahitian met him with a gift of hot roasted bananas, pineapple, and coconuts. Nothing, Darwin tells us, could be more delicious after walking in the burning sun than the milk of a fresh coconut.

Then there were the mouthwatering fish, silver and clean from the water, and freshwater prawns. Tahitians, swimming like otters through the chambered lava-rock cavities of inland ravines, netted fish and cooked them immediately. Drinking with the Tahitians was comical: alcohol, introduced by Europeans, had already taken vicious hold over many, and some of the Tahitians left standing joined temperance societies run by missionaries. Darwin carried with him a hip flask and offered a sip here and there (though he really approved of their customary temperance). Each time a Tahitian raised Darwin's flask to their lips, they would mutter—like an incantation to ward off evil—a single word: "missionary."

On one memorable inland expedition on the island, Darwin and the Tahitians happened on huge banks of mountain banana, with plants over twenty feet high, the fruit ripened and heavy with dense, creamy banana. Making a bed of a light wood from the flowering tree *Hibiscus tiliaceus*, whose blossoms darken from yellow to deep apricot during the course of the day, the Tahitians prepared a fire. Darwin felt a sharp surge of pride when he succeeded in setting fire to the hibiscus wood, as it required skill and practice, and he had learned well from the Tahitians. Stones "the size of cricket bats" were laid on top of Darwin's fire: within ten minutes the hibiscus had vanished and the stones were hot.

In parcels of banana leaves the islanders individually wrapped marbled beef, fish, stout bananas, and "the tops of the wild arum" (taro). These green parcels were placed on top of the hot stones, and more hot stones laid carefully on top. Dug earth was piled over. Within fifteen minutes the meal was ready and washed down with fresh water drunk from coconut shells.

As Darwin sat there in the deep ravine, eating hot, sweet banana, the other men eating and talking about him, he gazed with new eyes on Tahiti and saw an edible landscape. His journey on the *Beagle* had taught him to look on landscapes in a new way, no longer so much as a European but as someone who must survive in it and who, when times were good, should take pleasure in eating what it offered. This richly generous, edible landscape was one in which he saw no less than man himself beginning.

He looked at the thick litter of uneaten bananas on the forest floor. Close by where he sat was wild taro, whose roots he knew by now could be baked and tasted good. The young green shoots of taro leaves, which tasted even better than spinach, lay on his plate. Wild yam treaded its way across the forest floor. Mingling and twining and springing up about were liliaceous ti plants, symbols of good luck (ti leaves make up hula skirts), with their waxy, tiny lanterns of flowers. Those same flowers sprang from a starchy rhizome that sweetened as the plant matured and which looked like, as Darwin fondly described it, "a huge log of wood." When roasted, it became treacle-sweet.

Under the wild fruits and vegetation ran a narrow stream, eels and crayfish in its bright cool water. It was all so beautiful, Darwin thought, his plate forgotten now on his lap, more beautiful, perhaps, than the temperate zones of Europe. And it was then, Darwin wrote, "that I felt the force of the remark, that man, at least savage man, with his reasoning powers only partially developed, is the child of the tropics." Darwin had found his Eden and taken another step toward his theory of evolution—a journey that was to cost him much. when he presented his ideas about evolution and the origins of man to his closest friend, the brilliant botanist J. D. Hooker, Darwin said it was "like confessing a murder," so challenging were his ideas.

Pork Curry with Fei (Bananas) and Sweet Potatoes

4 tbsp. oil	3 cloves
½ lb. pork, diced	200 ml. coconut milk
2 small sweet potatoes, peeled	1 tsp. vanilla seeds
2 cloves garlic, pulped	sea salt
2 tbsp. curry powder	freshly ground black pepper
1 fei (or other cooking bananas, like plantain or matoke), peeled and halved	1 papaya, seeds removed and cut into large chunks
1 cinnamon stick	juice of 1 freshly squeezed lime

Heat 2 tablespoons of oil in a skillet and fry the pork for about 15 minutes. Remove from the oil and drain the pork pieces on kitchen roll. Clean the skillet.

Bring water to a boil in a large saucepan. Cut the sweet potato into large chunks and cook in the water for about 10 minutes. When they yield to a fork, drain them and then let them dry in the pan on the still-warm stove.

In the frying pan heat a further 2 tablespoons of oil and fry the garlic, curry powder, fei (bananas), cinnamon stick, and cloves. Add the coconut milk and bring to a boil. Add the vanilla seeds and the pork. Simmer for 5 more minutes and add sea salt and black pepper. Now add the sweet potato and cook for a further 2 minutes, stirring the curry. Finally, add the papaya. Warm and then sprinkle with the lime juice. Serve.

Banana Poe

8 fei (unpeeled cooking bananas)

1 large banana leaf (if none
available, use a large sheet of
grease-proof paper that you can
double fold)

1 tbsp. softened butter

1 cup manioc starch (or 1 cup
arrowroot or cornstarch)

3 tbsp. brown sugar

1 vanilla bean

1 cup coconut milk

Preheat the oven to 170 degrees centigrade. Place the bananas in a large deep saucepan, fill to cover the bananas (skins still on), and bring to a boil. Simmer for 15 minutes. Meanwhile, if you have managed to get hold of a banana leaf, then heat it in the oven. When it is warm, spread it with butter. If you are using grease-proof paper, then double fold it and warm it in the oven. Spread butter over it.

Remove the bananas from the water and dry them on kitchen roll. Peel and place in a bowl. Using a fork, begin to mash the bananas, making a rough puree. Now add the manioc starch/arrowroot/cornstarch and the sugar and mix. Scrape the vanilla seeds from inside the bean and add these to your mash (keep the bean for later).

When this is all mixed through, arrange the mash in the middle of the banana leaf/grease-proof paper. Wrap the banana leaf/grease-proof paper tightly around the banana poe.

Place the poe on a baking tray and cook for 40 minutes in the oven. Remove from the oven, slip the poe out of its banana leaf casing, and place in a dish. Add the coconut milk and mix. Cool and then enjoy.

THE MANY APPETITES OF ALBERT EINSTEIN

Albert Einstein and his first wife, Mileva Marić, enjoyed a gradually deepening romance when they first met as fellow students at Zurich University; they loved discussing ideas and drinking fresh coffee together. Einstein even characterized his relationship with Mileva this way, signing off one letter as from "your good colleague and fellow coffee-guzzler." When he wrote to her on August 10, 1899, he said, "We understand one another's dark souls so well, and also drinking coffee and eating sausages etc." Einstein's stomach was a sure way to get to his heart, and it is perhaps not coincidental that this was one of the main ways his mother showed her affection for him. Pauline often sent food parcels to her student son, packed with cakes and pastries, and Mileva noted "what a magnificent effect" their arrival had on him: Einstein walked proudly through the streets, with eyes only on the package in his hands. Otherwise Einstein subsisted on an allowance of 100 Swiss francs each month, sent to the "little professor" by his aunt Julie in Genoa. He enjoyed tobacco—a few years later his smoking habits were described as repulsive—but did not drink alcohol and usually dined in temperance restaurants. Often he was reduced to snatching a slice of tart from a bakery and bolting it in his room. His uneven diet has been blamed for the stomach problems that dogged him throughout his life, what Mileva was to call his "famous ailment."

Enjoying a semibachelor existence, living apart from Mileva before their marriage, Einstein lived in chambers in Berne, offering private tuition in maths and physics (he also busked with his violin). Students arrived at his coffee- and pipe tobacco–scented digs, to Einstein's booming "Come in!" Einstein formed an impromptu intellectual discussion circle with his colleagues Solovine and Habicht; they read scientific papers and debated over them, while dipping into honey, fruit, and cups of tea. If tea were not rousing enough, they also sustained their debate with drafts of black Turkish coffee and hard-boiled eggs. Einstein's enthusiasm for food was to be immortalized in a cartoon by Solovine, showing his curly-haired bust under a decorative arch of sausages. Sausage in any form seemed to be an Einstein family weakness; Albert liked to tease his sister Maja about her passion for hot dogs—an unfortunate one, given that she was also a vegetarian. Einstein issued a decree that the hot dog should now be classed as a vegetable. Science, though, could always capture his attention more than food, as when his debating friends decided to fork out and buy him very expensive caviar on his birthday. They loved to see the rapturous way in which Einstein responded to new, delicious, and novel food. Einstein, however, was caught up in Galileo's principle of inertia, and Habicht and Solovine watched him talk, gesticulate, and carelessly shovel caviar into his mouth. Eventually, one of them regained his voice and pointed out what Einstein had done. "Well," he said, "if you offer gourmet foods to peasants like me, you know they won't appreciate it." He deserved indigestion.

Indeed, shared indigestion at a dinner party led him to tell Mileva "how closely knit our psychic and physiological lives are." Mileva was an accomplished cook, and when they eventually married in Berne County Hall in January 1903, one of his first reports on their marriage unromantically endorses her as a good cook.

The marriage seemed to blossom only for a short time, though the Einsteins had two sons, Hans Albert and Eduard. A gifted musician, Eduard—called Tete, meaning "little"—was also a troubled child and was eventually to be diagnosed with schizophrenia when he reached twenty. Feeding Eduard was also not easy, as he tended to pick at his food—until, that is, Mileva started to make Bircher muesli for him. She advised her old friend Helene Savić to feed this to one of her ailing children (incidentally, Helene was rumored to have adopted the Einsteins' first illegitimate child, Lieserl).

Breakfast for the Einstein Family

Mileva recommends making Bircher muesli in roughly the following way:

1 heaped tbsp. oatmeal	2 or 3 unskinned apples, grated
2 tbsp. water	1 tbsp. crushed almonds
1 tbsp. condensed milk	2 tbsp. crushed walnuts and hazelnuts
Juice of ½ lemon	

Overnight, soak the oatmeal in water. The next morning, add the condensed milk, lemon, and apple. Sprinkle with the almonds, walnuts, and hazelnuts. Eat it right away.

Marriage to Einstein soured; Mileva felt starved of love and was ferociously jealous of Einstein's wandering eye. She kept her emotions hidden beneath a "plastercast," expressionless face. There were no more dark coffee, discussion, and sausages; the most they shared together was a perfunctory sandwich. Einstein was sometimes startled into affection again, as when he discovered she had packed ham and apples for a train journey for him; he felt a real tenderness for her on that cramped, sweaty late-night train to Brussels. Food always warmed his heart.

Albert and Mileva gradually grew apart, however, in the course of their marriage and were separated from each other from 1914 onward, Mileva moving back to Zurich with their two sons. Fatally, by 1912 Einstein was in renewed contact with woman who was to become Mrs. Einstein number two, his cousin, curvy Elsa, who liked chocolates too, too much and had such poor eyesight that one story has it she thought an orchid table decoration was a salad and helped herself to a plateful of it.

Einstein met up with Elsa secretly in Berlin—he was still married to Mileva. Elsa loved cooking, and both she and Einstein, premarriage, when he was having an affair with her, delighted in her home cooking; it was almost a metaphor for their consumption of each other and for the life they wished they had together. There was a stolen intimacy, an extra degree of infidelity, in their talk about food. Elsa loved feeding him; she was both passionate and maternal, cooking him mushrooms and watching him eat: "How much I like all these things and how gratefully I accept it from you!" he wrote to her. Elsa posted him packets of goose scratchings—tasty morsels of crackling in her letters—and he assured her that this moved him more than any beautiful poem she might care to recite for him: "you pinch me with your letter but stroke me with goose cracklings. Just now I have one in my beak and think with delight of the dear cook." He followed this with: "I know what the psychologists would make of that but I am not ashamed." Her goose cracklings appealed, he said, to the "the primitive part" of his character.

Goose Crackling (. . . a fatty love potion)

fatty skin of 1 goose
white wine vinegar
sea salt

Cook the goose skin in boiling water for 15 minutes. Next, drain and cool. Preheat the oven to 240 degrees centigrade. Pat the goose skin dry. Now rub the goose skin all over with white wine vinegar. Cut the goose skin into very thin strips. Place the goose strips on a rack and cook for about 15 minutes, but keep peeking in the oven. They may cook more quickly, and you don't want blackened crackling: that wouldn't impress Einstein. When the crackling has cooled, sprinkle it with sea salt.

After a good few years of marriage, though, Einstein's ardor for Elsa's food cooled. Elsa had to shout and shout and shout for him to come for his supper, and he'd drift toward the table as if he was sleepwalking. He ate mechanically from his bowl, with glazed eyes. So much for the romantic promise of goose crackling. Even so, at such times as unexpected visitors called, he was kind to his shy stepdaughter, Margot, who darted under the table; Einstein obligingly covered her further with a white tablecloth until the visitors had left.

Elsa found the ideal compromise between Einstein's philandering and her chocolate addiction: in later years, amorous women could gain access to Einstein by bribing Elsa with chocolate creams or, in the case of one of his mistresses, a statuesque Austrian blond called Margarete Lebach, with homemade vanilla pastries, so good that Einstein said they would make the angels sing.

Vanilla Pastries to Win a Place in Einstein's Bed

125 g. all-purpose flour
pinch of sea salt
100 g. ground almonds or
   hazelnuts

75 g. confectioner's sugar
100 g. butter, cold and cut into
   little pieces
2 tbsp. vanilla sugar

Sift the all-purpose flour into a large mixing bowl. Add the sea salt and almond or hazelnut flour. Add 25 grams of confectioner's sugar. Combine. Now add the tiny pieces of butter and, using your hands, work this into a smooth dough. There should be no gobbets of butter visible, but don't overwork the dough. Cover and refrigerate for a couple of hours.

Preheat the oven to 200 degrees centigrade. Dust a surface with all-purpose flour; you will shape the vanilla pastries on this. Form the dough into a long thin sausage shape with a 2-centimeter circumference. Now slice this long sausage into much smaller sausages about 6 centimeters in length. Shape the tips of these into points and curl each unbaked vanilla pastry into a half-moon shape. You should have about 20 crescents. Place these on a baking tray and put them in the hot oven. Bake for about 10 minutes, until each has turned golden brown. Combine the confectioner's and vanilla sugars. Remove the vanilla pastries from the oven and, while they are hot, dip each in the sugars. Enjoy them warm and imagine you are in Einstein's arms . . .

PRAWNS IN SPACE: MEN ON THE MOON

The food training required for astronauts is daunting; when fourteen of NASA's finest astronauts, among them Neil Armstrong and Buzz Aldrin, were sent to the air force's tropical survival school in Panama, classroom teaching was rapidly supplanted by real-life survival tests. Equipped with Air Force Manual 64-5, hopefully titled *Survival*, they were let loose to live off the lands of Panama. Movement, the manual instructs, may be a sign of edibility: and why be fussy . . . after all, we regularly ingest insects in our daily food. But, with a papery sigh, the manual goes on to concede that if you are really that squeamish about insect fare, then you should keep your eyes peeled for pangolins, mice, bats, and monkeys. Toads, however, should be overlooked. Then there are pages of advice on what to do to entertain "natives" should you meet them, including an encouragement to involve them in games with string. It's not difficult to envisage how, in certain unexpected circumstance, this might all come in handy on the moon. And anyway, it was excellent team-building work. The NASA team set out, Manual 64-5 at the ready, but . . . nothing seemed to move at all. There was a brief and unsuccessful struggle with some minnows in a pond, but it would have taken a truckload of minnows to feed their empty stomachs. Eventually, their good fortune returned in the shape of an iguana; at last, there was something savory on the evening menu.

Prior to the Apollo 11 flight, the team were kept in a germ-free environment, cooked for by Lew Hartzell, a former bakery manager and ordinary seaman who had learned to cook on tugboats run by the merchant marine. Edges of finesse had been added to Lew's catering experience when he learned to craft tomatoes into roses when working for gentler clientele on yachts. But here he was now, an employee of the catering business who had secured the contract for the Kennedy Spacecraft Center, shopping personally for tidbits for the space teams, true to his remit that the astronauts were "meat-and-potato men"—simple and solid the astronauts' fare would be. Steak was served with such terrible regularity—fried, braised, grilled—that Neil Armstrong complained to his wife Janet, "Why is it *always* steak?" Indeed, the very first American in space, Alan Shepard, breakfasted on a tasty filet mignon, topped up with orange juice and tea, before being roughed up by doctors supposedly doing a health check and then being transported to the launch pad of Freedom 7 in the sort of jittery, loose-socketed vehicle more fitted to moving our bovine friends. Oh, the glamour. Endless steak must have been a bit trying too for Michael Collins, who was a skilled cook himself, learning to appreciate more complex and delicious food such as slow-cooked and glassily dark beef bourguignon or sumptuous coq au vin during his time as a fighter pilot in France.

Breakfast on the day of the Apollo 11 launch was scheduled for a brisk 5 a.m. start; Lew had had an unusual night's sleep: he'd proven to be too big for the bed he was allotted in astronaut Gordon Cooper's bedroom and had tossed and turned, finally falling asleep at an eye-watering 2:30 a.m. He shook himself down and checked out the VIP viewing stand, mixing up a fresh batch of lemonade, setting the table, getting the meat out of the fridge, and lining up the eggs. Everyone knew this day would make history. Cocoa Beach was packed with sightseers. The astronauts were on what's called a "low-residue" diet, which meant that Lew had been cutting down on the amount of butter he used in cooking and striking milk from the menu entirely. The astronauts began to trickle into the room, looking deliberately casual, from 5 a.m. onward; Lee was going to start cooking the steaks only when they arrived but was dishing it up with "straight-dough" bread rather than the more indulgent hot biscuits that might have filled tummies. Fried steaks and eggs came in a stream out of Lew's kitchen as the astronauts ate their last Earth meal. There was definitely something ritualistic about the consumption of steak before moon flights, as if in the modern-world man needs testosterone-fueled steak before he can make it to the stars. Even Alan Shepard also had a filet mignon for breakfast before setting off in Freedom 7.

Lunch was a dehydrated one for Collins, Buzz Aldrin, and Armstrong as Apollo 11 hurtled through space toward the pockmarked moon. Very touchingly, Buzz (whose mother was unbelievably called Marian Moon) had amassed a whole pile of symbolic mementoes, such as rings or badges, taken from the bold and brave astronauts who had sacrificed their lives for the space race. If his dead brothers couldn't make it to the moon, Buzz was determined to make a relic representing them land there. He had other, more pragmatic things to deal with first, though. All three men were relieved not to have been space sick and were pretty peckish when it was time for their first Apollo meal. On the Gemini trip, Buzz had gotten used to squirting food into his mouth with a tube, so he was delighted by the civility of Apollo when, after rehydrating dry foodstuffs with a hot-water gun, they could eat with cutlery—in this case, a spoon. He recalled the joy but also the problems a spoon caused: "eating with a spoon was a much trickier activity without gravity; any crumbs from your pineapple fruitcakes could float around just about anywhere in the cabin. But I liked it better than simply squirting food into my mouth, as Jim Lovell and I had done on our Gemini 12 mission."

Ironically, the astronauts were paid not a cent more for their bravery in being fired into space—in fact, they were charged board and lodging rates for the eight days they spent in space on Apollo 11. By implication, then, the food should be up to scratch. Collins tells us in his memoirs, "While they are discussing West Crater and Cat's Paw and other mysteries, I am making like a French chef in the lower equipment bay." He hummed cheerfully while he pumped hot water through his hot-water gun into the dehydrated cream of chicken soup. There was even a knack to this, and Collins kneaded the bag to blend the soup, nipped off the end with his surgical scissors, and then sucked "up the ambrosia" through a small tube. He radioed Houston pretending to be a restaurant reviewer declaring that the chef should be congratulated and that he'd award him three spoons; Houston was perplexed. Then Collins started thinking about mariners and their rum rations. Briefly, he rooted about in the storage boxes with a torch to see if someone has stowed cognac there or a Jules Verne–style bottle of Chambertin. No such luck. On Apollo 8 they had a better time of it; after a surprise real turkey dinner (instead of dehydrated fare) with gravy and cranberry sauce, Deke Slayton produced three miniatures of brandy in celebration, only to be told sternly by Frank Borman to put them back.

Also on the menu for the eight-day mission to the moon was salmon salad, Picassoesque peanut cubes, more cubes of cinnamon bread, and the noisome snack, bacon squares. Wet pack foods, like frankfurters, were ready to go. Freeze-dried prawn cocktail was Buzz's favorite, and the prawns were selected to be tiny enough to be squeezed out of the bag containing them, after they had been rehydrated with a cold-water gun; the freeze-dried chicken salad, though, was unappetizingly gritty. Michael Collins realized that a tube of coffee felt comfortingly terrestrial; coffee was part of the circadian rhythms of day and made him feel the old traditions of Earth time and Earth eating return to him. The hydrogen in the water, though, made them fart, and Buzz suggested Apollo 11 didn't need thrusters; they could just fart their way to the moon. *Almost* everything had been thought of; afterward, they might clean their teeth with edible toothpaste. Some unaccountable moments hadn't occurred to the scientists in Houston, though: Buzz and Neil were delayed in stepping out onto the moon because, in their dry runs at leaving the craft, they hadn't factored in the extra time it would take to put away their dirty dishes after their space meal.

Cinnamon Bread

FOR THE BASIC DOUGH

¼ cup warm water
2 packs active yeast
¾ cup milk
2 eggs
3 tbsp. runny honey

½ cup sugar
generous pinch of sea salt
1 cup raisins
6 scant cups all-purpose flour
½ cup butter, melted

FOR THE CINNAMON FILLING

6 tbsp. soft butter
½ cup demerara sugar

2 tsp. ground cinnamon

TO GLAZE

2 tbsp. melted butter
1 tbsp. demerara sugar, mixed with
  2 tsp. cinnamon

Pour the warm water into a small jug, sprinkle on the yeast, and put in a warm place for 10 minutes until the mixture foams. Now heat the milk rapidly in a small pan, then leave to cool. Get a large mixing bowl and pour the foamy yeast and water mixture into it. Beat the eggs with the honey and add this. Now add the milk, sugar, and sea salt. Pour in the cup of raisins. Place a sieve over the bowl and sieve 2 cups of flour into the mixture. Add the melted butter and then a sieve cup of flour at a time into the dough, mixing it through with your hands until a soft, pliable dough forms. Leave this to rest for 5 minutes, flour a surface lightly, and then knead the dough for about 10 minutes until it is elastic and puffs and blisters. Put the dough in a buttered bowl and cover with a clean tea towel. Leave the dough in a warm place to rise. This will take about 2 hours.

After this time, punch the dough back down and then return it to the bowl, cover, and put back in its warm hiding place for another 30 minutes.

Preheat the oven to 180 degrees centigrade and flour a flat surface for preparing the loaf. Butter a loaf tin. Using a mortar and pestle, combine the butter, demerara sugar, and cinnamon into a paste. On the floured surface, shape the dough into a rectangle the same length as the loaf tin. Spread with the cinnamon-butter-sugar paste. Now roll the dough into a log shape, sealing the top and bottom. Place this seam-side down in the loaf tin. Brush with the butter and dust with the remaining demerara sugar and cinnamon. Bake for about 45 minutes, until the base of the loaf sounds hollow when tapped. When cooled, but not too cooled, eat warm with a cup of coffee and enjoy those circadian rhythms.

Prawns-in-Space Cocktail

¼ lb. shelled Atlantic prawns
2 tbsp. mayonnaise
1 dessert spoon Worcestershire sauce
1 tsp. Tabasco
½ tsp. paprika
freshly ground black pepper

sea salt
½ head of crunchy green lettuce,
    thinly sliced
1 avocado, cut into 1-inch chunks
3 scallions, finely chopped
pinch of cayenne

In a bowl, mix together the prawns, mayonnaise, Worcestershire sauce, Tabasco, paprika, black pepper, and sea salt. Arrange the lettuce in the base of a glass bowl and place the avocado and scallions on top. Slap the prawn cocktail mix on top and sprinkle with cayenne pepper. Then, if you feel like it, cram it all down a tube and then suck it out!

After walking on the monochromatic moon, back in their little metallic, spider-like lunar module, the moon dust fell from the astronauts' boots onto the floor; incredibly, moon dust has a smell. The astronauts tried to place it. Did it smell of gunpowder or the smoky trail of a firecracker? It was weird, almost metallic; Armstrong said it has a "wet ashes smell." Then, among the moon dust, Neil and Buzz snacked on fruit punch and cocktail sausages.

4

Dining with the Outlaws

If you are what you eat, could we all be dictators too? This chapter investigates the unusual appetites of these men with something to hide. The roll call: Adolf Hitler; Tito; Augusto Pinochet; Saddam Hussein; Benito Mussolini; Josef Stalin; Juan Perón; Chairman Mao.

HERR HITLER MADE THE COFFEE:
SERVING UP ADOLF AND EVA

Dictators aren't the great gluttons one would hope. Closest to pigginess is Stalin (but it usually is *just* pig, and a Georgian one at that). Napoleon was a bolter, spending only minutes on his beans; Franco was a potato obsessive; Mao fixated on Hunan home cooking; Mussolini was a milk addict who tried to ban pasta (a stunning idea in Italy); Sophia Loren did get Tito into the kitchen, but, like Slobodan Milošević, he could never see past cabbage. Idi Amin may seem a tad on the experimental side in eating his enemies, but, reputedly, they were generally homegrown fellow Ugandans.

My point? Dictators are homely eaters. When it comes to grub, they're conservatives. Saddam's old favorites Quality Street and Mateus rosé may seem un-Iraqi, but his affection is unwavering, schoolboyish almost. They even found Bounty bar wrappers in the infamous Tikriti bunker.

So how does Hitler fit in? Well, he does in the sense that throughout World War II this evil mastermind commanded the Third Reich and dominated Europe on a diet of creamed potatoes and two fried eggs *OR* ravioli with cheese *and* apple cake, washed down with Fachinger mineral water. Conservative has it. The limit of Hitler's passions was a baked potato and a dollop of cream cheese, drenched in unrefined linseed oil, knocked back with a caraway tea.

But then again, Hitler doesn't quite fit the dictator mold. Not quite. Yes, this architect of horror was a vegetarian. But . . . the vegetarians don't want him, and who blames them? Gandhi and Tolstoy fit more with the vegetarian ethic. Why, veggies plead, should they be landed with this bad boy of vegetarianism? It wasn't as if Adolf made the slightest effort to convert Germany to vegetarianism; societies promoting vegetarianism were forbidden to organize. The Gestapo confiscated books containing vegetarians. Vegetarians had to meet in secret cabals (imagine them whispering the password, "Tofu," in darkened Berlin doorways).

All this, and yet in an article, "At Home with the Führer" which appeared in May 1937, the German populace was told, " Hitler's [diet consists] of soup, eggs, vegetables and mineral water, although he occasionally relishes a slice of ham and relieves the tediousness of his diet with such delicacies as caviar." While this sounds like a slice of ham too far for some vegetarians, unfortunately he remains, defiantly, in their camp.

For most of his adult life, Hitler privately extolled vegetarianism. Bad teeth and a short life he attributed to a diet low in polenta (polenta explained why gleaming-toothed Bulgarians enjoyed long lives). Camels and elephants, he said, were better than lions. Why? Because they were herbivores, silly! His most ardent hope was that his ladder-climbing dog, Blondi, would become a confirmed vegetarian. Though he was cowed by the prospect of losing the National Socialist popular vote if he made Germany vegetarian, Hitler delighted in mocking the "carrion-eaters" who joined him at table in his usual haunts: the Osteria Bavaria in Munich's Schellingstrasse (where Unity Mitford spied on him and, eventually, dined with him, recording their conversations in red ink in her diary—non-Hitler days were in blue or black ink); the tea room at his mountain getaway, Obersalzberg; or, as Hitler coined it, the "Merry Chancellor's Restaurant" (ho! ho!) at the Chancellery. Throughout the 1940s, Hitler's personal cooks made it their mission to slip meat into his supper. First offender was Krümel (Crumbs). A notice above the kitchen door blazoned, "Wer Krümel nicht ehrt, ist den Kuchen nicht wert!" (If of Crumbs no heed you take, then you don't deserve the cake!). Hitler usually rumbled Krümel's tricks and eventually insisted Krümel only cook him gruel and mashed potatoes (a cow's leg being harder to hide in these). Later came Frau von Exner. A secret smoker to boot, Exner popped the odd bone into Adolf's soup to fatten him up. When it was discovered that she had Jewish blood, she was dismissed as Hitler's cook (although, tragically, terribly, he offered to have her family

"Aryanized"). Meantime, Hitler's lady admirers continued to tuck into hard-core German food such as leberknödel (a bread loaf-shaped liver dumpling). Indeed, Hitler himself always had to struggle to turn down a leberknödel—or Eva Braun in a floating, beribboned Wagnerian nightie. Hitler liked his ladies as he liked his food: rustic . . . he loathed red nail polish, lipstick, and perfume and advised Eva Braun to use a face mask of raw veal—oh, and to wear chamois leather underwear. Calves in crates and shots at chamois clearly didn't keep Adolf up at night.

However, Hitler couldn't bear rustic, honest questions at dinner, as when one brave soul, Henriette von Schirach, blurted, "My Führer, I saw a train full of deported Jews in Amsterdam the other day. Those poor people—they look terrible. I'm sure they're being very badly treated. Do you know about it? Do you allow it?" Hitler's secretary, Traudl Junge, noted the painful silence. Hitler rose to his feet and said goodnight. Frau von Schirach was hurried back to Vienna. Nor was Hitler so keen on "rustic" that he could tolerate as a mistress one peasant girl whom he ditched after a visit to the Berlin Opera because she bellowed at him, "Hey, Adolf, listen!"

Like some vegetarians, Hitler occasionally erred. Dione Lucas, a chef who cooked for Hitler in Hamburg, documented Hitler's early fondness for stuffed squab. His biographers have nosed out his most intimate moments with Bavarian sausages and cured ham. And—in no better place than Eva's diaries—do we find just such a slip. But note the tedious fidelity to teetotalism.

A First Date with Hitler

September of any year after 1932 would always be a red-letter time for Eva Braun. Her private diaries provide a dreamy account of her first formal date with the Führer. This was perhaps the first date of *all* first dates. Hitler pushed the boat out for Eva, abandoning his modest eating habits in order to impress her. There is a chilling, girlish romanticism to Eva's diaries; she records exactly what she wore that first night—a close-fitting blue pullover—and was starry-eyed about their first supper: "The dinner was wonderful for he is the most charming host you can imagine."

Firstly, Hitler served up hors d'oeuvres with Russian caviar—"The best," he chuckled to Eva, "Little Father Stalin can send us!" This was followed by delicate, fresh salmon and then woodcock "which was so tender that it melted on your tongue" and was not in the slightest too "gamey." Roguishly enough, Hitler didn't touch the ice-cold Chablis . . . or the Perrier-Jouet . . . or the Haute Sauterne. Eva had to do all the drinking. The final act of chivalry was that Hitler made the coffee while Eva lay on the sofa and talked and talked and talked. She woke up in bed. But whose? Her choice of a pullover was unexpectedly appropriate, as Hitler's customary come-on line to her was, "Aren't you too hot in those clothes?" Eva's signal to strip.

Stuffed Squab

A squab is a young pigeon. Woodcock is now an endangered species, and I almost faced arrest trying to acquire it. Look out your needle and thread!

4 squabs (boned—but with thigh and wing bones remaining)
6 chicken livers
7 oz. butter
8 tbsp. Calvados (plus 3 to 4 tbsp. for basting the squab)
2 oz. shiitake mushrooms, sliced (they were his allies, after all!)
juice of 1 lemon
crushed black peppercorns
sea salt

2 cloves garlic, crushed
2 oz. cooked tongue, finely chopped
2 cooking apples (skinned, cored, and cut into ¼-inch slices—allow these to dry)
1 oz. all-purpose flour
2 tsp. brown sugar
½ cup green pistachio nuts, shelled
4 tbsp. double cream
½ oz. truffles, chopped
1 tbsp. fresh tarragon leaves, chopped.

Salt and pepper the squabs all over and set aside. Arrange these spread-eagled on a wooden board, ready for stuffing. To prepare the stuffing, in a heavy-bottomed frying pan brown the chicken livers in 1 ounce of butter. Add 4 tablespoons of Calvados and set fire to this: the Calvados will extinguish itself when the alcohol content has evaporated. Remove and drain the chicken liver. When cooled, finely slice the livers.

Now add 2 ounces of butter to the pan. Heat till the butter bubbles and then add sliced shiitake mushrooms, a teaspoon of lemon juice, a pinch of black pepper and sea salt, and the crushed garlic. Fry quickly for 2 minutes. Add the tongue and the sliced livers.

Dust the apples with all-purpose flour. Gently sauté the sliced apple in a further 1 ounce of butter and the brown sugar. Next mix the apples and the shelled pistachios with the other stuffing ingredients. Place a core of stuffing on the center of each squab and shape the meat around the stuffing. Seal the squab by sewing the skin together. Each squab should now be bound with string.

Melt 3 ounces of butter in a heavy-based sauté pan. When hot, arrange the squab in the pan. Place a lid on the sauté pan and brown the squab gently till they become golden all over. Now flame the squab with the further 4 tablespoons of Calvados. Preheat the oven to 190 degrees centigrade. When hot, place the squab on a roasting tin and cook for about 45 minutes. Baste the squab once or twice with Calvados, turning the birds so they cook evenly. Next set aside the squab and remove the string. Leave them to rest.

Now you're going to make the gravy. Place the roasting tin over a medium heat. Into the tin stir the double cream, scraping up the sticky caramelized juices. Add the truffles and tarragon. Season with crushed black pepper and sea salt.

To serve, spoon the gravy over the squab. Lie back and think of Eva.

THE HUNGRY HUNGARIAN: MARSHAL TITO

Evelyn Waugh thought he was a woman disguised as a dictator. Hmmm . . . Or was he the "love child" of Winston Churchill? Had he nicked the identity papers of a deceased Croat prisoner of war? Could he rightfully call some Hungarian noble-man "Daddy"? All that one could be sure of was that a revolutionary going by the name of Josip Broz became "Marshal Tito," Yugoslavia's very own Great Dictator, in 1934. However, Tito's food affiliations reveal him as undoubtedly Yugoslavian.

It appears to be the case that Josip was born in 1892 in Kumrovec, a valley in the highlands of the Zagorje district of Croatia. His father was Croatian and his mother a Slovenian called Marija Javeršek. Prior to the First World War, a shameful 80 percent of Croatian peasant children died before the age of fifteen—Josip was one of the lucky ones. Nevertheless, bread was so scarce that Tito's mother had to lock the larder on her children, and when they begged for a slice of bread from visiting rela-tives, Marija whipped them soundly. She was in a gentler mood, though, when star-vation drove Tito to cook his brothers and sisters a meal one feast day. Their parents were out, and hanging from the rafters was a grinning, smoked pig's head that the family was hoarding for the New Year. Tito unhooked the head and dropped it into a pan of boiling water. Trying to make a sauce, he poured in some flour; then, after a few hours, the children feasted on the head. But it was so greasy that one by one they all became sick, and the parents returning to green-faced, groaning children.

The clearest markers of Tito's beginnings lie in his food tastes. He never got over the first, original tastes of his childhood: his mother's chicken soup with homemade noodles and the pastries she crafted, the best of which was štrukli, a sumptuous cottage cheese strudel. Indeed, so true was Tito to Hungarian food that he dragged his favorite cook, a Hungarian lady, off a train packed with scared, sallow-skinned fellow deportees; that night they celebrated with pheasant soup. Often at state banquets Tito sighed with disenchantment over the lobster bisque . . .

Chicken Soup with Noodles

2 onions, finely sliced	2 pints rich, dark chicken stock
2 tbsp. butter	6 carrots, sliced
1 stalk celery, finely sliced	2 to 3 parsnips, sliced
1 chicken, cut into sections	5 potatoes, quartered
2 cloves garlic, crushed	quarter cabbage, finely sliced
2 bay leaves	3 tbsp. parsley, finely chopped
1 tbsp. whole black pepper, lightly crushed	1 bowl dried noodles

Chicken Soup with Noodles (*continued*)

Soften the onions in the butter in a large, deep soup pan. After a few minutes, add the celery and sweat the celery along with the onion. When the onions are a light golden color, brown the chicken sections in the butter. Add the crushed garlic and fry the creamy garlic gently for a minute. Salt lightly, add the bay leaves, and add the tablespoon of lightly crushed peppercorns. Next, pour over the chicken stock. Add the carrots and parsnip. Bring it to a boil. Simmer on a medium heat until the chicken is cooked. Then add the quartered potatoes and the cabbage and simmer slowly until cooked thoroughly. Three minutes before serving, add the parsley and the noodles. Cook until well done.

Štrukli for a Benign Dictator

FOR THE DOUGH

4 cups all-purpose flour
1 tsp. sea salt
1 egg, beaten

2 tbsp. olive oil
100 ml. lukewarm water

FOR THE CHEESE FILLING

5 cups fresh cottage cheese
2 tbsp. butter, melted
4 eggs, beaten

⅓ cup bread crumbs
½ cup sour cream
sea salt

Begin by making the štrukli dough. Sieve the flour and salt into a deep mixing bowl no less than three times. Using a fork to mix the dough, add the beaten egg and the oil. The dough should now appear crumbly. Slowly add the warm water, using your fingers to work it together, until you are eventually kneading the dough. It should become pliable and firm. Transfer the dough into a lightly oiled bowl, cover it with a clean tea towel, and leave it to rise in a warm place for 30 minutes.

While the dough is resting, make the cheesy, crumby, and slightly sour štrukli filling. Empty the cottage cheese into a mixing bowl. Add 2 melted tablespoons of butter. Mix the beaten eggs with the bread crumbs. Add them to the cottage cheese and then add the sour cream. Mix well.

Preheat the oven to 200 degrees centigrade. Butter a large ovenproof baking dish.

Flour a clean, smooth dish towel ready for rolling out the dough. Divide the dough into three; shape each third into a rectangular shape and then roll each out to the thickness of ⅓ centimeter. Brush one of the rectangles with melted butter. Now spread a quarter of the sour cheesy filling over the rectangle—leave

Štrukli for a Benign Dictator (*continued*)

about a 1-inch edge on all sides. Use the dish towel to roll up the štrukli. Pinch the ends closed and then, using the side of your hand or a plate, divide the štrukli into sections of about 3 inches in length; thus these individual štrukli sections will be sealed, but not divided from each other. Place your first completed štrukli "necklace" into the baking dish. Repeat this process with the other two dough rectangles. Once all three are lined up in the baking dish, tip the remaining quarter of the filling over the top of the štrukli. Bake in the oven for about 45 minutes, until the štrukli is golden brown.

Tito was never partial to outlandish, "foreign" food. While he was quite happy to accept the gift of a pair of elephants from Indira Gandhi to join the giraffes in his private island zoo on Brioni, he dreaded eating at Indian state functions. He asked his social secretary to smuggle plates of Croatian peasant food to him before a banquet in Delhi, in the hope that this would enable him to politely restrict himself to only a few mouthfuls of Indian nosh. Even when Tito seemed on safe territory eating Georgian food with Stalin, Stalin made him drink so much that, when he managed to crawl his way back into his dacha, he vomited down his shirt sleeve, returning all those pickled cucumbers and kievs and spoonfuls of red caviar.

Plagued by stomach-churning, strange delicacies on foreign trips, Tito, like most dictators, may justifiably have felt as if someone was trying to poison him. If the Indian government weren't trying to choke him with chilies, the Chinese were offering him plates of sparrows (he managed to get out of eating these by saying they counted as the proletariat of the bird kingdom and so were indigestible to a Communist), the Koreans were plying him with brandy bottles lithe with alcohol-pickled snakes or sneaking dog onto the lunch menu. At one meal in Pyongyang in the company of Kim Il-sung, it was noted that the Yugoslavs were avoiding a rich meat stew. "No woof woof," their hosts hastily assured them. No wonder Tito liked meat on the bone—at least it could be traced to its source.

One might have thought that Tito's Red Army training in the Soviet Union of the 1930s would have taught him to endure hardship (one of the endurance tests was to stand up to the neck in freezing water, naked and unflinching). The lean years of imprisonment for Communist agitation a decade earlier had, in a sense, only fortified Tito's culinary conservatism. Turnip soup, beans, and bread hardly expand your eating or social horizons. Even his first wife, Polka, left him.

Tito behaved true to character on a state visit to Paris in the late 1970s. Most of us, given the opportunity to stay in a luxurious hotel in southern France, would salivate at the prospect of the culinary delights on offer. But not Tito. His party took over the whole hotel and requested cabbage soup, sausage, and boiled meat for breakfast (Tito was always up and working by 6 a.m.), an eight-course lunch, an afternoon snack of cheesecakes, and, of course, a variety of thick soups in the evening. On top of that, they left without paying the bill.

Tito, however, was nothing if not convivial when it came to food. Bedecked in one of his gaudy uniforms (white in summer, field gray in winter), whether aboard his yacht *Galeb* or at his hunting lodge in Bled, Tito approached communal dining with good humor and panache. In self-mockery, Tito told his guests that he was "not lucky with suits," regaling them with the story of having slept overnight in a farm shed. A cow that had mistaken him for a pile of salt and decided to dine on his suit rudely awakened him. Our chess-loving dictator would smoke one of the hundred and twenty or so cigarettes he went through a day, his dog Tigar at his side, and indulge his partisans with ten-course banquets. Bread and plates of fish were handed round (Tito fed his fish to Tigar) accompanied by delicious prošek wine specially conveyed from Hvar. Tito was never a heavy drinker and rigorously avoided šljivovica, the popular Yugoslavian tipple of plum brandy. In the end, Tito was a whiskey and Coke man.

In the later years it was not partisans who shared Tito's supper but Hollywood glitterati like Gina Lollobrigida, Jackie Kennedy, and Sophia Loren, perhaps in testimony to the three hundred films movie-buff Tito liked to watch each year. Richard Burton and Elizabeth Taylor were given a tour of his private zoo. Burton was a particularly favored guest, having played Marshall Tito in the 1973 film *Sutjeska* (which involved Tito being rescued by his dog).

Sophia Loren got Tito hooked on pasta during her two-week stay, and Tito loved experimenting in the kitchen with her, emerging as an eager and docile kitchen assistant. Reputedly Tito himself was an excellent cook, treating his family to a specialty he liked to prepare of sausages, salami, and garlic. As a host, he tried his best: the Windsors were served Hungarian cheese spiced with roseate paprika, Gina Lollobrigida was treated to fish soup, and perhaps in some misplaced cultural reference to the paddy fields of Vietnam, Ho Chi Minh was served risotto.

But Tito never forgot his mother's pies and thick soups, and in this shows what could almost amount to a predilection among Yugoslavian dictators for their own national cuisine. For instance, cabbage is a much-loved staple of the Yugoslavian diet—Slobodan Milošević was most partial to turkey stuffed with cabbage and reportedly claims that prison food was fit only for the likes of Tigar.

TEA AND CAKES WITH AUGUSTO PINOCHET

I may be the only person alive who has spent time longingly wondering which cakes Chilean dictator Augusto Pinochet went for on his famed tea parties with Margaret Thatcher. Devon scones? Crumpets? Brandy snaps? The culinary rites that were performed behind the white walls of Margaret's house at Chester Square, Belgravia, may be forever lost. Perhaps I will never know.

Sporting his favorite shaded glasses, Pinochet enjoyed a variety of London town treats on his visits to Britain. Margaret's teas weren't all that was on the menu. He mulled over ties in Piccadilly, was spotted in Harrods, Fortnum and Mason, the River Café. During his seventeen-year-long dictatorship, Augusto liked to call in on Britain in October, on time to celebrate Margaret's birthday, and took pleasure in selecting special flowers, chocolates, and candies to send her on the auspicious day. Autumnal Britain must have seemed so delightful, all very different from that ghastly occasion when, en route to visit those ogres of corruption, the Marcos family in the Philippines, he got stuck in Fiji and was fed only sandwiches and pelted with eggs and tomatoes.

Pinochet, though, was never a great one for exploring the pleasure principle. The making of this dictator can be traced back to his mother forbidding ice cream in case the milky oozing soiled the strange mock-military sailor suits the boy Pinochet wore.

This self-conscious puritanism was later bolstered by Pinochet's abhorrence of alcohol (even this makes you sigh longingly for good old Allende and his healthy passion for Chivas Regal whiskey and dinner parties).

Eventually, the coziness of Pinochet's trips to London was rudely interrupted in 1998 when he was detained in Britain and faced extradition to Spain. Poor Augusto was holed up at Everglades, a rented mansion in Wentworth in Surrey (his supporters paid £10,000 a month to keep him in style). In *Statecraft*, Margaret Thatcher refers to visiting him at Wentworth: "I visited him twice at the modest rented house on the Wentworth Estate just outside London where he was kept under close guard." (p. 271). Only Lady Thatcher could manage to make Everglades sound like a housing estate in Slough.

During this period of privation, our Chilean dictator was attended to by his Chilean cook, bodyguards, and butler. Perhaps, at this time, Pinochet roundly cursed Margaret's custard slice for his predicament. Perhaps he returned to memories of Chilean food. This may be why his bodyguards were spotted in the local supermarket, Waitrose, buying chicken and sweet corn to make pastel de choclo, a baked Chilean dish with a sweet crust.

Pastel de Choclo

2 tbsp. sunflower oil
½ tbsp. paprika
2 onions, finely chopped
1 lb. minced steak
2 tbsp. fresh parsley, chopped
2 tsp. oregano

CORN TOPPING
3 cups corn kernels
¾ cup cream
sea salt
freshly ground black pepper
about 10 leaves fresh green basil
1 cup grated fresh Parmesan cheese
17 black olives, pitted

2 heaped tsp. ground cumin
sea salt
freshly ground black pepper
¼ cup chicken stock
½ cup raisins, softened in a little
    water

6 eggs, hard-boiled (but so that the
    yolk will remain slightly soft), cut into
    eighths
2 chicken breasts, cooked and diced
4 finely shredded scallions
½ tsp. granulated sugar

In a frying pan, warm the sunflower oil. Add the paprika and stir into the oil until the oil is has taken on the rich, roseate hues of the paprika. Add the onion and sauté for about 10 minutes until it is translucent. Add the steak mince and brown. Now add the parsley, oregano, cumin, salt, and pepper. Pour the chicken stock over, add the raisins, and set to one side. Preheat the oven to 230 degrees centigrade.

In a food processor, blend the corn, cream, and black pepper. Heat a dry frying pan and cook the corn mixture until it darkens in color, stirring to prevent it from sticking. Salt and pepper. Finally, tear the basil leaves and add the Parmesan to the corn. Set to one side.

TO ASSEMBLE
In individual ovenproof bowls place 3 tablespoons of the steak mince mixture, 1 or 2 olives, some chopped egg, a small amount of chicken, and shredded scallions. Top with at least 3 tablespoons of the corn topping. Ensure that the corn topping covers the filling. Dust with a little sugar. Bake in the oven for 10 to 15 minutes. Turn on the grill and finish the pastel del choclos by browning them under the grill.

SADDAM HUSSEIN AND THE CARP CONNECTION

Healthy eater Saddam Hussein liked to eat lobster, shrimp, very fresh fish, lean meats, and yogurts and cheeses. Unlike Tito, Saddam loved salads and fresh fruit. Stories abound about his food being flown in twice a week, then x-rayed by nuclear scientists, checking for radiation contamination or doses of poison (it is also rumored that Saddam wore bulletproof hats). Planes transported sides of lamb and beef carefully trimmed of all their fat, fresh shrimp, live lobsters, and his favorite olives picked from the Golan Heights. According to General Wafic Samarai, Saddam's former head of intelligence, Saddam loved to spit out the pips, claiming that this would be "the way I will one day spit out the Israelis from their land."

The al Himaya, Saddam's personal bodyguards, supervised while a team of chefs trained in European cuisine, cooked up his meals. A food taster took the first bite; obviously Saddam couldn't count on his resident soothsayer to predict whether poison was on the menu. Ironically enough, Saddam's food taster, Hanna Geogo (the son of one of his chefs) had thrived on Saddam's suppers until Saddam's enraged son, Udai, killed him publicly at a banquet attended by foreign dignitaries. The wife of Egyptian president Hosni Mubarak must have paused between courses when she witnessed Udai gun down the food taster. The story goes that Udai had blamed Geogo for fixing Saddam up with blond Samira Shabandar, who had become the second Mrs. Hussein in 1986. Fun-loving Udai also fed the minister for health to a pack of ravenous dogs.

In Saddam's many palaces, the staff went through the ruse of preparing three meals a day for him, pretending Saddam was in residence to fool his many enemies—he never stayed more than one night in one place. Remember all those body doubles as well. If he turned up for a meal in a restaurant in downtown Baghdad, a flock of security staff descended on the kitchens, insisting on Saddam's orders that all cooking utensils be scrubbed clean. There is, then, a fastidiousness to Saddam's eating habits that no amount of urban myth about him tucking into Quality Street can ignore. After all, it was Saddam who said, "If we are satisfied only by food, we become worms or poultry." True to this vein of thought, Saddam liked to eat modest portions, naively accompanying his meals with a glass of Mateus rosé. Dear me. Apparently, he also drank Old Parr whiskey, and did *you* know he is rumored to have had as many as four wives in total?

Workaholic Saddam used to rise from his small cot (oh yes) at 5 a.m., don his crimson bathrobe, drink coffee in his room—purportedly filled with books on Stalin—and follow a rigorous model of personal hygiene. He manicured his nails, brushed his teeth with Colgate, regularly dyed his mustache satin black, and washed with Lux soap. Hussein famously recommended that one (especially if "one" was female) bathe twice a day. According to his reasoning, this was because:

"It's not appropriate for someone to attend a gathering or to be with his children with his body odor trailing behind him emitting sweet or stinky smell mixed with perspiration." Such fastidiousness may be accounted for by Saddam's humble Tikriti origins. He grew up in a traditional Iraqi mud brick hut, animals in close proximity, with no electricity or running water. Saddam had to become a hustler at a young age, stealing chickens and eggs to feed the family, selling watermelons at the roadside. According to one Saddam biographer, Said Aburish, Saddam's family were one of those social groupings known as *ili baklyu bi al khamsah*; in other words, they ate with all five fingers, as they had no eating utensils. They gathered around a communal pot, eating with their hands largely meatless meals based on the staple rice.

Five-Finger Tikriti Rice

1 cup brown lentils	2 tsp. cumin
1 tbsp. butter	2 tsp. sea salt
2 tbsp. olive oil	1 tbsp. tomato puree
1 cup rice	freshly ground black pepper
2 cardamom pods	1 onion, finely sliced

Clean the brown lentils in running water, then put them in a saucepan with a cup of water. Bring them to a boil and then cover, lower the heat, and cook for about 20 minutes, until the water is absorbed. Drain. Clean the pan, place it on a low heat, and add the butter and 1 tablespoon of the olive oil. Empty the cup of rice into the oil and stir to coat the rice in the buttery oil. Now add the cardamom, cumin, salt, tomato puree, and black pepper, stirring these through the grains of rice. Add the lentils and stir through. Now add two cups of hot water (use the same-size cup you used for the rice), stir, and cover the pan. Bring to a boil, then lower the heat and leave until the rice has absorbed the water—this will take about 15 minutes. Meanwhile, in a shallow frying pan, heat the remaining tablespoon of olive oil and fry the onion slices until they are golden brown. Drain the oniony oil into the pan of lentils and rice, reserving the onion for decoration.

Saddam's passion for fish reappeared at different points. As a young man he used a popular teenage Iraqi method of catching fish by lobbing an explosive device into the water. Later, he stocked the artificial lakes that surrounded his palace at Tharthar with fish and fished there with King Hussein of Jordan in the eighties. He loved swimming in the Tigris; when his family was young, he could be spotted picnicking on the riverbank with them. The fish dishes of sixty-four-year-old

Ayyub al-Obeidi, owner of a Baghdad restaurant in Abu Nawwas Street, were a favorite with Saddam: "Saddam loved my fish. He used to send his guards to order from me two or three times a week." The last time Saddam ordered fish from Ayyub was in April 2003, two months before the regime collapsed.

The Hussein family was particularly hooked on masguf, a delicious Tigris River fish (a type of carp) and Baghdadi specialty that is grilled over palm fronds and a wood fire. In fact, in 1989, Ayyub traveled to the village where Saddam was born, Awjah, to prepare masguf for Queen Noor of Jordan and Mrs. Hussein (first wife Sajida). Ayyub claimed that while Saddam loved fish, he preferred "small fish"—does this have an ominous ring to it? Arguably, Saddam's fondness for finned creatures cemented his relationship with erstwhile ally and gourmand Jacques Chirac. "Mon ami, Saddam" was visited in Iraq in 1975 by Chirac, then prime minister for Giscard d'Estaing's government. Saddam and Jacques made a happy couple when in 1975, they shared masguf at Ben Geogheahan after negotiating fighter aircraft sales and set up a program whereby France would help Iraq to develop its nuclear capacity.

Masguf

Masguf is definitely suited to an outdoors life—try it when you're camping out or on the run. Or if President Chirac is due to swing by for a beer. You will need a whole, fresh carp and a barbecue fish grill for holding your carp in place. Palm fronts and brushwood are recommended instead of charcoal for your fire.

1 large, freshwater carp (get the fishmonger
   to scale and gut the carp, and also to cut
   along the back of the carp and open it up
   so that the fish can be spread out flat)

DRESSING
freshly quartered lemons
sea salt

Build an open wood fire and, when it is lovely and hot, you are ready to cook masguf. Rub both the fish and the fish grill with olive oil. Sprinkle with sea salt. Barbecue the carp as follows: place the carp flat in a two-sided fish barbecue grill and cook upright alongside the fire. This means it will take longer to cook but will taste deliciously of wood smoke—without being at all burned—using this slow-cooking method. It will take about 30 to 45 minutes to cook. Turn the fish grill to cook both the skin of the carp and the fleshy inner fish.

   Eat with your fingers, squeeze fresh lemon juice onto the chunks of carp, and crumble fresh sea salt onto the crunchy, sweet skin. Eat with bread and salad, ideally in the early twilight on a warm evening by the bank of a river.

Saddam also paid a visit to France, which was marked by, among other excesses, gastronomic delights. Orly Airport was bedecked with the eagle of Saladin, a national emblem of Iraq. Champagne and French cocktail sandwiches were on hand. After dining out for several days at state banquets, Chirac's wooing of oil-rich, thirty-eight-year-old Saddam was topped off by a weekend at the exclusive Oustau de Baumanière in Provence, courtesy of famous French chef Raymond Thullier (Chirac also courted Deng Xiaoping there).

Saddam "glowed like a peacock," Thullier claimed, basking in the attention Chirac paid him. They were like "bride and bridegroom" as they sipped coffee together. However, Saddam couldn't resist the opportunity to return the favor, inviting Chirac to a banquet at Marigny Palace which nestles alongside Elysée. Guess what was on the menu? You've got it, Iraqi carp barbecued over open fires—masguf! However, the carp connection doesn't stop there. Fishy as it may seem, Chirac is reported to have developed what amounts to an addiction for masguf carp, and Saddam had to arrange for one and a half tons of masguf to be transported by air to Paris as a gift for Chirac.

In a sense, few things illustrate Saddam's fall from grace more than the tuck that lay around him when he was surprised in his last hiding place by U.S. forces. Our fallen dictator's last meal was uncovered near the jerry-built shack where Saddam hid. As one might expect, he was found near Tikrit, near the banks of the Tigris. Of companions, there was no sign. Just honey, pistachio nuts, a nearly empty cardboard box of Bounty bars, and a half-consumed bowl of tomato salad lay abandoned on a table in the outdoor kitchen . . .

Bunker Tomato Salad

sea salt
1 clove garlic
6 really juicy, aromatic, dark-red
   medium-size tomatoes (if you can
   only find the palely anemic Dutch
   tomato, then put this salad on hold)

½ tbsp. fresh mint leaves, torn
1 tbsp. flat-leaf parsley, shredded
4 spring onions, minced
2 tbsp. lemon juice
2 tbsp. olive oil
freshly ground black pepper

Sprinkle sea salt (a generous pinch) into your salad bowl. Take the clove of garlic and, with your fingers, crush the garlic against the base of the bowl and the small pile of sea salt, pressing the garlic into the salt so that a faint trail of garlic oil (mixed with crumbly salt) begins to ooze out. Small craters of garlic and salt will also break off; wipe these around the lower third of the bowl, coating it in garlicky oil and sea salt. Next, roughly chop the tomatoes and put them in the bowl, stirring once to mop up the garlic. Add the mint, parsley, and onions. Toss and then add the lemon, olive oil, and black pepper. Serve.

BENITO MUSSOLINI BANS PASTA

Like Franco, Benito Mussolini was a bit of a bore when it came to food. Firstly, he didn't really each much of anything with any gusto. In fact, he rarely ate. Although, like Napoleon, he spent only a few minutes on a meal, he didn't have Napoleon's grand food superstitions or sense of social bonhomie. Secondly, he was very bossy about what everyone else in Italy should eat. Who can blame his last mistress, Claretta Petacci, for whinging and lying around in bed all day eating chocolate? Chocolate was probably the more exciting bedtime companion. At one point, when he was dictator of Italy, he personally endorsed a specific brand of chocolate in the newspapers for Perugina confectionery. The advertisement cited Mussolini's words (typically, barking at the company in question): "I tell you, and I authorize you to respect it, that your chocolate is truly exquisite."

Mussolini always liked to be tucked up in bed early. Sober as a judge. And then he just couldn't resist linking food to virility. This is where he got the bright idea to ban pasta. Pasta made you lazy, slothful, and gloomy. It wasn't "masculine" and meant that Italian blokes wouldn't be physically ready for war. Yes, the Dictator of Italy banned pasta. Do you think that a deft political move?

Benito was the first of three children born in 1883 to blacksmith-cum-socialist-journalist Allesandro Mussolini and schoolteacher Rosa. The family lived in considerable poverty near the little town of Predappio in the Emilio Romagna region of Italy (ironically considered the birthplace of pasta and coined "Italy's food basket"). Dad was careless with money, and it fell upon hardworking Rosa to bring home the bacon. Benito had to sleep in the dingy, smoky kitchen with his younger brother. The Mussolinis made their own wine, and the family diet consisted of soup and black bread, supplemented by meat on Sundays.

It is hardly surprising that Benito grew into a troubled and troublesome youth—he had difficulties with speech and was pronounced dumb in his early years. At school, he was a notorious bully; he stabbed one fellow student. Ironically enough, Benito's expulsion from school at around the tender age of ten was partly the result of his leading role in organizing a food riot in protest at the quality of grub served in the school's dining hall.

When young, Mussolini had a liking for alcohol (this couldn't continue later in life due to stomach problems—milk became his preferred tipple). He was fond of a frappé of Chianti, Angostura bitters, and strawberry sherbet. Incidentally, at the end of the Second World War, one hapless Giuseppe Marscone was lynched by a mob in Rome, infuriated by the fact that he had ordered Mussolini's favorite frappé.

Mussolini's Strawberry Frappé

1¼ lb. strawberries   Chianti
1 pint water   crushed ice
2 cups sugar   1 lemon, sliced
2 lemons, squeezed   mint leaves, torn
Angostura bitters   frosted glasses

Cook the strawberries and water together for 10 minutes and then sieve.

Combine with the sugar and the lemon juice. Cool and freeze gently to a light mush. To make one drink, pour ½ teaspoon of Angostura bitters into a frosted cocktail glass and turn the glass quickly, allowing the Angostura to glaze or coat the glass. Next, in a cocktail mixer, shake together ½ cup of the strawberry mush with a glass of Chianti for 30 seconds. Put a spoonful of crushed ice into the cocktail glass. Pour this luscious mixture into the chilled, Angostura-laced glass. Garnish with a slice of lemon and a few mint leaves.

Mussolini had lots of peculiarly disparate jobs as a young man—he worked variously as a laborer on the building site of a chocolate factory; a butcher's boy; he even made a sparse living as a fortune teller! He worked also as a schoolteacher, a job he did very badly, bribing the children with sweets in order to keep them quiet.

Like Queen Elizabeth I, he disliked eating in company. He adhered to a strict diet, and it may be that the pleasure he apparently took in his own company was a move to conceal the real extent of his gastric problems. However, there may be other reasons for this. Mussolini's rough upbringing didn't exactly lend itself to good dining etiquette, and his table manners were such an embarrassment that a civil servant was given the job of teaching him how to behave and eat in politer society. His dress sense was also questionable, as he liked to step out in canary-yellow-colored shoes, a histrionic bowler hat, and a butterfly collar.

Despite his wealth, our Italian dictator was remarkably abstemious. He was fond of saying that no one should waste more than ten minutes a day on eating. Doubtless, this can't have helped the state of his stomach ulcers. His diet became increasingly liquid in later life, and he needed to drink three liters of milk daily and liked to supplement this with fruit at least six times a day. Depressingly enough for the Italians, he often urged that they adopt his own austerity.

Black Bread

2½ tsp. dried active yeast
¼ pint lukewarm water
2 tsp. dark muscovado sugar
½ tsp. ground ginger
¾ pint hot water
2 oz. 80 to 90% dark chocolate, crumbled
4 tbsp. dark molasses or black treacle

6 oz. dark bread crumbs, lightly browned
12 oz. rye flour
6 oz. strong white flour
¼ tsp. fennel seeds
1½ tsp. caraway seeds
2 tsp. sea salt
3 tbsp. melted butter

FOR THE GLAZE
1 egg yolk, beaten

Add the yeast to ¼ pint of lukewarm water and then add the 2 teaspoons of muscovado sugar and the half teaspoon of ground ginger. Put this in a warm place and leave it for 10 minutes—it will develop a foamy "head" as the yeast comes alive. Meanwhile, in a mixing bowl, combine the ¾ pint of hot water with the chocolate and gloopy molasses. Stir vigorously until the chocolate melts into the water and molasses. Add the bread crumbs and mix thoroughly. Add the yeast mixture and stir. In another, larger bowl, sieve the rye flour and the strong white flour. Add the fennel and caraway seeds and the sea salt. Gradually, using your hands to mix them together, combine the wet and dry ingredients until a stiff dough forms; loosen it by kneading in the 3 tablespoons of butter. Oil a bowl and put the bread dough into it, cover with a clean towel, and put this in a warm place to rise for an hour and a half; it will double in size.

Preheat the oven to 220 degrees centigrade.

Lightly flour a surface and turn the dough out onto it. Shape the dough into a round loaf and, using a sharp knife, score a crisscross into the top. Put the loaf on an oiled baking tray, cover it, and return it to the warm spot to rise for a further 45 minutes. It will again increase in size.

Finally, brush the surface of the bread with the egg yolk in order to glaze it. Bake in the oven for 20 minutes at 220 degrees centigrade and then lower the heat to 180 degrees. It is ready to remove from the oven when the base makes a hollow sound when tapped.

Egg and Cheese Dumpling Soup

3 eggs plus 1 egg yolk, beaten
1 cup freshly grated Parmesan
  cheese
1 cup white bread crumbs
2 oz. butter, softened
¼ tsp. freshly grated nutmeg

1 tbsp. parsley
1 tsp. fresh thyme, crumbled
pinch of sea salt
pinch of freshly ground black pepper
2 pints rich, dark homemade beef
  stock

FOR THE GARNISH
1 cup freshly grated Parmesan cheese

In a bowl, combine the beaten eggs, the cup of Parmesan, the bread crumbs, butter, nutmeg, parsley, thyme, salt, and black pepper until this forms a sticky paste. In a deep saucepan, bring the beef stock to a boil. When the beef stock is boiling, put the paste into a potato ricer and press down so that strings of the dumpling mixture drop into the bubbling broth. Repeat until you have used all the dumpling mixture. Now, turn down the beef broth to a simmer and let the soup cook for just under 10 minutes. Serve with a generous stack of Parmesan cheese on top.

DINNER WITH STALIN

Apart from learning how to stand naked up to the neck in icy water, Tito also learned a few lessons in high living during his time in the Soviet Union. Communism and fine dining were not incompatible—at least for those high up in the Communist Party. As he observed, "in Stalin's circle of friends they all enjoyed wine and song, but were not interested in women." It seems strangely appropriate that Lenin chose a culinary metaphor when he gloomily predicted Russia's future under Stalin's control: "That cook will concoct nothing but peppery dishes!" Gone were the good old days when Lenin and Stalin enjoyed a pancake party together.

Totalitarianism was a hungry business, and Stalin never stopped eating and toasting his way through the long years of his dictatorship. Successor Nikita Khrushchev ruefully observed, "I don't think there has ever been a leader of comparable responsibilities who wasted more time than Stalin did just sitting around the dinner table eating and drinking." Georgian food predominated at Stalin's nocturnal banquets; as with all our dictators, there was a distinct nationalism to Stalin's eating habits. Beria's wife earned Stalin's gratitude by making walnut jam and sending it to Stalin, to remind him of his mother's Georgian jam. Strangely enough, food even links Vladimir Putin to Stalin's table—his grandfather had worked as Lenin's cook in Gorky and was then inherited as Stalin's chef after Lenin's death.

In the 1930s it was customary for Stalin and family to occupy rooms in the Kremlin during the week. The food had improved from the early postrevolution days when Lenin and Trotsky had chewed their way through incommodious barley stews and had despaired over yet another plate of red caviar. Soups, Russian hors d'oeuvres, lamb, and salted fish dishes (Stalin liked herrings) were delivered up to the Stalins' Kremlin pad.

Lemon-growing Stalin also liked to dine at his dacha, holding long, delicious brunches in the late afternoon. According to his daughter Svetlana he was never a hands-on gardener, but would march about once every month or so with a pair of shears, officiously clipping the odd bush. Like his later successor, Yeltsin, Stalin enjoyed a good hunt—hare at nighttime with a rifle and, by day, hawks, with a double-barreled rifle. The Stalin family liked to have picnics in the woods when they visited Stalin's dacha at Zubalovo: shashlyks (kebabs) sizzled and browned, dripping their fat into the open cooking fires, and Stalin sent his daughter, Svetlana, into the poultry yard to hunt out pheasant and guinea fowl eggs that he could then cook in the hot ashes of the fire. Stalin loved eating kebabs on holiday, firing up the barbecue on trips to the steamy shores of the Black Sea. In fact, kebabs were the meat of celebration in September 1949 when Stalin and his sidekick Beria tucked into fragrant, juicy barbecued shashlyks as they made merry over Russian advances in the development of the A-bomb. Stalin was also a passionate devotee of game—small, plump quails, guinea fowl, duck. Nikita Khrushchev (did you know he worked in the coal mines as a child?) remembered shooting ducks with Stalin, which they then brought to the kitchen and feasted on while tactics about Hitler were discussed.

Shashlyks

2 lb. boneless leg or shoulder of lamb

FOR THE MARINADE

2 onions, peeled and pureed	1 tsp. soft brown sugar
3 cloves garlic, pulped	2 tsp. ground cumin
1 tbsp. olive oil	freshly ground black pepper
1 tbsp. lemon juice	1 tsp. sea salt

FOR THE KEBABS
2 onions, cut into chunks

TO GARNISH

4 tomatoes, quartered	pinch of sumac
2 lemons, quartered	freshly ground black pepper
8 whole scallions	sea salt

Cut the lamb into 1½-inch chunks. Leave some fat on, but trim off excess. Put the lamb in a large bowl with the marinade ingredients and leave at room temperature for at least 4 hours—if you want to marinate overnight, then this has to be in the fridge.

Heat the barbecue until the coals become white. Thread the lamb chunks onto skewers, alternating the chunks of meat with the chunks of onion, pressing them tightly together. Grill the kebabs and serve with the garnish.

Stalin held terrifying late-night dinner parties—his idea of noisome fun was to throw tomatoes at his drunken colleagues. In fact many of "Uncle Joe's" chief party tricks seem to have involved throwing—orange peel at children, biscuits into tea, champagne corks into the dessert. What bonhomie. Pepper vodka toast followed pepper vodka toast in a terrible Mexican wave of revelry—on top of the Crimean champagne, as many as thirty toasts could occur at one sitting. About twenty-four courses could offer some lining for the stomach. Political allies sat nauseated and drunk, still trying to watch their words as Tito's betrayal was mooted or the Vatican was declared a tool of capitalism.

Stalin could be quite sneaky about booze. Although stories abound about his supposed alcoholism, Khrushchev claimed that the flask of vodka Stalin quaffed from was really filled with water and that Stalin switched his vodka for white wine during toasts. The cad. Stalin liked to stock his table with precious and delicious Georgian wines in his later years, poured into tiny, traditional glasses for guests. There was a legion of bottles on the table, but Stalin would not necessarily take so much as a sip, watching with dark pleasure as his guests sweated and drank and wished to hold their heads in their hands. Svetlana's letters present a less-than-cheerful vision of marital domesticity during the years when her mother, Nadezhda, the second Mrs. Stalin, was around. Her mother and father's relationship was a strained one and became particularly so when Stalin tried to encourage their children to drink wine at dinner, as was the Caucasus style. They fell out spectacularly over a few dinners (Nadezhda was to kill herself—or be killed by Stalin—after a Kremlin dinner). After one banquet to celebrate the October Revolution, Stalin bellowed across the table, "Hey, you. Have a drink!" and she yelled back, "Don't you dare talk to me that way!" and stormed from the room. On one occasion, Stalin facetiously claimed that he was sending Trotsky into exile in Siberia on the grounds that it was apparent he was colluding with counterrevolutionaries because: "Trotsky drinks the wrong kind of whiskey!"

If you weren't already feeling queasy with vodka or jittering with fear as Stalin nibbled caviar off his golden knife, then "Uncle Joe" also liked to serve you at the table, as a mark of special recognition. In his ingratiating memoirs, Enver Hoxha recalls dining with Stalin in November 1949:

After the tête-à-tête talk I had with Comrade Stalin, we went into the house for dinner [. . .] Also present at the dinner were two Soviet generals, the one Stalin's aide-de-camp and the other my escort during my visit. Stalin talked, asked questions, cracked jokes with us [. . .] When we sat at the table he made jokes about the dishes. The way the dinner was served was very interesting. There was no waiter to serve us. A girl brought in all the food in dishes covered to keep them hot; she put the dishes on the table and left. Stalin got up, took the dish himself and, standing there, carved the chicken, then sat down and resumed his jokes.

"Let us begin," he said addressing me. "What are you waiting for? Do you think the waiters will come to serve us? There you have the dishes, take them, lift the lids and start eating, or you'll go supperless."

He laughed again heartily, that exhilarating laugh of his that went right to one's heart. From time to time he raised his glass and drank a toast. At one moment, Stalin's aide-de-camp, seeing that Stalin was taking another kind of drink from the table, made an attempt to stop him and told him not to mix his drinks. He did so as it was his duty to take care of Stalin. Stalin laughed and said that it would do no harm. But when the general insisted, Stalin replied to him in a tone half angry, half in fun:

"Leave me in peace, don't pester me like Tito!" and looked me right in the eye, laughing. We all laughed.

By the end of the dinner he showed me a fruit and said: "Have you ever tasted this kind of fruit?" "No," I said, "I've never seen it. How is it eaten?" He told me its name. It was an Indian or tropical fruit. He took it, peeled it and gave it to me. "Try it," he said, "my hands are clean." And I was reminded of the fine custom of our people who, while talking, peel the apple and give it to the guest to eat.

Surreptitiously, Stalin also encouraged ever-hungry Khrushchev to try dishes before he did—was he being polite? Or was Khrushchev an unofficial food taster? Stalin often dished up for guests a special stew called Aragvi, named after the Aragvi River in Georgia. Aragvi consisted of a spicy stew of lamb, tomatoes, potatoes, and aubergine.

Aragvi

3 oz. butter	2 tsp. dried cumin
1 tbsp. olive oil	1 tsp. dried ginger
1½ lb. lamb	1 tsp. mint
4 onions, finely chopped	1 stick cinnamon
2 garlic cloves, crushed	3 tbsp. chopped, fresh parsley
1½ tbsp. all-purpose flour	salt and black pepper
2 tbsp. tomato puree	2 pints rich, homemade lamb or
8 tomatoes, chopped	chicken stock
1 tbsp. cayenne	5 medium-size potatoes, peeled and
½ tsp. saffron stems	quartered
1 tsp. tarragon	¼ lb. green beans
1 tsp. dried cilantro	1 aubergine, chopped

Heat the butter and the olive oil in a deep pan. Dice the lamb and fry in the oil until it is nicely browned. Add finely chopped onion and go on stewing until the onion is golden, translucent, and starting to "bleed" its golden color. Add the garlic, all-purpose flour, and tomato puree and cook for 30 seconds, stirring constantly. Add the chopped tomatoes and fry for a further 30 seconds. Now add the cayenne, saffron, tarragon, cilantro, cumin, ginger, mint, cinnamon, parsley, salt, and black pepper. Add the stock and cook on a gentle simmer for 1½ hours. Next add the potatoes, green beans, and aubergine and cook for a further 45 minutes.
Serve with sour cream, finely shredded scallions, and crusty bread.

Stalin helped everyone to soup at his fifty-fifth birthday party, serving soup to his guests. On the menu was shchi (translated as "liquid meat"—Turgenev writes a wonderful short story of this title), consisting of cabbage soup and then veal. But

Stalin, in Georgian peasant style, ate his shchi from the bowl, piercing the meat with his fork. Yes, Stalin liked soups. So much so that the affection he bore for his mistress Zhenya was apparent in the fact that she was forgiven for polishing off his onion soup. Stalin liked to eat his soup according to Georgian custom, as Mikoyan recollected: "He ate at least twice as much as I did [. . .] He took a deep plate, mixed two soups in it, then in a country custom that I knew from my own village, crumbled bread into the hot soup and covered it all by another plate—and then ate it all up to the end." Stalin had appallingly bad teeth, and soup probably slipped down very well. He could only eat the ripest, squishiest of fruit and the tenderest meat.

Apparently both Hitler and Stalin liked to check the cutlery in advance of a banquet. Stalin's piece de resistance for trying to charm guests was to feed them suckling pig. This is what he tried on Churchill at a secret summit meeting during the Second World War. After all, roast bear had worked with the Poles.

Gochi (Georgian Roast Suckling Pig)

The smaller the pig, the more succulent it is . . .

2 tbsp. sea salt
1 tbsp. freshly ground black pepper
½ cup olive oil

One 10-lb. pig, quartered and with the head removed but retained

Preheat the oven to 250 degrees centigrade. Mix together the salt, pepper, and olive oil. Rub the pig all over with the seasoned oil. Put an apple in the pig's mouth to stop it closing while roasting and wrap napkins of aluminum foil around its ears so that they don't burn. Assemble the pig quarters around the head and roast in the oven, undisturbed, for 1½ to 2 hours (until when the skin and flesh is pierced, the juices run clear). About 15 minutes before the pig is fully roasted, remove the foil from the ears so that they can brown.

Given that Khrushchev had unwittingly functioned as Stalin's food taster, there seems to be a strange justice in Khrushchev's presence at dinner on the night Stalin suffered his fatal stroke. Stalin had been drinking—but apparently only "light wine"—a far cry from the tales that abound of him beating his servants with a cane after drinking bottles of capitalist hooch and Scotch whiskey from his battered Red Army mug. But perhaps he was the lush that rumor has made him. Demonic twentieth-century dictators are always re-created as creatures of excess; either of profound frugality in appetite or a having wolfish appetites to match their lupine tempers.

PUCHERO FOR THE SHIRTLESS ONES: JUAN AND EVITA PERÓN

It must be suspected that a sober old straitlaced dictator like Franco would have been appalled by the reputation of the woman behind the Argentinian dictator, Juan Perón. The powerful Eva "Evita" Perón called in on Franco when she represented Argentinian interests in a tour of Europe. She had an audience with Pope Pius XII, was decorated by Franco, and was the target of several hostile, left-wing demonstrations. Meantime, Evita worried about her waistline in Paris and sent one of her maids down into the kitchens of the Ritz to give the chef specific instructions about her food: it mustn't be so rich!

Given the poverty of her youth and sexual compromise of her past, Eva left even her pro-fascist hosts with mixed feelings. In fact, an apocryphal tale of a dinner Evita shared with Franco allows us an interesting glimpse of Franco's prudish acerbity. As they dined together at a Madrid restaurant, some other diners shouted "Puta!" "Puta!" at Eva Perón. She asked Franco why they were calling her a whore. Franco's reply was, "Never mind, Senora. I've been retired for years, but they still call me General."

Undoubtedly, Eva's beginnings were marked by compromise. She was born, the youngest of five children, in dreary, fly-blown Los Toldos a couple of hundred miles from Buenos Aires. While the children didn't starve, they would have eaten the same poor diet repetitively: puchero, a soupish, drizzly stew of sausages, scraps of meat, rice, and root vegetables. As it became thicker, it became the main course too . . .

Puchero (. . . enough for a small crowd)

2 tbsp. olive oil
3 onions, finely chopped
6 cloves garlic, crushed
6 scallions, chopped
4 tomatoes, chopped
2 tsp. cumin
½ tsp. saffron strands
1 tsp. sea salt
1 tsp. freshly ground black pepper
1 bunch cilantro, finely chopped
3 onions, quartered
1 lb. beef shank, still on the bone
1½ lb. pork spareribs, split into
    individual ribs

1 small chicken
2 lb. cassava, peeled and diced
½ winter squash, deseeded and
    diced roughly
2 carrots, peeled and roughly
    chopped
4 corn on the cob, cut into thick
    slices
4 large potatoes, peeled and cut
    into quarters
1 bunch of Swiss chard or green
    cabbage, finely sliced
salt and pepper

Puchero (*continued*)

Heat the oil and then add the first 3 onions and half the garlic. Fry these gently for 10 minutes until the onion is a deep gold color. Now add the chopped scallions, tomatoes, cumin, saffron, 1 teaspoon of sea salt, and a teaspoon of black pepper. Cook these for a further 6 minutes and then add half of the cilantro. Turn down the heat and simmer gently for 15 minutes; then cool and reserve for later.

Now put the next lot of 3 onions, the rest of the garlic, the remaining cilantro, the shank, ribs, and whole chicken into a deep stockpot. Cover with cold water, bring to a boil, and cook over a medium heat for 1½ hours. When this time is up, remove the chicken, drain it, and strip it of all flesh. Chop up the breasts. Keep to the side.

Now add the chunks of cassava, squash, carrots, corn, potatoes, and cabbage.

Cook for 30 minutes, then add the chicken meat and the tomato sauce to the puchero; cook for 5 more minutes, salt and pepper, and serve. Drink the broth first, then eat a plate of the meat and vegetables.

At Eva's funeral, the poor who came to pay their respects were given puchero, cooked by the army and served up in huge pots—it was free.

No more puchero after marriage to Juan Perón! The charismatic Juan was a good six feet in height and cultivated a cult of machismo useful for impressing the Argentinian working men he dictated to—the eulogized "shirtless ones." Scotch and soda was his drink, although he liked to wax lyrical after too much coarse red wine. He carried a hunting knife and liked to eat scorching hot barbecue with his fingers. Times had changed for Eva—instead of being one of the poor, ragged children straining for a glimpse of unattainable wealth, she could now demonstrate largesse. She handed out food packages that held bread studded with raisins, bottles of cider, a picture of the beaming faces of Dictator Juan and Dictatress Evita wishing Happy Christmas to the "shirtless ones."

The Peróns showed their style in a truly South American fashion—through throwing lavish and grand barbecues. Instead of using their state residence, the Palacio Unzué, they entertained guests at their second home in Olivos, a mile or two north of Buenos Aires. They opened up the grounds to ambitious provincial wheeler-dealers, and Evita, in charmingly feminine fashion, saw to the baking of meat patties, the slicing of cold meats, the presentation of pickled partridge, and all the other customary delicacies that float in the wake of a real Argentinean barbecue.

Chapter 4

EATING BITTERNESS WITH CHAIRMAN MAO

An odd mix between brittle revolutionary zeal and boy-scoutish excess, Mao thought that remaining ever true to the greasy spicy Hunan food of his youth was common sense. Plus, oil was glamorous, a sign of wealth in hungry 1950s China. When he wasn't worrying about being poisoned or supping ginseng root boiled in water for his impotence, Mao enjoyed nothing better than pork with fatty bits—finished off with a puff on one of his terrible, woody Yanan cigarettes. Probably he tucked into this before a night of dancing with young nurses. The poor nurses jiggled about in Mao's arms, while he paced the floor rigidly, like a rather stiff attendee at an exercise class.

Nurses aside, Mao liked to nod off—his pillows were stuffed with buckwheat husks—on a wooden bed (anyone remember Saddam Hussein's cot?) before hopping off for a quick float down the Yong River. Mao dived into choppy, rough, or freezing waters—what the hell if there were sharks! Brisk has it. Ever since he chopped off his pigtail—that loathed symbol of homage to the Manchu dynasty—Mao prided himself on this type of vigorous intellectual and physical independence. Yet his needs were assiduously attended to: his food was flown in daily from the Great Mountain Farm in Beijing, his room was cooled by tubs of ice, and his temperature was raised by the country girls who could visit him there. Mao didn't like baths and managed to avoid having one for some twenty-five years; showers went the same way too. Instead he liked to be rubbed down with hot towels daily and massaged by handsome people. Sounds good?

Mao liked to eat just two meals a day—lunch at about 4 p.m. and a meatless "dinner" of red peppers and porridge or vegetables at around 3 a.m. Like Stalin, Mao was a dictator who invited nervous underlings to share his supper. He liked to spook you over the mains. Mao's erstwhile doctor, Zhisui Li, recalled one such occasion. Dictator and doctor sat down to a meal of lamb with leeks, some fish, and pork mixed with hot peppers—another top dish of Mao's. Li's heart sank at the amount of oil in every mouthful, and he secretly bemoaned the lack of soy sauce on the menu.

But Li had little time to concentrate on his sauces. The clock was ticking for Dr. Li—he was to suffer internal exile and be sent on one of Mao's reeducation programs. When Mao heard of minor potentates tucking in while the poor starved, they were sent on "diplomatic missions" to the countryside for a taste of poverty.

Our cunning dictator hinted just such a fate lay in wait for Dr. Li when he offered him bitter melon cooked with hot peppers. Li had never tried it before, and Mao roared with laughter as Li choked down the bitter, hot melon. "Everyone should taste some bitterness in his life," Mao chortled, "especially a person like you. You studied medicine and became a doctor. You have probably never eaten bitterness." Uh-oh.

Someone very close to Mao who had to eat more than a fair slice of bitterness was Mao's doomed second wife, Kai-hui. Abandoned along with their three children by Mao when he popped out to look after the Autumn Harvest Uprising in 1927 and never came back—he had married sulky wife number three, Gui-yuan, only four months later—Kai-hui remained deeply in love with him. She accounted for the absence of letters from him by imagining that floods, mountain ranges, armies, and the business of building a revolutionary force had interfered with his knocking on her door. Meanwhile, Mao was holed up pretty comfortably, enjoying the dietary concessions made to his rank, with plenty of beef in his soup, and entire chickens if required; drinking lots of milk, which is unusual in Chinese food culture; dining out on his favorite fish heads; and expressing his pleasure very pragmatically as, "I can eat a lot and shit a lot." Thanks for letting us know.

Kai-hui was ever luckless and was executed by anti-Communists for being Mao's wife: she refused to denounce or divorce him. She was paraded through the wintry streets of Changsha, bound with rope and in a thin blouse, before a cheerful, clapping crowd. After she was shot, her assassins went off for a bite of lunch, only to hear she was writhing in pain; they declared magnanimously that they'd deal with it after lunch. And true to their word, having wiped their lips, they went back and finished the job, shooting Kai-hui dead. Many, many, years after, tiny little packets of her writings, sealed in wax paper, were found in the rafters and walls of the flat in which she'd pined so long and hard for Mao. There were love poems there; letters unsent but addressed "To my beloved" and poignant references to meals made for Mao—she made special noodles to guarantee him long life on his birthday, saluting her vanished love. But they were never touched by him, a bit like Kai-hui herself. Although she had only received one letter for a year—in which Mao unromantically moaned about his feet—when the opportunity arose, in the form of a CCP inspector on his way to see Mao, Kai-hui thrust a jug of Mao's much-loved chili with fermented beans into his hands to take to Mao. Was there so much as a squeak of thanks from Mao? No.

The Chili-with-Fermented-Beans of Unrequited Love

6 fresh chilies (large if you seek
   mildness, but bird's-eye if you
   are being authentic!)
⅓ cup fermented black beans

2 tbsp. groundnut oil
1 tbsp. Chinese rice wine or dry sherry
2 tsp. rice vinegar
1 tbsp. sugar

Begin by chopping and then mincing the chilies; make sure you wash your hands thoroughly after touching them! Now wash and chop the fermented black beans. Warm the groundnut oil in a pan and fry the chilies and beans for about 2 minutes. Now pour on the Chinese rice wine or sherry and the vinegar. Let this simmer for another 2 minutes, then sprinkle on the sugar and stir until it dissolves.

Finally let this cool—it will keep for several weeks in the fridge and can be sent by the jar to someone who has forgotten all about you. They'll remember you after one spoonful!

Gui-yuan wasn't to fare much better; no matter how many delicious suppers of pig's trotters she made for Mao, he still treated her like an old suitcase, forcing her to lose—and I mean literally lose either through abandonment or death—all of the many children she bore him, one on the Long March; Mao compared her ability to have children to a hen that drops many eggs.

Fearsome Madame Mao, Jiang Qing, was wife number four. When they first lived together, Jiang developed a sudden interest in cooking, and although she wasn't keen on Mao's spicy tastes, these dishes appeared, lovingly prepared. Mao couldn't compromise reciprocally; when his retinue went into the forests of Beidaihe after fresh rain to gather bagfuls of blooming, autumn-brown mushrooms, Jiang Qing had the sense to enjoy the delicious, rich soup these made. Mao would never touch it. Jiang kept Mao supplied with endless cups of tea during intimate political meetings, eavesdropping as she wandered in with hot pepper snacks and bowls of nuts. Over the course of time, Madame Mao came to live in fear of her husband; he never let her off with being less than rigorous in her Communist self-examinations. But Jiang was tyrannical herself and quite happy to accuse and denounce anyone who displeased her; even the hapless individual who offended Jiang by washing and styling her hair wrongly was exposed as an enemy of the state.

When times were good, Mao supplemented his fatty pork dishes with the likes of his adored Wuchang silver carp. Symbolically, the carp meant good fortune (bad luck for the carp). Understandably, perhaps, Jiang Qing ate with him only once a week (and they had to use *her* chef, not his). Mao was always a bolter of his food, and would have tossed his chopsticks to the side before Jiang got past the first mouthful or two. She preferred to breakfast alone, picking at almond yogurt on toast, and considered herself far more sophisticated in culinary terms—after all, Jiang Qing had dined on the glories of those "Western" foods, pot roast and caviar, in the Soviet Union. Mao, in contrast, evoked the royal "we" to get out of eating Russian nosh: "It is not to our liking," he'd grumble. Brilliantly, he also deliberately failed to understand Russian ballet—"Why do they dance on their toes? It looks very uncomfortable," he queried. On top of that, he hated puffy Russian bed pillows, the nasty frozen fish his hosts kept serving him, and the fact that he couldn't spend any quality time on their weird pedestal toilets.

Wuchang Silver Carp

1 whole 2-lb. carp, cleaned and scaled, but with the head and tail left on
1 tbsp. fresh gingerroot, shredded
1 tbsp. groundnut oil
1 tsp. sesame oil
2 cloves garlic, finely sliced
1 tbsp. Chinese rice wine or dry sherry
4 scallions, minced
1 long red chili, minced
1 tbsp. light soy sauce

Set up a wok with a rack inside it. Fill it with about 2 inches of water; bring the water to a boil, and then place the carp on a plate. Pile the ginger on top, cover the pan, and steam for about 15 minutes.

Meanwhile, heat the mixed sesame oil and groundnut oil in a pan and brown the garlic slices. Cool and then combine this with the Chinese rice wine, scallions, red chili, and light soy sauce. When the fish is ready, pour some of this delicious dressing over the top and serve; keep a bowl of the sauce at the side for drizzling over the white flesh of the carp.

When Mao toured the backwaters of China in 1958, preparing his observations as fuel for the Great Leap Forward of the following year, he insisted on staying in local, rundown guesthouses, sticking to the roughly ground corn steamed buns that typified the peasant diet. By the early 1940s, Mao had realized that his own food consumption had to get the right PR spin. The Party, it was announced, forced food on the Communist inner circle. One official said: "Take Chairman Mao . . . the Party can order him to eat a chicken a day." And Mao could only obey. When, after dinner with Mao, one guileless female official was invited to return often to eat with him, she cheerfully commented, "So I'll come to you every Sunday to treat myself to a good meal!" Mao's smile became rigid. When tiger and deer meat were sent to Mao, he refused to try it—just as he refused to go to the lavish banquet held for his sixty-sixth birthday. His retinue sneaked into the banquet, though, drawn into betraying Maoist principles by the prospect of bird's-nest soup with baby doves. Restaurants became scarce in the Communist era, and Mao's home eating life—in one of the villas he adored—was more indulgent, in a number of small ways, than his public profile suggested. His rice had to be husked in a special way. Stir-fried food had to be served immediately. One poor, hapless type of fish he considered particularly tasty was brought 1,000 kilometers, alive, in an oxygenated bag of water to land up in his bowl. He didn't want to be offended by the smelly, foodie odors wafting out of his kitchens and so insisted that the food preparation be conducted at a safe distance from him. It was common to see servants racing across from building to building with plates of food for Mao's table, trying to get there before it cooled.

Loyal Communist workers were rewarded with chew-on-that treats during the Cultural Revolution. With all the largesse of a Big Brother, Mao presented mangoes to the workers. A strange fate befell these prized, dictator-blessed fruit; water in which they had been boiled was drunk as an enchanted elixir—mangoes even had altars consecrated to them! True to form, Mao himself gave up meat during the famine that followed—the terrible harvest of 1959—opting instead for bean curd. Eventually, even vegetables were in short supply. Tens of millions were to die of starvation in China. Mao was ruthless in the privations he expected ordinary Chinese to endure—when China invaded Korea in 1950, the Chinese army "volunteers" suffered terribly. Night blindness was brought on by lack of nutrition, and the Party advice was that they eat tadpoles and make soup from pine needles.

Things can't have been easy for Mao, though. Anyone who is a Red Menace should take heed. Again like Saddam, he had to have food flown in, forensically analyzed, and tested. There were the usual nervous food tasters hovering about. Like any Caesar, Mao kept an eye on his mushrooms, and who could blame him? For instance, there was the Bamboo Shoot Episode in Guangdong. Seven banquet tables had been set out in honor of Mao, but he wasn't particularly happy, as his hosts hoped he would eat Cantonese food, of which he was highly suspicious. But then the alarm was raised. The kitchens were sealed off: traces of cyanide had been found in the food! Hong Kong was in dangerously close proximity. Distrust and political intrigue smoldered. It was only after days of waiting that the laboratory announced cyanide had been found in the bamboo shoots—ho ho! It turned out that cyanide appears naturally (and in safe amounts) in bamboo shoots. So no fancy Cantonese mumbo jumbo for Mao. He'd stick to what he knew. Who could doubt the health benefits of pork belly? Only Dr. Li, and he was long gone, leaving Mao to devise his own healthy eating program. Mao claimed that pork braised in brown sauce made his brain work better and ate it twice monthly.

Mao took a roguish delight in gulping down shocking dainties that others found crazy to say the least—such as "Dragon Battling Tiger" (snake with wildcat). If this left him with a little touch of gas or a wince of heartburn, a sip of turtle soup restored his appetite. Were he still around, I'm sure Dr. Li would attest to Mao's sense of humor about food—but it's always at *the guest's* expense.

Pork in Brown Sauce

6 fresh, crisp spring onions
1 tbsp. corn flour, mixed with
   3 tbsp. water
3 tbsp. light soy sauce

5 tbsp. sugar
2 lean pork steaks
½ cup vegetable oil

Shred the spring onions and place half in the base of the dish in which you intend to serve the pork. Reserve the other half, as you will use this to garnish the cooked pork. In a smaller bowl, combine the corn flour and water mixture, the soy sauce, and the sugar. Place to one side. Next, shred the raw pork quite finely. Heat the oil in a wok and, when it is almost smoking, add the shredded pork. Stir-fry until it crisps up (about 2 minutes). Then add the corn flour, water, soy sauce, and sugar mixture. Stir-fry until fragrant and the color deepens slightly (about 2 minutes). Place this on top of the shredded scallions and garnish with the remaining scallions. Serve with plenty of rice. Follow with a cup of green tea!

Pork with Hot Peppers

½ tbsp. peanut oil
2 cloves of garlic, crushed
¾ lb. pork (slightly fatty), sliced
1 red pepper, sliced
2 tbsp. chili jam

1 tbsp. fish sauce
2 long red chilies, seeded and
   shredded lengthwise
1 fl. oz. chicken stock
25 to 30 leaves sweet basil (to taste)

Warm the peanut oil in a pan and stir-fry the crushed garlic. Slice the slightly fatty pork into thin shreds. Add the pork to the hot oil and garlic and stir-fry for 2 minutes or until it becomes crispy. Next, add the sliced red pepper and stir-fry until it is slightly cooked (about 1½ minutes). Add the chili jam, fish sauce, and chilies and stir-fry till done. Drizzle on some chicken stock and stir. Remove from the heat. At the last moment stir in the basil leaves—they should only wilt slightly and add a wonderful licorice/basil aroma and fragrance to the dish. Now serve.
   Bunches of fresh, sweet basil are available from any Chinese supermarket and are an absolute must for this recipe.

Bibliography

Aburish, Said and K. Saïd, *Saddam Hussein: The Politics of Revenge*. London: Bloomsbury, 2000.

Aitken, Jonathan, *Nixon: A Life*. Washington, DC: Regnery Publishing, 1996.

Aldrin, Buzz and Ken Abraham, *Magnificent Desolation: The Long Journey from the Moon*. London: Bloomsbury, 2010.

Aldrin, Buzz and Malcolm McConnell, *Men from Earth*. London: Bantam, 1989.

Allilueva, Svetlana, *Twenty Letters to a Friend*. London: Hutchinson, 1967.

Álvarez de Toledo, Lucia, *The Story of Che Guevara*. London: Quercus, 2011.

Anderson, Jon Lee, *Che Guevara: A Revolutionary Life*. London: Bantam Press, 1997.

Armstrong, Neil, Michael Collins, Buzz Aldrin, Gene Farmer, and Dora Jane Hamblin, *First on the Moon: A Voyage with Neil Armstrong, Michael Collins and Edwin F. Aldrin, Jr.* Boston: Little, Brown, 1970.

Aron, Leon Rabinovich, *Boris Yeltsin: A Revolutionary Life*. London: HarperCollins, 2001.

Bardach, Ann Louise, *Cuba Confidential: The Extraordinary Tragedy of Cuba, Its Revolution and Its Exiles*. London: Penguin, 2004.

Bedell, Sally Smith, *Grace and Power: The Private World of the Kennedy White House*. London: Aurum, 2005.

Bergen, Peter, *Holy War, Inc.: Inside the Secret World of Osama Bin Laden*. London: Weidenfeld & Nicolson, 2001.

———, *The Osama Bin Laden I Know: An Oral History of al-Qaeda's Leader*. New York: Free Press, 2006.

Biagi, Enzo, *Svetlana: The Inside Story*. London: Hodder & Stoughton, 1967.

Bodansky, Yossef, *Bin Laden: The Man Who Declared War on America.* Rocklin, CA: Great Britain: Forum, 1999.

Bourne, Peter G., *Castro: A Biography of Fidel Castro.* London: Macmillan, 1987.

Brian, Denis, *The Unexpected Einstein: The Real Man behind the Icon.* Hoboken: Wiley, 2005.

Brock, David, *The Seduction of Hillary Rodham.* New York: Free Press, 1996.

Brodie, Fawn McKay, *Richard Nixon: The Shaping of His Character.* New York: Norton, 1981.

Browne, Anthony Montague, *Long Sunset: Memoirs of Winston Churchill's Last Private Secretary.* London: Cassell, 1995.

Buckley, William F. Jr., *The Reagan I Knew.* New York: Basic Books, 2008.

Califano, Joseph A. Jr., *The Triumph and Tragedy of Lyndon Johnson: The White House Years.* New York: Simon & Schuster, 1991.

Callinicos, Luli, *Oliver Tambo: Beyond the Engeli Mountains.* Claremont, South Africa: David Philip; Johannesburg: Thorold's Africana Books, 2004.

Campbell, John and David Freeman, *Margaret Thatcher: Grocer's Daughter to Iron Lady.* London: Vintage Books, 2009.

Carpenter, Liz, *Ruffles and Flourishes.* College Station: Texas A&M University Press, 1993.

Carter, Jimmy, *Christmas in Plains.* New York: Simon and Schuster, 2001.

———, *A Remarkable Mother.* New York: Simon and Schuster, 2008.

———, *White House Diary.* New York: Farrar, Straus and Giroux, 2010.

Castro, Fidel, Deborah Shnookal, and Pedro Álvarez Tabío, *My Early Years.* Melbourne: Ocean Press, 1998.

Castro, Fidel, Ignacio Ramonet, and Andrew Hurley, *My Life.* London: Penguin, 2008.

Chang, Jung and Jon Halliday, *Mao: The Unknown Story.* London: Jonathan Cape, 2005.

Cherry-Garrard, Apsley, *The Worst Journey in the World: Antarctic 1910–13.* London: Picador, 1994.

Churchill, Winston, *My Early Life: A Roving Commission.* New York: Charles Scribner's Sons, 1958.

Churchill, Winston, Mary Soames, and Clementine Churchill, *Speaking for Themselves: The Personal Letters of Winston and Clementine Churchill.* London: Black Swan, 1999.

Clark, Ronald, *Lenin: The Man behind the Mask.* London: Faber, 1988.

Clinton, Bill, *My Life.* New York: Alfred A. Knopf, 2004.

Cockburn, Andrew, *Saddam Hussein: An American Obsession.* London: Verso, 2002.

Coll, Steve, *The Bin Ladens: The Story of a Family and Its Fortune.* London: Allen Lane, 2008.

Collins, Michael, *Carrying the Fire: An Astronaut's Journeys.* London: W. H. Allen, 1975.

Collins, Rodnell P., *Seventh Child: A Family Memoir of Malcolm X*. New York: Kensington Publishing, 1998.

Coltman, Leycester, *The Real Fidel Castro*. New Haven, CT: Yale University Press, 2003.

Coote, Colin R., *The Other Club*. London: Sidgwick and Jackson, 1971.

Coughlin, Con, *Saddam: The Secret Life*. London: Macmillan, 2002.

Cowger, Thomas W. and Sherwin Markman, editors, *Lyndon Johnson Remembered: An Intimate Portrait*. Lanham, MD: Rowman & Littlefield, 2003.

Crane, David, *Scott of the Antarctic*. London: Harper Perennial, 2006.

Dallek, Robert, *Flawed Giant: Lyndon Johnson and His Times, 1961–1973*. Oxford: Oxford University Press, 1998.

Darwin, Charles, *The Autobiography of Charles Darwin*. London: Watts, 1929.

Darwin, Emma, *A Century of Family Letters*. Cambridge: Cambridge University Press, 1904.

Davis, Patti, *Family Secrets: An Autobiography*. London: Sidgwick & Jackson, 1992.

Debenham, Frank, *In the Antarctic: Stories of Scott's Last Expedition*. London: Murray, 1952.

Dedijer, Vladimir, *Tito*. New York: Arno Press, 1972.

De-la-Noy, Michael, *Scott of the Antarctic*. Stroud: Sutton, 1997.

Deutscher, Isaac, *Lenin's Childhood*. London: Oxford University Press, 1970.

Diwakar, Ranganath Ramachandra, *My Encounter with Gandhi*. New Delhi: Gandhi Peace Foundation, 1989.

Djilas, Milovan, *Conversations with Stalin*. London: Rupert Hart-Davis, 1962.

———, *Tito: The Story from Inside*. London: Phoenix, 2000.

Dowdeswell, Evelyn, J. A. Dowdeswell, and Angela Seddon, *Scott of the Antarctic*. London: Raintree, 2012.

Dubois, Diana, *In Her Sister's Shadow: An Intimate Biography of Lee Radziwill*. Boston: Little, Brown, 1995.

Einstein, Albert, *The Collected Papers of Albert Einstein*. Princeton, NJ: Princeton University Press, 1987.

Ferris, Paul, *Dr. Freud: A Life*. London: Sinclair-Stevenson, 1997.

Fiennes, Ranulph, *Captain Scott*. London: Hodder & Stoughton, 2003.

Fischer, Louis, *The Life of Lenin*. New York: Harper and Row, 1965.

———, *The Life of Mahatma Gandhi*. London: Grafton, 1970.

Foss, Clive, *Juan and Eva Perón*. Stroud: Sutton, 2006.

Fox, Ralph, *Lenin: A Biography*. London: Victor Gollancz, 1933.

Fraser, Nicholas and Marysa Navarro, *Evita: The Real Lives of Eva Peron*. London: André Deutsch, 1996.

Fresquet, Rufo López, *My Fourteen Months with Castro*. Cleveland: World Publishing Co., 1966.

Freud, Martin, *Sigmund Freud: Man and Father*. New York: J. Aronson, 1983.

Gadea, Hilda, *Ernesto: A Memoir of Che Guevara*. London; New York: W. H. Allen, 1973.

Gallagher, Mary Barelli, *My Life with Jacqueline Kennedy*. London: Joseph, 1970.

Gandhi, Mahatma, *The Collected Works of Mahatma Gandhi, Vol. 1, 1884–1886*. Delhi: The Publications Division, Ministry of Information and Broadcasting, 1958.

Gandhi, Mahatma and Mahadev H. Desai, *An Autobiography, or, the Story of My Experiments with Truth*. Ahmedabad: Navajivan Publishing House, 1996.

Gardiner, George, *Margaret Thatcher: From Childhood to Leadership*. London: Kimber, 1975.

Gartner, John D., *In Search of Bill Clinton*. New York: St. Martin's Press, 2008.

Gilbert, Martin, *The Churchill War Papers: Never Surrender, Vol. 2, May 1940– December 1940*. London: Heinemann, 1994.

———, *The Churchill War Papers: The Stricken World, Vol. 4, 1917–1922*. London: Heinemann, 1975.

Godbold, E. Stanly, *Jimmy and Rosalynn Carter: The Georgia Years, 1924–1974*. New York; Oxford: Oxford University Press, 2010.

González, Luis J., *The Great Rebel: Che Guevara in Bolivia*. New York: Grove Press, 1969.

Gorbachev, Mikhail, *Mikhail Gorbachev: Memoirs*. London: Bantam, 1997.

Gorky, Maxim, *Days with Lenin*. London: M. Lawrence, 1933.

Gowers, Andrew and Tony Walker, *Behind the Myth: Yasser Arafat and the Palestinian Revolution*. London: W. H. Allen, 1990.

Gregory, James, *Goodbye Bafana. Nelson Mandela: My Prisoner, My Friend*. London: Headline, 1995.

Guevara, Che, *The Bolivian Diary of Ernesto Che Guevara*. New York: Pathfinder, 1994.

———, *Reminiscences of the Cuban Revolutionary War*. London: Allen & Unwin, 1968.

Guha, Ramachandra, *Gandhi Before India*. London: Penguin Books, 2014.

Guikovaty, Emile, *Tito*. Paris: Hachette, 1979.

Hickman, Tom, *Churchill's Bodyguard: The Authorised Biography of Walter H. Thompson*. Headline: London, 2005.

Highfield, Roger and Paul Carter, *The Private Lives of Albert Einstein*. London: Faber and Faber, 1993.

Hunt, James D., *Gandhi in London*. New Delhi: Promilla & Co., 1978.

Huxley, Elspeth, *Scott of the Antarctic*. London: Weidenfeld & Nicholson, 1977.

James, Daniel, *Ché Guevara: A Biography*. London: Allen, 1970.

Johnson, Lady Bird, *A White House Diary*. London: Weidenfeld & Nicolson, 1970.

Kelley, Kitty, *Jackie Oh!* New York: Ballantine Books, 1984.

———, *Nancy Reagan: The Unauthorised Biography*. London: Bantam, 1991.

Kennedy, Rose Fitzgerald, *Times to Remember: An Autobiography*. London: Collins, 1974.

Kessler, Ronald, *In the President's Secret Service: Behind the Scenes with Agents in the Line of Fire and the Presidents They Protect*. New York: Random House, 2010.

Kiernan, Thomas, *Yasir Arafat: The Man and the Myth*. London: Abacus, 1976.

King, Coretta Scott, *My Life with Martin Luther King, Jr.* London: Hodder and Stoughton, 1970.

King, Martin Luther Jr., *The Autobiography of Martin Luther King, Jr.* London: Little, Brown and Co., 1998.

Kornitzer, Bela, *The Real Nixon: An Intimate Biography.* New York: Rand McNally, 1960.

Krupskaya, Nadezhda Konstantinovna, *Memories of Lenin.* London: Lawrence and Wishart, 1970.

Landemare, Georgina, *Recipes from No. 10.* London: Collins, 1958.

Lawrence, T. E., *The Diary Kept by T. E. Lawrence while Travelling in Arabia during 1911.* Reading: Garnet, 1993.

———, *Oriental Assembly.* London: Williams and Norgate Ltd., 1947.

———, *Seven Pillars of Wisdom.* Fordingbridge: Castle Hill Press, 2003.

Leaming, Barbara, *Mrs. Kennedy: The Missing History of the Kennedy Years.* London: Weidenfeld & Nicolson, 2001.

Lewis, David, *King: A Biography.* Urbana: University of Illinois Press, 1978.

Li, Zhisui, Hongchao Dai, and Anne Thurston, *The Private Life of Chairman Mao: The Memoirs of Mao's Personal Physician.* London: Arrow, 1996.

Liebknecht, Wilhelm, *Karl Marx: Biographical Memoirs.* London: Journeyman Press, 1975.

Lockwood, Lee, *Castro's Cuba, Cuba's Fidel.* Boulder, CO: Westview, 1990.

Longuet, Jenny Marx, Laura Marx Lafargue, and Eleanor Marx Aveling, *The Daughters of Karl Marx: Family Correspondence, 1866–1898.* Edited by Olga Meier. Harmondsworth: Penguin, 1984.

Malcolm X and Alex Hayley, *The Autobiography of Malcolm X.* London: Penguin, 2001.

Mandela, Nelson, *Long Walk to Freedom: The Autobiography of Nelson Mandela.* London: Little, Brown, 1994.

Mandela, Winnie, *Part of My Soul Went with Him.* New York: W. W. Norton, 1984.

Maraniss, David, *First in His Class: The Biography of Bill Clinton.* New York: Touchstone, 1995.

Mazo, Earl, *Richard Nixon: A Political and Personal Portrait.* New York: Harper, 1959.

McCauley, Martin, *Gorbachev.* Harlow: Longman, 1998.

McGowan, Norman, *My Years with Churchill.* London: Souvenir Press, 1958.

Medvedev, Zhores, *Gorbachev.* Oxford: Basil Blackwell, 1988.

Meer, Fatima, *Higher than Hope: The Unauthorized Biography of Nelson Mandela.* London: Penguin, 1990.

Meir, Golda, *My Life: The Autobiography of Golda Meir.* London: Weidenfeld & Nicolson, 1975.

Meir, Menahem, *My Mother, Golda Meir.* New York: Arbor House, 1983

Meredith, Martin, *Nelson Mandela: A Biography.* London: Simon & Schuster, 2010.

Miller, Jonathan, *Freud: The Man, His World, His Influence.* London: Weidenfeld & Nicolson, 1972.

Montefiore, Simon Sebag, *Stalin: The Court of the Red Tsar*. London: Weidenfeld & Nicolson, 2003.

———, *Young Stalin*. Toronto: McArthur, 2007.

Moore, Charles, *Margaret Thatcher: The Authorized Biography*. London: Allen Lane, 2013.

Moran, Lord, *Winston Churchill: The Struggle for Survival 1940–1965*. London: Constable, 1966.

Morgan, Iwan, *Nixon*. London: Oxford University Press, 2002.

Morton, Andrew, *Monica's Story*. London: Michael O'Mara Books, 1999.

Mountevans, Edward, *South with Scott*. London: Collins, 1921.

Muravyova, L. and T. Sivolap-Kaftanova, *Lenin in London*. Moscow: Progress Publishers, 1983.

Nicolson, Juliet, *The Perfect Summer: Dancing into Shadow in 1911*. London: John Murray, 2006.

Nixon, Richard, *The Memoirs of Richard Nixon*. London: Sidgwick & Jackson, 1978.

Page, Joseph, *Perón, a Biography*. New York: Random House, 1983.

Parry, Dan, *Moon Shot: The Inside Story of the Mankind's Greatest Adventure*. London: Ebury Press, 2009.

Pawle, Gerald, *The War and Colonel Warden*. London: George G. Harrap & Co. Ltd., 1963.

Pearson, Michael, *Inessa: Lenin's Mistress*. London: Duckworth, 2001.

Perón, Eva, *In My Own Words*. Edinburgh: Mainstream, 1997.

Ponting, Herbert George, *The Great White South, or, With Scott in the Antarctic: Being an Account of Experiences with Captain Scott's South Pole Expedition and of the Nature Life of the Antarctic*. London: Duckworth, 1923.

Popović, Milan, editor, *In Albert's Shadow: The Life and Letters of Milena Marić, Einstein's First Wife*. Baltimore: Johns Hopkins University Press, 2003.

Quirk, Robert E., *Fidel Castro*. New York: Norton, 1993.

Radzinskiĭ, Ėdvard, *Stalin*. London: Sceptre, 1997.

Randal, Jonathan, *Osama: The Making of a Terrorist*. London: I. B. Tauris, 2005.

Ridley, Jasper Godwin, *Tito*. London: Constable, 1994.

Roazen, Paul, *Freud and His Followers*. New York: Da Capo Press, 1992.

Robinson, Adam, *Bin Laden: Behind the Mask of the Terrorist*. Edinburgh: Mainstream, 2001.

Rothman, Hal, *LBJ's Texas White House: "Our Heart's Home."* College Station: Texas A&M University Press, 2001.

Russell, Jan Jarboe, *Lady Bird: A Biography of Mrs. Johnson*. New York: Scribner, 1999.

Schefter, James, *The Race: The Definitive Story of America's Battle to Beat Russia to the Moon*. London: Century, 1999.

Scott, Robert Falcon, *Journals: Captain Scott's Last Expedition*, edited by Max Jones. Oxford: Oxford University Press, 2005.

————, *The Voyage of the 'Discovery.'* London: John Murray, 1929.

Service, Robert, *Lenin: A Biography*. Cambridge, MA: Harvard University Press, 2000.

————, *Stalin: A Biography*. London: Macmillan, 2004.

Shaw, Maud, *White House Nanny: My Years with Caroline and John Kennedy, Jr.* London: Leslie Frewin, 1966.

Sheehan, Sean, *Lenin*. London: Haus, 2010.

Shephard, Gillian, *The Real Iron Lady: Working with Margaret Thatcher*. London: Biteback Publishing Ltd., 2013.

Shub, David, *Lenin: A Biography*. Harmondsworth: Penguin Books, 1966.

Skierka, Volker, *Fidel Castro: A Biography*. Malden, MA: Polity Press, 2004.

Smith, Andrew, *Moondust: In Search of the Men Who Fell to Earth*. London: Bloomsbury, 2005.

Soames, Mary, *Clementine Churchill*. London: Doubleday, 2002.

Stelzer, Cita, *Dinner with Churchill: Policy Making at the Dinner Table*. London: Short Books, 2012.

Swift, Will, *Pat and Dick: The Nixons, an Intimate Portrait of a Marriage*. New York: Threshold Editions, 2014.

Tabori, Paul, editor, *The Private Life of Adolf Hitler: The Intimate Notes and Diary of Eva Braun*. London: Aldus, 1949.

Terrill, Ross, *Madame Mao: The White Boned Demon: A Biography of Madame Mao Zedong*. Stanford, CA: Stanford University Press, 1999.

Thatcher, Carol, *Below the Parapet: the Biography of Denis Thatcher*. London: Harper Collins, 1997.

————, *Diary of an Election: With Margaret Thatcher on the Campaign Trail*. London: Sidgwick and Jackson, 1983.

Thatcher, Margaret, *The Downing Street Years*. London: Harper Collins, 1993.

————, *Margaret Thatcher: The Autobiography*. London: Harper Press, 2013.

————, *The Path to Power*. London: Harper Press, 2011.

Thompson, W. H., *Beside the Bulldog: The Intimate Memoirs of Churchill's Bodyguard*. London: Apollo, 2003.

Thomson, Andrew, *Margaret Thatcher: The Woman Within*. Oxford: Isis, 1989.

Thomson, David, *Scott's Men*. London: Allen Lane, 1977.

Trapido, Anna, *Hunger for Freedom. The Story of Food in the Life of Nelson Mandela*. Auckland: Jacana Media, 2008.

Trotsky, Leon, *Leon Trotsky's My Life: An Attempt at an Autobiography*. London: Wellred Books, 2004.

Vasil'eva, Larisa Nikolaevna and Cathy Porter, *Kremlin Wives*. London: Weidenfeld & Nicolson, 1994.

Vivian, Octavia, *Coretta: The Story of Coretta Scott King*. Minneapolis: Fortress Press, 2006.

Walker, Steven, *Fidel Castro's Childhood: The Untold Story*. Leicester: Matador, 2012.

Walker, Tony, *Arafat: The Biography*. London: Virgin, 2003.

Wapshott, Nicholas, *Ronald Reagan and Margaret Thatcher: A Political Marriage*. New York: Sentinel, 2007.

West, J. B. and Mary Lynn Kotz, *Upstairs at the White House: My Life with the First Ladies*. London: W. H. Allen, 1974.

Wheen, Francis, *Karl Marx*. London: Fourth Estate, 1999.

Williams, Beryl, *Lenin*. Harlow: Longman, 2000.

Wollheim, Richard, *Freud*. London: Fontana, 1991.

Wood, Allen, *Karl Marx*. London: Routledge & Kegan Paul, 1981.

Yeltsin, Boris, *Midnight Diaries*. London: Weidenfeld & Nicolson, 2000.

———, *The View from the Kremlin*. London: Harper Collins, 1994.

Yeltsin, Boris and Michael Glenny, *Against the Grain: An Autobiography*. London: Cape, 1990.

Young, Hugo, *The Iron Lady: A Biography of Margaret Thatcher*. New York: Farrar Strauss Giroux, 1989.

Zverev, Vasiliĭ and Boris Lunkov, *Vladimir Ilyich Lenin: Pages from His Life*. Moscow: Novosti, 1990.

JOURNALS AND ARTICLES

Brocklesby, Eddie, "Nan's Kitchen at No. 10," *The Serpentine*, Autumn 2003, p. 3 and p. 22. http://www.serpentine.org.uk/data/files/pages/serpentimes/autumn03.pdf.

Comyn, Marian, "My Recollections of Karl Marx," *The Nineteeth Century and After*, vol. 91, January 1922.

Miller, Arthur, "My Dinner with Castro," *The Guardian*, January 24, 2004. http://www.theguardian.com/books/2004/jan/24/biography.cuba.

Yaacov, "Golda's Kitchen," Israeli National Archives blogspot, Sunday, December 2, 2012. http://israelsdocuments.blogspot.co.uk/2012/12/golda-kitchen.html.

Index